The *Stolpersteine* and the Commemoration of Life, Death and Government

A Philosophical Archaeology

Lars Östman

PETER LANG
Oxford • Bern • Berlin • Bruxelles • Frankfurt am Main • New York • Wien

Bibliographic information published by Die Deutsche Nationalbibliothek.
Die Deutsche Nationalbibliothek lists this publication in the Deutsche National-bibliografie; detailed bibliographic data is available on the Internet at http://dnb.d-nb.de.

A catalogue record for this book is available from the British Library.

Library of Congress Control Number: 2017958909

Cover image: Photograph by Lars Östman.

Cover design by Peter Lang Ltd.

ISBN 978-3-0343-1958-4 (print) • ISBN 978-1-78874-076-0 (ePDF)
ISBN 978-1-78874-077-7 (ePub) • ISBN 978-1-78874-078-4 (mobi)

Wabernstrasse 40, CH-3007 Bern, Switzerland
info@peterlang.com, www.peterlang.com, www.peterlang.net

This publication has been peer reviewed.

Printed in Germany

Es ist ein Versuch, sich gleichsam a posteriori eine Vergangenheit zu geben, aus der man stammen möchte, im Gegensatz zu der, aus der man stammt – immer ein gefährlicher Versuch, weil es so schwer ist, eine Grenze im Verneinen des Vergangenen zu finden, und weil die zweiten Naturen meistens schwächlicher als die ersten sind. Es bleibt zu häufig bei einem Erkennen des Guten, ohne es zu thun, weil man auch das Bessere kennt, ohne es thun zu können. Aber hier und da gelingt der Sieg doch, und es gibt sogar für die Kämpfenden, für die, welche sich der kritischen Historie zum Leben bedienen, einen merkwürdigen Trost: nämlich zu wissen, daß auch jene erste Natur irgendwann einmal eine zweite Natur war und daß jede siegende zweite Natur zu einer ersten wird.

— FRIEDRICH NIETZSCHE, *Unzeitgemässe Betrachtungen* (1872)

Voi che vivete sicuri
Nelle vostre tiepide case,
Voi che trovate tornando a sera
Il cibo caldo e visi amici:
Considerate se questo è un uomo
Che lavora nel fango
Che non conosce pace
Che lotta per mezzo pane
Che muore per un sì o per un no.
Considerate se questa è una donna,
Senza capelli e senza nome
Senza più forza di ricordare
Vuoti gli occhi e freddo il grembo
Come una rana d'inverno.
Meditate che questo è stato:
Vi comando queste parole.
Scolpitele nel vostro cuore
Stando in casa andando per via,
Coricandovi, alzandovi;
Ripetetele ai vostri figli.
O vi si sfaccia la casa,
La malattia vi impedisca,
I vostri nati torcano il viso da voi.

— PRIMO LEVI, *Se questo è un uomo* (1947)

Contents

Figures

Acknowledgements

I submitted a preliminary version of this book for the requirements of the PhD degree at the University of Copenhagen, Denmark, September 2014.

An article discussing the overall issues of the present book was published as: Östman, L. (2015). 'The 'Stolpersteine' between Commemoration and Biopolitics'. In M. Lytje, T. K. Nielsen, M. O. Jørgensen (eds), *Challenging Ideas: Theory and Empirical Research in the Social Sciences and Humanities*, pp. 43–65. Newcastle upon Tyne: Cambridge Scholars Publishing.

Some of the analyses in Chapter 2 were published as: Östman, L. (2013). 'Philosophical Archaeology as Method in the Humanities. A Comment on Cultural Memory and the Problem of History', *Danish Yearbook of Philosophy*, no. 46 (2011), pp. 81–103. Copenhagen: Museum Tusculanums Forlag.

Some sections from Chapter 6 are also being published as: Östman, L. (2017). 'Stolpersteine in Light of Roman Archaic Religion'. In L. B. Christensen, J. T. Jensen (eds), *Religion and Material Culture: Defining Religion, Religious Elements and Cultural Memory on the Basis of Objects, Architecture and Space. Proceedings of an International Conference held at the Centre for Bible and Cultural Memory (BiCuM), University of Copenhagen and the National Museum of Denmark, Research & Exhibition, Danish Prehistory, Copenhagen, May 6–8, 2011*, pp. 341–61. Antiquité et sciences humaines, III. Turnhout: Brepols Publishers.

My sincere thanks to all the publishers who allowed me to reproduce this material.

Every effort has been made to trace copyright holders and to obtain their permission for the use of copyright material. The author apologizes for any errors or omissions in the above list and would be grateful for notification of any corrections that should be incorporated in future reprints or editions of this book.

This book would not have been possible without the kind help and support from dear friends: Dr Gert Sørensen, Professor Jesper Høgenhaven, Professor Rüdiger Schmitt. I also wish to thank my editor at Peter Lang, Dr Laurel Plapp, for her continuous encouragement.

INTRODUCTION

Working Philosophically with Commemoration

Apart from the Roman Empire, there is perhaps no single regime that has received as much attention as the Third Reich. Even today, it appears to be true that the former is 'a revolution that will ever be remembered, and is still felt by the nations of the earth', as Edward Gibbon writes in his grand œuvre *The Decline and Fall of the Roman Empire* from 1776 (vol. I: 31). As for the latter, this was the first form of government to have placed the extermination of millions of civilians at the core of its politics, constituting 'an administrative process carried out by bureaucrats in a network of offices spanning a continent', as Raul Hilberg wrote in the preface of his classic work from 1985 (1996: vol. 1, ix).

New research concerning the historical circumstances of the Third Reich keeps appearing: new archaeological findings, yet another mass grave, another document confirming the deportation of yet another group of citizens and so on, may shed new light on a particular region, on its citizens, its culture and also on how, why and when this region fell into the hands of the Third Reich – even why some welcomed it. Perhaps further historical investigation may also show that a particularly Western European focus has resulted in the neglect of the Eastern European dimension of the Third Reich's politics, as Timothy Snyder (2010) has underlined, for instance. Despite different scholarly interests, new historical details about the victims seldom change the overall picture. Already Hilberg's book specifies who the victims were and where they were living when their lives were brutally taken from them (1985: vol. 3, 1212).

The general picture, thus, has remained the same for decades. In any case, as the historian Eric Hobsbawm rhetorically asks in his *The Age of Extremes*: 'What does statistical exactitude mean, where the orders of magnitude are so astronomic? Would the horror of the holocaust be any less if historians concluded that it exterminated not six millions […] but five or even four?' (1995: 43). Although it is certainly an impressive work, the first published volume of the multivolume *Encyclopedia of Camps and Ghettos 1933–1945* is unlikely to change the general picture of the Third Reich but, rather, strongly to reinforce it. Rather than produce new historical knowledge, what is important in research such as Snyder's and in reflections such as Hobsbawm's is that they change and challenge our existing knowledge and discuss the facts at hand. This is necessary, Snyder writes at the end of an article, because 'memory has made some odd departures from history, at a time when history is needed more than ever' (2009: 8).

In many ways, which will become clear over the pages to come, Snyder's statement structures the core of the present book's intention. If the historical examination of the Third Reich's exterminations can be safely declared as completed, further work could, for example, continue to focus on how these are commemorated and to investigate the relation between history and memory, in performing something like a philosophical archaeology of this relation and, perhaps, conflict. Such an archaeology would then invite the question of contemporaneity, by asking how the present relates to the past and in what the nature of memory's departure from history consists.

An extraordinary example of such historical commemoration is found in the *Stolpersteine* [Stumbling Stones]. Since the beginning of the 1990s, throughout the European continent and even beyond, the German artist Gunter Demnig has continued to install one small Stolperstein (96 × 96 × 100 mm), similar to a cobblestone, for each of the victims of the Third Reich, whether from Germany or elsewhere. Most often by installing the Stolperstein in front of the individual victim's last self-chosen *Wohnort* [place of residence] – although sometimes the victim's workplace is chosen as a location, instead – this act constitutes itself as an ongoing project of commemoration. As at November 2015, as the homepage of <http://www.stolpersteine.eu> advises, 55,000 Stolpersteine have been installed. Setting aside the Berlin *Denkmal für die ermordeten Juden Europas* [Memorial to the Murdered Jews of Europe (see Figure 1)], the Stolpersteine collectively constitute the world's largest monument for victims of the Third Reich.

Figure 1. *Denkmal für die ermordeten Juden Europas* [Memorial to the Murdered Jews of Europe].

It is certainly commendable that a monument should aim at individualizing the victims, to mark the lives they once lived in the city or in the countryside. Victimhood, as defined by the Stolpersteine, is all-inclusive: the stones do not distinguish between, nor do they specify, Jews, homosexuals, communists, Sinti and Roma or any other group. Rather, they follow the principle of 'one human being – one stone – one fate' (Demnig 2015: 3).[1] Instead of any religious, political, or sexual identification, what unites the victims is their humanity. Perhaps the greatest human catastrophe suddenly appears at our feet. The victims were just like you and me. They lived here; they walked here where today you and I live and walk. The 'Stolpersteine-landscape' marks a cartography of past life in the midst of present life.

1 All translations are my own unless otherwise noted.

Nonetheless, when it comes to this kind of commemoration, a difficult question presents itself, which of course applies not only to the Stolpersteine but for commemoration in general: namely, how is it possible to commemorate the annihilation of a human being who was subjected to something far worse than murder? Can annihilation still be captured in legal or ethical terms, or is the reality of the exterminations beyond such conceptualizations? The commemorative task is how the condition of extreme inhumanity can be remembered while still respecting the humanity of the victims. The risk could be that if the victim's humanity is commemorated, the fact of his or her annihilation will be forgotten. And if the fact of the victim's annihilation is forgotten, the importance and, indeed, ethical obligation to commemorate the victim's humanity cannot be fulfilled – at least, not if one believes that commemoration of the victims of the Third Reich must stand upon the soil of history.

The aim of this book is to investigate how the Stolpersteine relate commemoratively, politically and ethically to the Third Reich and its victims, which will be done by describing and interpreting the Stolpersteine philosophically. The scope is to investigate not merely the problem between history and memory, but also the Stolpersteine's particular political and ethical problems and challenges. How, if at all, do the Stolpersteine acknowledge that the exterminations by far exceed what can be grasped juridically and ethically, religiously and politically? To what extent do the Stolpersteine help in commemorating the victims of National Socialism and to what extent is this form of commemoration based upon history? These questions become all the more acute and important from the fact that many fundamental institutions, from NATO to the EU, from international law to human rights, from the Western welfare state to its educational systems, etc., have Auschwitz as their implicit point of departure and *primus motor*. Auschwitz, in this way, fundamentally continues to structure our Western communities. For this reason, it matters how victims of totalitarianism are commemorated. History matters.

This book has as its main theoretical frame the work of Giorgio Agamben, and in particular his *homo sacer* project. Agamben is among the first scholars – if not the only scholar – to have attempted to conceptualize the philosophical problems in the politics of the Third Reich and of its victims, something that is at the core of the Stolpersteine. The chapters of this book will first identify a specific problem in the Stolpersteine monument and, then, discuss it philosophically. The book is therefore structured according to the form of commemoration one finds in the Stolpersteine, letting the monument dictate the following philosophical discussions and analyses, rather than the other way around.

Not much has been written about the Stolpersteine, in spite of them being the world's second largest monument for victims of the Third Reich. That which has been written is mainly concerned with the biographies of those deported and annihilated, or with providing regional information regarding the respective city at the time of deportation, such as Rainer Radies' edited volume *Zehn Jahre Stolpersteine für Stuttgart* [*Ten Years of Stumbling Stones for Stuttgart*] (2013). Online databases such as Jstor and Project Muse, for instance, the largest databases for research in the European languages of Dutch, Portuguese, Spanish, French, Italian, German, and also for English, the largest language represented, do not list many articles. The Stolpersteine have yet found no place in the *Vierteljahrshefte für Zeitgeschichte* [Quarterly Journal of Contemporary History], one of the largest German journals. In general, the Stolpersteine have only reached the arts and humanities as a part of larger and more general discussions, mentioning them *en passant* in relation to other monuments, themes, or topics.

However, quite recently, in 2014, Petra T. Fritsche published her *Stolpersteine – Das Gedächtnis einer Straße* [*Stumbling Stones – The Memory of a Street*]. In her monograph, Fritsche places the Stolpersteine in the history of German *Vergangenheitsbewältigung* [coming to terms with the past] and, in particular, she addresses the impact these monuments have on public life [Öffentlichkeit]. The scope and purpose of my book is different from Fritsche's and other similar work. Not only would yet another investigation focusing only on forms of commemoration be more or less a repetition of Fritsche's book and other cultural memory scholarship, but it would also fail to acknowledge other and no less central dimensions of the Stolpersteine that have still not been discussed or analysed. In this book, I will argue that many of these problems have an interesting philosophical core.

It is the task of any research to deliver critical analysis. Nothing seems more evident and, yet, nothing is more difficult when it comes to critical reflection on the Third Reich's deportation and extermination of millions of human beings and how this is commemorated. 'How is it possible', Ulrike Schrader asks in her article about the Stolpersteine, 'to criticize what is generally considered to be a good "contribution to the debate on National Socialism"?' (2006: 174). Yet, it is just as true, Schrader wrote a few lines before, that to simply jump on the 'running train of enthusiasm' (2006: 174), would be too easy.

If scholarly and intellectual principles are not preserved, the possibility to come closer to an understanding of the Third Reich and the form of victimhood it produced could fade away. Just as problematic, our ethical obligation to the maxim 'never again Auschwitz' could lose its footing. Commemoration would then jeopardize – despite all its good intentions – the representation of Auschwitz's historical reality, and the reality of the victims' fate could hence run the risk of being forgotten.

It is my opinion that only by relating the historical reality behind the Stolpersteine may the monument's attempt at commemorating this event be discussed. Because, from an ethical point of view, the task of such a monument must be understood on its success – as well as failure – to somehow give witness to Auschwitz, that is, to present the victims' humanity amid Auschwitz's inhumanity in which the victims found themselves. If the reality of Auschwitz is somehow absent, the risk is that Auschwitz will not only be forgotten but, far worse from a commemorative point of view, that Auschwitz's extremeness fails to be tightly woven into the fates of its victims. As a consequence, the fates of the victims of the Third Reich would be normalized, simply yet another group – however awful – of victims of exterminations. Correspondingly, if the reality of Auschwitz somehow stands apart, the risk evidently is that what is commemorated is the inhumanity of the Third Reich, at the cost of the humanity of the victims.

Throughout the present book, the representational character of the Stolpersteine will gradually reveal itself, presenting an outline of the relation between memory and history, between the form of commemoration in the Stolpersteine (memory) and the victims who were deported and exterminated by the Third Reich (fact). How do the Stolpersteine govern the streets and landscapes upon which they are installed? What is the relation between Stolpersteine and citizens, man and monument? How is it possible to understand the point at which the voluntary servitude of individuals comes into contact with the power of monuments, and is there, in the end, any free choice of commemoration, something that appears to be so important considering that the Stolpersteine are placed right in front of people's residences?

CHAPTER I

Stumbling upon Victims of National Socialism

Individualizing the Victim

This first chapter aims to present and analyse the Stolpersteine as they are found on the European continent of commemoration. Central to the discussion is how the monuments describe the individual victim, and how his or her life and annihilation are characterized.

The Stolpersteine comprise 'an art project for Europe', as stated on Demnig's homepage, and commemorate victims of the Third Reich. Although such a commemoration is far from unusual in Germany, or even more widely in Europe, the Stolpersteine are not quite ordinary, a fact that is also true with respect to the very first steps of the commemoration project. On 16 December 1992, when Demnig installed the first Stolperstein, this was done in front of Cologne's town hall 'in an art event for the deportation of Sinti and Roma' (Fings (ed.) 2007: 12). This act of commemoration was initially illegal, because Demnig had not obtained the required permission from the state of Cologne for his installation – and would not acquire this until eight years later, in 2000. Even the installation of Stolpersteine in Berlin in 1996 happened illegally (Fings (ed.) 2007: 13).

Regarding this aspect of civil disobedience in Demnig's commemorative project, Kirsten Serup-Bilfeldt writes that Demnig, from the bottom of his heart, is a 'defiantly convinced old *Achtundsechziger* [a person from the generation of 1968]' (2004: 155, italics added). Demnig therefore believes, as Serup-Bilfeldt explains, that in the end his project of commemoration 'is left to confrontation', before concluding that this is 'also an inheritance of the '68-generation' (Serup-Bilfeldt 2004: 156). Today, permission to install the monument is most often granted automatically in Germany, but Demnig still travels all over Europe laying down Stolpersteine, since December 2005 with the assistance of his friend Michael Friedländer (Franke 2008).

The monuments replace one or more of the standard, usually smaller, granite cobblestones; at other times, Demnig needs to make a hole in the asphalt using machinery. Each Stolperstein measures 96 × 96 × 100 mm and, since March 2015, costs 120 Euros. However, what is bought is really the sponsorship [*Patentschaft*]: 'The states accept the Stolpersteine as gift [...]' (Demnig 2002: 19). Each stone is made of cement, with an engraved brass plate displaying a short text with the victim's name and other biographical details on its surface. The name itself, Stolpersteine, is probably intended metaphorically in the following sense: 'He who does not stumble, does not walk', as one researcher put it (Rönnerper (ed.) 2010: 7). The Stolpersteine are installed in front of the last self-chosen place of residence of the Third Reich victim in question, or sometimes in front of the building where the victim worked or carried out some other kind of activity.

In cases where the old address corresponds to the contemporary one, the Stolpersteine are laid as close to the existing property as possible, though still on public ground (see Figure 2). Sometimes, a property owner may also agree to have a Stolperstein installed on his private property. Any person or organization who wishes to have one or several of these monuments installed at an address where a victim or victims lived can invest in the Stolpersteine. Although the state, in theory, could also purchase these monuments, this project particularly tries to address different kinds of NGOs, from Jewish communities to groups of contemporary neighbours, inhabitants of the respective streets, or simply any individual citizen with an interest in commemorating victims of the Third Reich.

The Stolpersteine homepage advises that, as of November 2015, 55,000 stones have been installed at approximately 1,600 locations. The monuments are present in Germany (of which more than 7,000 are in Berlin) but, in addition, in Austria, Belgium, France, Greece, Italy, Croatia, Luxemburg, the Netherlands, Poland, Romania, Russia, Switzerland, Slovakia, Slovenia, the Czech Republic, Ukraine and Hungary victims now have Stolpersteine in their memory (Demnig 2015: 1). Norway is the only Scandinavian country to have the monument, with its first Stolpersteine installed in 2010 and more added in 2012 in Oslo, Trondheim and Larvik (Slettholm 2011).

Figure 2. Stolperstein. Jewish Quarter, Rome, May 2012.

In Denmark, *Rambam – Selskabet for Dansk Jødisk Historie* [Rambam Society for Danish Jewish History] was in charge of organizing the installation of eighty Stolpersteine as soon as sufficient funding was provided, according to their homepage on 29 November 2011. However, as of January 2014 the project seems to have been cancelled and remains so. In terms of covered urban space (currently 550 m^2) the Stolpersteine constitute the world's second largest monument for victims of the Third Reich, only exceeded by the Berlin Memorial to the Murdered Jews of Europe. Continuously increasing and crossing nationalities, nations, cities, languages, religions, political conviction and sexual orientation, it would also seem to be the most ambitious monument.

A curious fact, obvious to anyone stumbling across these monuments when walking through a European city or landscape, is that the Stolpersteine are not always placed in front of a house but are sometimes in the middle of nowhere or, just as strangely, in front of a playground or a school. This might seem peculiar, as the idea was, as mentioned above, to install the monument where the deportee lived or worked. However, puzzlement quickly dissolves if one considers the quite extreme historicism embedded in the Stolpersteine: a stone that is positioned away from a contemporary house or building exists simply because it corresponds to the previous location of a home or workplace that no longer exists. Many houses were destroyed during the war, both in Berlin and Germany as well as in other European cities and towns all over the continent, leaving entire parts, even whole areas of urban space, devastated. Similarly, many streets, roads, houses and addresses that existed in the 1930s and 1940s do not exist anymore. New streets and roads, new playgrounds and schools have found their way into the urban and sometimes rural landscape; others have disappeared. It is not the present but the past that outlines the Stolpersteine cartography – urban as well as rural.

The Stolpersteine enjoy great popularity. Already about ten years ago, on 4 October 2005, Demnig was awarded the *Verdienstorden der Bundesrepublik Deutschland* – also known as the *Bundesverdienstkreuz* [the Federal Service Cross] – a medal awarded by the state of Germany. The same year, Demnig received the Obermayer German Jewish History Award from the United States (Richarz 2008: 336). Demnig has been awarded over twelve medals for his work on the Stolpersteine, including the European Citizens' Prize and, most recently, the state of Königstein presented the Eugen-Kogon Award to Demnig. The monument has even found its way into popular culture: in November 2010, the Stolpersteine figured in a key story in the popular German television series *Lindenstraße* (episode 1302, for 16:45 minutes). The episode depicted a kind and elderly woman who was trying to organize the installation of Stolpersteine, and a rich, rather blunt, businessman who preferred not to have these monuments installed in front of his building.

In real life, the monuments meet with little resistance, and they are only seldom vandalized. However, one city is not at all thrilled by this innovative memorial: in November 2003, Munich refused Demnig permission to install Stolpersteine and, in contrast to the project's early days, this time Demnig did not undertake an act of civil disobedience. The central arguments concerned the victims losing their dignity when walked upon. The best-known opponent of the Stolpersteine was Charlotte Knobloch, former President of the Zentralrat der Juden in Deutschland [Central Counsel of Jews in Germany], Vice President of the European Jewish Congress and of the World Jewish Congress. In an interview given the year after the affair to the largest South German newspaper, *Süddeutsche Zeitung*, Knobloch declared that it was '"unbearable" to read the names of murdered Jews on plates in the ground and to "walk around" on them' (Goebel 2004). Today, Munich still has no Stolpersteine on public ground, neither for Jewish nor other victims.

In Berlin, the former headquarters of the Third Reich government and today still the capital, the Stolpersteine, of course, constitute a special case: 'Between 1996 and 2004', Jennifer Jordan wrote ten years ago, '350 stones were set in the sidewalks of the district of Friedrichshain-Kreuzberg alone, with the aim of eventually installing a stone for each of the 2000 people from these districts who died at the hands of the Nazis' (2006: 192). Friedrichshain-Kreuzberg, crossing the former borders of East and West Berlin, cover about 20 km^2. With the proclaimed goal of installing one stone for each of the 2,000 deportees, this will amount to one stone every 100 m^2.

Berlin did not always contain most of the stones: 'Up to the end of 2006 most of the memorial stones had been laid in Hamburg (1,600), Cologne (1,400) and Berlin (1,300)' (Richarz 2008: 334). Today, however, the picture is different: according to the cities' respective Stolpersteine webpages, Hamburg has 5,223 stones, Cologne 2,164, and Berlin 7,283 (all accessed August 2017).

The Stolpersteine specifically commemorate Third Reich deportations of Jews, Sinti and Roma, the politically persecuted, homosexuals, Jehovah's Witnesses and victims of the Euthanasia Programme. Probably the vast majority of victims do, in fact, belong to one or even several of these groups. However, the Stolpersteine homepage informs its readers of a hitherto unprecedented level of inclusiveness: 'The artist Gunter Demnig commemorates the victims of the NS era'. This statement suggests not only that commemoration from part of the Stolpersteine concerns the entire period of National Socialist government from 1933 to 1945, but also that even if a person's deportation (and, most likely, annihilation) in one way or another can be related to the government of the Third Reich in the years 1933 to 1945, a Stolperstein may be installed for this individual. Also, victims who do not belong to the groups listed by the Stolpersteine may still have a stone installed in his or her memory, such as, for instance, resistance members or those who the Third Reich called asocials. The Stolpersteine, thus, are simply a monument for any civilian, throughout Europe and beyond, who fell victim at the hands of the Third Reich. Thus, the engraving on a Stolperstein contains no trace of victim's membership group.

Moreover, an alteration in the project's charter (which appeared when the homepage underwent modernization sometime during 2012) redefines victimhood in extremely broad terms: '[...] in the end all human beings who had to suffer under this regime'. In the end it appears that the Stolpersteine define deportation not only as being deported from the home or workplace but even as the ultimate deportation *unto* death or the deportation *from* life as such. In this way, not only victims who perished in the camps can be commemorated, but also those who were forbidden to work due to National Socialist restrictions against, for instance, Jews and communists.

The Stolpersteine might be considered provocative: not only do they proclaim to be an artistic commemorative monument; they even seem, at the same time, unsuited for current categories of understanding and analysis – politically as well as commemoratively. They do not limit themselves to a certain group or to specific victims and, moreover, they do not describe the event via the usual terms 'Holocaust' or 'Shoah'; instead, the homepage simply speaks of *Opfer des Nationalsozialismus* [victims of National Socialism] (Demnig 2015: 3).

What is rather extraordinary and interesting regarding the Stolpersteine is that victimhood is identified as the very beginning of a process that could – and, in many cases, did – lead to annihilation. In specifying that deportation not only must be conceived as being deportation from the home but also even as the ultimate deportation *unto* death or the deportation *from* life as such, the specific personal aspect of National Socialism presents itself. The Stolpersteine specify not only the historical circumstances, in terms of time and place, but also call attention to the actual victim in question.

For instance, although the founding father of philosophical phenomenology, Edmund Husserl, was not killed by the NS government, a Stolperstein is nonetheless installed for him because he suffered disbarment and a travel ban. The Stolperstein for Husserl that meets one at the University of Freiburg has the following text displayed on it (see Figure 3):

HIER LEHRTE
EDMUND HUSSERL
JG.1859
BERUFSVERBOT 1933
AUSREISEVERBOT
GEDEMÜTIGT/ENTRECHTET
TOT 27.4.1938

[HERE TAUGHT
EDMUND HUSSERL
BORN 1859
DISBARMENT 1933
TRAVEL BAN
HUMILIATED/DISENFRANCHISED
DEAD 27.4.1938]

Interestingly, Husserl has yet another Stolpersteine, which concerns the deportation from his home. Two Stolpersteine are installed in memory of Husserl and his wife, Malvine, and are found in front of the couple's house in Freiburg's Lorettostraße 40 substituting, in Husserl's case, *hier lehrte* [here taught] with *hier wohnte* [here lived].

Figure 3. Stolperstein. Freiburg, December 2013. Photo courtesy of Anne Louise Nielsen.

It is to be regretted that the two Stolpersteine confront the pedestrians of Freiburg with a rather inaccurate account of events. Contrary to what the Stolperstein suggests, the fact that Husserl is dead [*tot*] has nothing to do with the Third Reich (although both he and his wife were deported from their home). Husserl, in fact, died of pleurisy, following a serious fall. Despite this unhappy confusion of events, via the term *entrechtet* [disenfranchised] the Stolpersteine nonetheless underline that Third Reich victimhood concerns not only annihilation but also the fact that the victim's normal life and status as a citizen were suspended. The point to which the Stolpersteine refer in this and similar cases is quite refined: in their commemorative strategy, the focus is not only on life's actual ending but, also, on its potential ending. Such a potential ending, according to the Stolpersteine, begins with deportation from one's home or workplace, or with disbarment and a travel ban. One could say that deportation – whether unto death or from life – is the first step towards potential annihilation. Deportation from the home and the normal sphere of quotidian life is what, to the Stolpersteine, opens the door to the camp.

It is striking that the number of Third Reich civilian victims is rather difficult to establish, and that it can seemingly only be obtained by combining different studies that seldom share any common ground in terms of whom to include in the different victim groups and categories. In fact, on many occasions the total death tolls cannot be seen apart from definitions of Holocaust or Shoah (Niewyk and Nicosia 2000: 45–50). There seems to be little interest from scholars in stating the death toll for civilians *qua* civilians, that is, regardless of any group affiliation (religious, national, sexual, or other). Whoever is to be included in the Holocaust – while reserving Shoah for Jewish victims – and beyond any discussion of the legitimation of these two concepts for a correct conceptualization of victimhood and extermination in the Third Reich, it is clear that the Stolpersteine are freed from such considerations.

The Stolpersteine demand no physical, sexual, ethnic, political or any other criteria of qualification. Questions such as whether he or she was killed on grounds of anti-Semitism, euthanasia, sexual orientation or something else become less important. Being civilian and being deported are the only two criteria for representation in the Stolperstein monument. It is important to understand that this redefinition of victimhood by the Stolpersteine is done by placing the challenge of commemoration into another arena: more than redefining Holocaust, Shoah or even genocide or racism, the monument places each human being in the arena of that single victim's humanity and individuality.

One could say that the Stolpersteine reflect the historian Eric Hobsbawm's point of view in his *The Age of Extremes*, which was mentioned in the introduction to this book: 'What does statistical exactitude mean, where the orders of magnitude are so astronomic? Would the horror of the holocaust be any less if historians concluded that it exterminated not six millions [...] but five or even four?' (Hobsbawm 1995: 43). The answer from the Stolpersteine would be that they have no concept of magnitude as such. Rather, the monument places the humanitarian catastrophe of extermination and annihilation on the level of the individual for whom – as one could say in a Hobsbawm manner – the catastrophe is independent of its totality.

On the homepage, the large degree of victim inclusion and individuality is confirmed, explaining that also victims beyond the borders of Europe are to be included (Demnig 2015: 1). The Stolpersteine project recognizes that the Second World War was a war that for the first time was waged to a large extent against civilians – even beyond the nation state itself. The victims are therefore not, so to say, deported once again from their home in order to be commemorated far away, perhaps even a country that today is foreign or a city with victims who are unknown to them. Instead, the Stolpersteine cement memory in the very ground and land, place and time from where the individual victim was originally taken, and replace this victim in the community among, perhaps, other Stolpersteine. The Stolpersteine symbolically recreate the lost community on the very same soil from where they were deported.

Although the strategy the monument has chosen in order to underline the horror of the exterminations is not to try and symbolize its magnitude but, instead, to underline the individual catastrophe, the larger historical context does not disappear – at least not according to Demnig, who said in an interview: '[E]ach personal stone also symbolizes the victim's context [...] since, in fact, all necessary stones cannot be installed. In Cologne, whole rows of houses would then have to be paved with Stolpersteine' (2002: 14). Following Demnig, one little stone of 96 × 96 × 100 mm succeeds better in representing the exterminations and their context than does, for instance, the 19,000 m^2 Berlin Memorial to the Murdered Jews of Europe.

The ethics of the Stolpersteine seems to be that one can relate to another human being. Who can relate to six million? To twenty million? Therefore, because Demnig cannot install one Stolperstein for each and every individual victim, the project must remain symbolic. As a consequence, the decision as to which victims actually get a stone must likewise remain symbolic. To Ulrike Schrader, a central question therefore presents itself: 'Who establishes this limit and what is it based on?' (2006: 180).

The Hierarchy of Death

An example of individualized commemoration on the part of the Stolpersteine is seen when examining the webpage for the monuments in Berlin. It describes who the victims were, specifically where they are commemorated and, most importantly for this chapter, it also opens up the possibility of discussing one of the central issues of the Stolpersteine that Schrader mentioned: the criteria of differentiation between individual victims.

On the Berlin homepage for the Stolpersteine, one can conduct an *erweiterte Suche* [advanced search] showing the following categories for Berlin victims currently represented by a Stolperstein: 'Jews or Jewish origin; member of forbidden political party or resistance; pretext of physical or mental disabilities; pretext of homosexual acts; Sinti and Roma; Jehovah's Witnesses, Bible researcher.' Even if these groups and categories structure the sum of victims, every single individual is also represented on the homepage, where one can read the respective engravings and sometimes even view specific Stolpersteine in question, which is the case for the Arons, for example. If further information about the individual is available – the homepage calls this 'biographical text' [*Biografietext*] – it is presented with the appropriate sources. As of August 2017, the homepage for the Berlin Stolpersteine advises that it has been possible to establish biographical texts for 3,648 persons.

There is a listing of thirteen sources for the establishment of these biographies. The list is divided into two categories: one of only Jewish victims and another that also includes non-Jewish victims. The first category contains seven sources, the two most significant being *Gedenkbuch: Opfer der Verfolgung der Juden unter der nationalsozialistischen Gewaltherrschaft in Deutschland 1933–1945, Bd. I–IV* [*Remembrance Book: Victims of the Persecution of the Jews during the National Socialist Tyranny in Germany 1933–1945, Vol. I–IV*] published by the Bundesarchiv in 2006 and available online, and the *Yad Vashem-Datenbank* [*Yad Vashem Database*], likewise available online. The second category contains six sources, on both non-Jewish and Jewish victims: *Berliner Adressbücher* [*Berlin Address Books*],

Bundesarchiv [*Federal Archive*], *Brandenburgisches Landeshauptarchiv* [*Brandenburg Central State Archive*], *Landesamt für Bürger- und Ordnungsangelegenheiten Berlin* [*The State Office for Residents' and Regulatory Affairs in Berlin*], *Landesarchiv Berlin* [*Archives of the Land Berlin*] and *Internationale Suchdienst (ITS)* [*International Tracing Service (ITS)*] in Bad Arolsen.

Sometimes the information on the victims is very scarce, as for instance in the case of Johanna Berg, about whom practically nothing is known. For a number of others, however, much information is provided, not least due to several sources, as in the case of Emil Louis Liepmannssohn – the Berlin Stolpersteine homepage even displays a copy of Liepmannssohn's driver's licence.

Despite the fact that the Stolpersteine declare to be for all victims, in 2008 Professor Emeritus at University of Hamburg Monika Richarz, referred to above, wrote that 'the vast majority of stones are dedicated to murdered Jews [...]' (2008: 327). A look at the home page for the Berlin Stolpersteine confirms Richarz's analysis in that city. As of August 2017, 6,797 of Berlin's 7,283 Stolpersteine are for Jews or those of Jewish origin, which amounts to 93 per cent. Sponsors to Berlin Stolpersteine evidently have very specific demands and they seem to prefer Jewish victims, although, as one can read in the online Anne Frank Guide, just before the Olympic Games began in 1936, 'all the Roma and Sinti in and around Berlin were rounded up (about 600) and put into a concentration camp'. As of August 2017, only one single sponsorship for a Stolperstein in Berlin has been bought for these approximately 600 Roma and Sinti – or 0.7 per cent. This is the stone of Johann 'Rukeli' Trollmann, a boxer.

Against this background, it is interesting to remember that Demnig himself has criticized traditional monuments for being able only to 'commemorate the victims on a general level, and in addition, many of them are dedicated only to a particular group of victims', as he is quoted in Richarz's article (Demnig in Richarz 2008: 327). Nonetheless, some scholars continue to believe that the Stolpersteine are only for Jewish victims, thereby confusing the intention behind the Stolpersteine with the reality of sponsors' free choice and market forces; Sonja Georgi, for instance, examines 'the "stumbling stones" placed in front of houses formerly inhabited by

Jewish residents' (2011: 29), and while it remains perfectly true that the monuments really are installed in front of former Jewish homes, they are not exclusively installed here as Georgi seems to believe.

Richarz tries to explain in the following way why non-Jewish victims have not enjoyed the same attention as Jewish victims in the Stolpersteine project: 'This is not only because of the large number of Jewish victims in the big cities but it is also because of the particular commitment of institutions and individuals who are prepared to devote their time and energy as coordinators for the project' (Richarz 2008: 334). It is not unlikely that Richarz is right in arguing that since many Jews were deported from Berlin, it is only natural that attention on their fates receives more attention than others. Nonetheless, it appears less convincing that the *particular* commitment of institutions and individuals should automatically concern Jewish victims.

A similar tendency is found in Michal Imort, when he notes that of course 'Demnig knows that he cannot create individual Stumbling Blocks for every one of the six million Jewish victims across Europe, or even for the 55,000 deported from Berlin alone' (2010: 236). Imort sympathizes with this impossibility because it helps illustrate 'the unfathomable magnitude of the Holocaust' (2010: 236). As Demnig himself expressed in an interview, the project can only 'be a gesture' (2002: 13f. cf. Richarz 2008: 328). However, if this impossibility is underlined by the extent of the deportations and exterminations, why limit the mention to Jewish victims rather than extend it to victims, which is even the primary rationale of the Stolpersteine, in contrast to so many other monuments? This would have underlined Imort's own point further and, hence, brought forward what is unique about the Stolpersteine: they are for every individual victim in every country, city and village rather than for one particular group, in one particular country, in one particular city, at one particular place.

Instead of discussing the unique idea of victim inclusiveness of the Stolpersteine – the victim as such – the literature on the subject focuses mainly on Jewish victims, and mainly German–Jewish ones. While, of course, it is completely legitimate to analyse Stolpersteine for Jewish victims, it is surprising that scholars such as Richarz and Imort do not mention that the engravings on the Stolpersteine do not claim anything about the individual victim's religious, political, racial, or sexual belonging but, rather, identify each victim as a human being who had a name and a home. A more reasonable explanation for why sponsors of the Stolpersteine have chosen Jewish victims rather than others thus seems relevant, setting aside, of course, those cases where the sponsors are directly affiliated with the victim in question.

Jewish victims constitute the largest group of civil victims in Germany, and all in all the second largest in the Second World War. Between 160,000 and 180,000 out of 214,000 Jews in Germany proper (1937 borders) who had remained in Germany were exterminated (USHMM). But the most central reason for a larger focus on Jewish victimhood, following the example from Berlin, could be that for no group other than the Jews was anything like an *Endlösung* [Final Solution] planned. The Jews were exterminated because they were Jews, and although this could also be said concerning, for instance, communists and homosexuals, who were exterminated because of their political and sexual orientation, respectively, the extent of this did not lead to anything alike the *Endlösung*. The Jewish victims are simply paradigmatic of Third Reich extermination.

To these circumstances, one might add that the identity of a Jewish victim is, all things considered, still easier to establish than for other victims, due to well-structured Jewish communities, plus reasonable political and research environments that are lacking for other groups. In the research that leads to the installation of the Stolpersteine – performed by laymen and other non-professionals – easily accessible sources are all the more crucial. For, as mentioned, with the exception of situations in which sponsors of the Stolpersteine are related to or otherwise directly personally involved in the matter, the probability is considerable that the victim whose fate is easiest to research will draw more attention than for a victim whose fate is more difficult to establish.

Reflecting on the commemoration in Germany, examples of groups that do not have this kind of apparatus or enthusiasm behind them are not hard to find. Victims of the Euthanasia Programme, homosexuals and the Sinti and Roma, for instance, constitute such victims. It was not until 10 November 2011 that the German government decided to establish a *Gedenkort für die Opfer der NS Euthanasie Morde* [Memorial Site for the Victims of the National Socialist Euthanasia Programme]. As for the homosexuals, this particular group did not possess a recognized organization, its members were not well organized and they did their best to hide rather than be seen. The *Denkmal für die im Nationalsozialismus verfolgten Homosexuellen* [Memorial to the Homosexuals Persecuted under the National Socialist Regime] was not installed until 27 May 2008, inaugurated by Berlin's mayor, Klaus Wowereit. The Sinti and Roma culture does not have a conception of residence in the sense of dwelling and living in a house or in an apartment, so official records are much harder to trace (if they exist at all) and their citizenship is even harder to establish. The *Denkmal für die im Nationalsozialismus ermordeten Sinti und Roma Europas* [Memorial to the Sinti and Roma Victims of National Socialism] was not installed until 24 October 2012, inaugurated by Kanzler Angela Merkel and Bundespräsident Joachim Gauck (Knittel 2010). For the Stolpersteine project, these circumstances regarding the Sinti and Roma are all the more crucial, because the precondition for the Stolpersteine is *who* the particular victim was and *where* he or she lived.

What has been made clear by the Stolpersteine is the refutation of group identification concerning the individual victim: 'one human being – one stone – one fate' is the principle of commemoration (Demnig 2015: 3). But why, then, for instance, does the homepage for the Berlin Stolpersteine identify the victims by the group to which they belong? Why is there this possibility for selection? The fact of the matter is that, by avoiding group identification, the Stolpersteine have also avoided the critique saying that, despite that they are meant to be an all-inclusive monument, they are *de facto* a monument for Jewish victims, as Richarz describes above. Such critique would only be applicable if one were to accept the principle of group identification, which is precisely to what the Stolpersteine object.

At least two consequences can be drawn from these circumstances: first, that in contrast to many other, more traditional, monuments the Stolpersteine testify to a gap between principles of installation and actual installation or, in other words, between all victims and the individual victim getting a monument. Secondly, since the maker of the Stolpersteine does not decide on the actual installation, any kind of statistics or preference for some victims says not only something about access to and availability of information, but even points to a fundamental problem concerning the decision on who gets a stone.

Ulrike Schrader underlines this problem in the following way: 'It must be regulated who assigns the names of the victim for the respective sponsors. The Düsseldorfer example shows that this procedure can overstep the limits of piety: here, sponsors could "select a victim" who, according to victim group, age and gender is assortedly [*sortiert*] "offered" for sale' (Schrader 2006: 178). Schrader is certainly right in her 'discrete' hint that this kind of *Sortierung* is indeed reminiscent of what happened to the victims – however, to Schrader at least, perhaps not in the most appropriate fashion. The result could very well be, Schrader explains, that neither do principles exist concerning who *in particular* will obtain a Stolperstein nor who is in charge of making this decision: 'The naming memory' [*Das namentliche Gedenken*], Schrader writes, 'leads to an over-identification with one victim to the exclusion of all others [...]' (2006: 178). Principles of decision seem at best left to the desire and will of a buyers' market. It appears to be an open question whether this is a problem that relates specifically to the Stolpersteine and their idea of commemoration as such or, in the end, to those who sponsor the monument. It is not easy to determine how far the circumstances of market forces and preferences are actually part of the Stolpersteine and their form of commemoration, and who in the end is the carrier of such responsibility.

Petra T. Fritsche in her 2014 book *Stolpersteine – Das Gedächtnis einer Straße* [*Stumbling Stones – The Memory of a Street*] tries to meet Schrader's objections in the article mentioned above and discusses the critique of the *Paten* [sponsorships] and 'what or who constitutes a "victim"' (Fritsche 2014: 322). However, Fritsche fails to deal with Schrader's fundamental point, which, in the end, is less about the problems in identifying each and every single victim and more about the whole process of *selection* to which the Düssseldorfer example so brutally testified. Fritsche, whose book opens with a foreword by the artist Demnig himself, does not mention the Düssseldorfer case although it is at the core of Schrader's article. Instead, Fritsche makes it clear that the person having better 'artistic ideas', quoting Jacqueline Aslan from the Amadeu Antonio-Stiftung, should realize these and 'not point the finger at Demnig' (Fritsche 2014: 324).

Even though the Stolperstein monument's idea of commemorating victims *qua* victims and not as Jews, communists, homosexuals, Sinti and

Roma, or as any other overall category, the current state of affairs shows just how difficult this really is in practice. The best intentions to create knowledge about, and monuments for, the individual victim may very well happen at the cost of some other victim. However, is it not always the case that the preference for and selection of something specific always already logically implies that something else *ipso facto* has not been chosen? The Italian historian Enzo Traverso explains that these circumstances are not unknown. Rather, they actually define the memory practice: 'in the realms of the past – real or invented – where ritualized practises are constructed, it tends to strengthen the cohesion of a group or of a society, that is, to legitimize some institutions and include some values within society' (Traverso 2004: 9). To Traverso, this is what constitutes 'the political use of the past' (2004: 10). However, it is not impossible to argue that precisely by pushing forward such considerations and dilemmas the Stolpersteine are actually doing what they were intended to do: to make us stumble upon Auschwitz.

The Five Fates

According to the Stolpersteine homepage, the engraved text on the brass plate covering the Stolperstein is formatted to show the following five points:

1) A STOLPERSTEIN carries most often the heading: HERE LIVED [*HIER WOHNTE*]. Further possibilities are: HERE LEARNED or HERE TAUGHT; HERE WORKED; HERE PRACTISED (for instance, regarding physicians), and HERE RESIDED [*HIER LEBTE*] (for instance, regarding institutional care). Stones without any heading are also possible. The following facts [*Daten*] must be researched for *the inscription*:
2) Name, surname (if relevant, also maiden name)
3) Year of birth
4) Year of deportation and location
5) Descriptions [*Angaben*] of fate. [numerals added] (Demnig 2015: 4)

The first four points do not pose any considerable problems, as they simply concern the victim's name, address and deportation details. Point 5, the description of fate, is the most interesting. This point is more directly connected with what happened to the victim in question, and thus concerns the historical foundation for the person whose name and dwelling are being commemorated, that is, individual victimhood in the era of the Third Reich. Point 5, therefore, must be considered as core in the Stolperstein monument.

The homepage explains the following five fates that can be selected:

> Possible descriptions of fate are: DEAD [*TOT*] or MURDERED [*ERMORDET*]; for unclear cases: FATE UNKNOWN. Instead of suicide we write ESCAPED IN DEATH [*FLUCHT IN DEN TOD*]. We do not use the concept 'missing' [*verschollen*], and just as rare is the concept 'death' [*Tod*] since this suggests a natural death. Equally rare is the use of the concept 'Emigration' or 'left the country' [*Auswanderung*]. Instead, we write ESCAPED [*FLUCHT*] + YEAR + TARGET COUNTRY. (Demnig 2015: 4)

The sponsor of a Stolperstein decides on the complete wording of the stone in question though a limitation in the sponsorship is specified: 'Gunter Demnig reserves the ultimate right to decide on the formulation of the inscriptions' (Demnig 2015: 4).

In the following, seven Stolpersteine have been selected in order to discuss these different fates in detail. The first Stolperstein is the famous stone of the German philosopher Edith Stein, assistant to Edmund Husserl (in his turn likewise famous for his gifted apprentice, Martin Heidegger). Stein's stone is installed in Freiburg and once also appeared on the Stolpersteine homepage:

HIER WOHNTE
DR. EDITH STEIN
JG. 1891
FLUCHT 1938/HOLLAND
LAGER WESTBROCK 1942
ERMORDET 1942 IN
AUSCHWITZ

[HERE LIVED
DR. EDITH STEIN
BORN 1891

ESCAPED 1938/HOLLAND
CAMP WESTBROCK 1942
MURDERED 1942 IN
AUSCHWITZ]

The second Stolperstein is Anne Frank's, placed in Aachen's Pastorplatz. Frank was a young girl who became famous for her posthumously published Dutch-language *Diary of a Young Girl* (1947):

HIER WOHNTE
ANNE FRANK
JG. 1929
FLUCHT 1934 HOLLAND
INTERNIERT WESTERBORK
DEPORTIERT 1944
BERGEN-BELSEN
ERMORDET MÄRZ 1945

[HERE LIVED
ANNE FRANK
BORN 1929
ESCAPED 1934 HOLLAND
INTERNED WESTERBORK
DEPORTED 1944
BERGEN-BELSEN
MURDERED MARCH 1945]

The third Stolperstein of interest is Max Bloch's on Freiburg's Reichsgrafenstraße 16:

HIER WOHNTE
MAX BLOCH
JAHRGANG 1894
FLUCHT SCHWEIZ/FRANKREICH
NIZZA
MISSHANDELT GESTAPO
TOT 14.12.1943

[HERE LIVED
MAX BLOCH

BORN 1894
ESCAPED SWITZERLAND/FRANCE
NIZZA
MALTREATED GESTAPO
DEAD 14.12.1943]

The fourth Stolperstein is Hans Pollack's on Berlin's Aachener Straße 27:

HIER WOHNTE
HANS POLLACK
JG. 1890
VERSTECKT GELEBT
VERHAFTET
FLUCHT IN DEN TOD
27.9.1943 IM
POLIZEIGEFÄNGNIS
DRESDEN

[HERE LIVED
HANS POLLACK
BORN 1890
LIVED IN HIDING
ARRESTED
ESCAPED IN DEATH
27.9.1943 IN
POLICE CUSTODY
DRESDEN]

The fifth Stolperstein is Max Pander's, installed on Bochum's Bongardstraße:

HIER WOHNTE
MAX PANDER
JG. 1891
DEPORTIERT
AUSCHWITZ
???

[HERE LIVED
MAX PANDER

BORN 1891
DEPORTED
AUSCHWITZ
???]

The sixth Stolperstein is Bertha Oppenheimer's on Schulgasse 3 in Schriesheim:

HIER WOHNTE
BERTHA OPPENHEIMER
GEB. KARLSBERG
JG. 1869
UNFREIWILLIG VERZOGEN
1938 DARMSTADT
FLUCHT 1939
USA
ÜBERLEBT

[HERE LIVED
BERTHA OPPENHEIMER
MAIDEN NAME KARLSBERG
BORN 1869
INVOLUNTARY REMOVAL
1938 DARMSTADT
ESCAPED 1939
USA
SURVIVED]

The five points mentioned above do not, as can be seen, represent a complete list of contents from which a prospective sponsor of a Stolperstein must select; yet they do contain the most necessary pieces of information. For instance, to add that Oppenheimer survived is not mandatory, but is something the sponsor of the stone wished, just as with the addition that Pollack lived in hiding. The seventh and last stone relevant to the coming analysis represents one of the most unusual examples of additional self-chosen information – even breaking with what is, perhaps, the most mandatory point of specifying, that is, *hier wohnte* [here lived]. The Stolperstein is Johann 'Rukeli' Trollmann's in Berlin, which was briefly mentioned above. His stone reads:

HIER BOXTE
JOHANN 'RUKELI'
TROLLMANN
JG. 1907
1933 DEUTSCHER MEISTER
HALBSCHWERGEWICHT
1942 KZ NEUENGAMME
ERSCHLAGEN 1944
KZ WITTENBERGE

[HERE BOXED
JOHANN 'RUKELI'
TROLLMANN
BORN 1907
1933 GERMAN CHAMPION
LIGHT HEAVYWEIGHT
1942 KZ NEUENGAMME
KILLED 1944
KZ WITTENBERGE]

The purpose for the rest of this chapter is to begin the discussion that even though all victims of the National Socialist government were deported and in most cases annihilated in one way or the other (shot, gassed, beaten to death, left to starve, left to die of illness, etc.), in the engravings the Stolpersteine provides an individualized and differentiated description of each victim's fate. Relevant questions are whether such a strategy of differentiation makes sense at all – despite its laudable and, indeed, appealing idea. To what extent is the individualized commemoration, as found in each Stolperstein, able to live up to the task of commemorating victims of the Third Reich, that is, to represent the memory of the victims' humanity while not forgetting the history of Auschwitz and the extreme inhumanity to which the victims were reduced?

Even though both Stein's and Frank's annihilation, what the Stolpersteine call 'fate', is rendered with the same term *ermordet* [murdered], some differences exist on which it is relevant to reflect. Although one could argue that Stein's death was different from Frank's, because the latter died of typhoid fever, such a line of argument nonetheless evokes a certain unease. First, typhoid fever was a disease that could be cured with a fairly simple vaccine, invented in 1930 by the Polish biologist Rudolf Weigl. Nonetheless, Frank was left to die. Might it not seem more reasonable to argue that although Frank was not gassed, she was annihilated, no less than Stein? Following this brutal logic, it is not unlikely that such reasoning lay behind the idea of leaving typhoid fever and other diseases untreated in Frank's camp, Bergen-Belsen, and in many other camps as well. The annihilation of Stein and Frank was in both cases a direct consequence of Third Reich politics. Any difference in method – gas or disease – seems irrelevant and beside the point. By describing the fates of Stein and Frank with the same term (murdered [*ermordet*]), in these two cases the Stolpersteine represent such a line of argument.

On other occasions, the logic in the inscriptions appears less consistent. One could ask, for instance, why Bloch's fate is described by the term 'dead' [*tot*]. Marlis Meckel writes in her 2006 book, the *Stolpersteine in Freiburg*, that Bloch was severely tortured: 'Among other things, during interrogation, both of his eyes were put out. On 14 December 1943, he died at the age of forty-nine in Nizza as a consequence of these assaults' (Meckel 2006: 210). In this example, in what does the difference, on the premises of the Stolpersteine, between *tot* [dead] and *ermordet* [murdered] actually consist? If the direct annihilation of Stein, in comparison with the more indirect one of Frank, is described by the same term *ermordet* [murdered], would it not then – again on the premises of the Stolpersteine, at least – have made more sense also to describe Bloch's fate as *ermordet* [murdered] since he was tortured to death? Or, on the other hand, to have described Frank's fate as dead [*tot*]?

Turning to Pollack's Stolperstein, a closer look reveals that it tries to address the difficult task of how to describe the fate of those victims who killed themselves. Can these victims be said to be victims of annihilation proper or do they, as the exception proving the rule, testify to at least one fate that somehow managed to escape the horrors of the Third Reich? Pollack's suicide is rendered by the euphemism 'escaped in death' [*Flucht in den Tod*]. But is it unfortunate in the same sense as in the case of Bloch? It does seem hard to argue, however, that the possibility of suicide really existed for these victims. Rather, victims such as Pollack had been deprived of such an option. Whatever the specific reason was for the fifty-three-year-old man to choose to end his life, one must admit that, all things considered, this was likely to be more closely linked to the life conditions forced upon him by the Third Reich and a specific government than would normally be the case with a suicide; especially considering that at the time he killed himself he was being kept in a Dresden detention cell. Nonetheless, in contrast to Stein, Frank and Bloch, Pollack did die by his own hand. It is not at all impossible, therefore, that the Stolpersteine, via such an inscription, try to symbolize the fate of a victim who took control over his own death – and therefore life – by avoiding the use of the term suicide in favour of escaped in death. More than Pollack's killing himself, which can be regarded as a case of proper suicide, it was, rather, an escape.

It is important to note that the description of Pollack's fate, in contrast to Stein's, Frank's and Bloch's, is rendered neither in juridical nor ethical terms but, instead, in quite poetical terms. Furthermore, the horror of the circumstances under which Pollack spent his last days is expressed to the full by the euphemism that he 'preferred death over life'. In any case, answering the question of who actually killed Pollack is not easy. Although the Third Reich had indeed deprived the victims of a proper life and death, one of the few things of which it could not deprive the victims was the moment in which they chose to kill themselves. If anything, this expresses the horror of the Third Reich: the victim's last attempt to grasp for humanity is constituted by the moment in which the victim makes the ultimate decision and commits suicide.

When it comes to the fates of Oppenheimer and Pander, the Stolpersteine have chosen a vocabulary from a different sphere: 'Fate unknown' (displayed with three question marks (???)) and 'Escaped' (instead of emigration). The explanation – which is only partial – seems: 'Just as rare is our use of the concept "Emigration" or "left the country" [*Auswanderung*]. Instead we write ESCAPED [*FLUCHT*] + YEAR + TARGET COUNTRY' (Demnig 2015: 4). Since it is known that Oppenheimer survived in the USA, no problems really exist regarding the description of her fate. The logic behind Pander's fate is likewise rather straightforward: what happened to Pander is unknown, hence the engraving of three question marks on his Stolperstein. However, to a certain extent one could also describe the '???' as a poetical formulation, similar to 'escaped in death';

because, in this way, the Stolpersteine once again provoke reflection about what actually happened to Pander. Like the Unknown Soldier, for the Stolpersteine the victim whose fate is unknown becomes the strange hero in the commemorative act.

German contemporary law speaks of someone as *Verschollen* [missing]. A rather surprising circumstance is that the law on *Verschollenheit* goes back to the National Socialist government, which passed a decree on the matter in 1939: *Gesetz über die Verschollenheit, die Todeserklärung und die Feststellung der Todeszeit* [Law on Absence, Declaration of Death and the Establishment of the Time of Death]:

(1) 'Missing' corresponds to a person whose abode [*Aufenthalt*] has been unknown for a long period of time, with no news indicating whether the person is alive or dead, such that, under the circumstances, real doubt concerning the person's survival can be established [*begründet werden*].
(2) 'Missing' does not correspond to a person whose death under the circumstances is not questionable'. (RGBL, 4 July 1939, Teil I, 1186, cit. in ALEX)

The Stolpersteine project's unwillingness to use the exact juridical category of missing persons ('We do not use the concept "missing" [*verschollen*]' (Demnig 2015: 4)), appear to carry perhaps, too strong an association. The Stolpersteine project seems intentionally to distance itself from any kind of affiliation with Third Reich vocabulary. Most importantly, the Stolpersteine distance themselves from any reference to a state of normality – even though the law on missing persons seems quite harmless, even reasonable, thus featuring in contemporary German law. The Stolpersteine project asserts that 'missing' does not indicate that a person's disappearance is the direct result of government actions, something that is naturally a crucial fact in this matter. Nonetheless, on 17 November 2003 Demnig installed Stolpersteine for Edith Frank and Emma Anker in Neuruppin. The engravings state that the victims were 'missing'.

Reflecting the Solpersteine's insistence on disassociating themselves from any reference to a state of normality and of law, Trollmann's stone also testifies simply to his fate as *erschlagen* [killed]. So, when the Stolpersteine refrain from the use of juridical terminology and instead make use of poetical formulations such as 'escaped in death' and '???', it appears that they are doing their best to avoid any vocabulary suggestive of normality (albeit not always with success, and not always consistently). The purpose of the next chapter is therefore to discuss the term *ermordet* [murder]. Does this particular juridical term not presuppose that which on other accounts and other stones precisely has been stated to not exist – that is, some kind of normality – and what justifies the use of non-juridical, poetical formulations? However, before embarking on this discussion, it is necessary to mention a few other central aspects regarding the Stolpersteine.

Although the Stolpersteine insist on a high level of differentiation, some differences are left unmentioned on the monuments. Stein and Frank were annihilated because they were Jews, and for no other reason. They had committed no crime and were found guilty of nothing, certainly in no court of law. In contrast to other German memorials, information about these victims is not provided. For instance, contrary to the Memorial to the Murdered Jews of Europe, Memorial Site for the Victims of the National Socialist Euthanasia Programme, Memorial to the Homosexuals Persecuted under the National Socialist Regime and Memorial to the Sinti and Roma Victims of National Socialism, which all clearly state and specify who the victims were by placing them in a group, information on who the individual victim was is unrevealed to the pedestrian stumbling upon the Stolpersteine. The monuments contain no trace of whether the victim was Jewish, a victim of euthanasia, a homosexual, a Sinti and Roma, etc. Thus, the general picture remains the same: readers of the Stolperstein engravings are given an aphoristic biographical tale containing the victim's name, age and fate but not the reason the Third Reich annihilated him or her. What could the reason be for the Stolpersteine not mentioning religious, national, sexual, or any other form of belonging? After all, the reasons the victims were exterminated were to do with *who* they were in terms of group belonging, not because of *what* they had done.

The commemorative principle behind the Stolpersteine is, as pointed out above, 'one human being – one stone – one fate' (Demnig 2015: 3). This is an idea of commemoration that places the gigantic Third Reich mass exterminations on the level of the individual victim's catastrophe, where what unites the victims is name and dwelling rather than anything else. However, this strategy of distinction and differentiation does run the risk of separating what, the first time around, was said should not be separated – the victims. Because, contrary to former and more traditional monuments, the separation does not happen in terms of group belonging but involves instead differentiation in terms of annihilation and extermination as such, via the wish to individualize the different fates of different victims, that is, some were murdered, others escaped in death, etc.

It is possible to argue that the Stolpersteine represent a dilemma: the heading *hier wohnte* [here lived] and, in particular, the name of each individual victim, is what indeed succeeds in commemorating the humanity of the victims. Nonetheless, the fifth point (the indication of fate) just as quickly redistributes the victim in a Hell of different deaths. Even though is it clear that no one but you carries your name and your dwelling, the Stolpersteine insist that a fundamental distinction can be made between extermination and annihilation following poetical, ethical and juridical conceptualizations. Not only is it difficult to determine the success of such a differentiation based on the principles presented by the Stolpersteine project and Demnig (this was Schrader's point, mentioned above), something to which the difference in fate between, for instance, Stein and Bloch testifies. The question is also whether it makes any sense to claim the existence of such a differentiation in terms of extermination. Do the Stolpersteine succeed in the task of being a monument for victims of the Third Reich when they maintain that some were 'more' annihilated than others, some 'less'? Some were 'murdered', while others 'escaped in death'? And, just as strange, is it really a proper presentation of individuality to state that a victim was murdered when three others, and in the end millions, were also murdered following the logic of the Stolpersteine? The five fates appear to contain an unnecessary qualitative difference, which once more redistributes the quantity of victims in terms of a hierarchy of death.

The challenge of the Stolpersteine seems clear: they are confronted with the difficult task of commemorating the victim's humanity, which hopefully nobody questions, while at the same time referring to the inhumanity – paradigmatically represented by Auschwitz – under which the victim was annihilated, one way or the other. Since the inscription on the Stolperstein is also a *description* of the victim's fate (Demnig speaks of *Daten* [facts] (2015: 4)) this is somehow meant to produce a statement that can answer to what happened to a particular victim, now being commemorated. This historical referentiality is not only reasonable, as the victims were historical beings who once existed. Via the monument's repeated statements of historical facts, such as date of birth, and by specifying when the victim was annihilated, the Stolpersteine *causa sui* must also be held responsible for such historical proclamations. The *primus motor* in the Stolpersteine is to insist and underline that the Third Reich exterminations are a historical fact that involved real human beings who had a name, lived in a home and were annihilated, and that these facts are commemorated correspondingly.

The inscription on the Stolperstein therefore carries a double task, one ethical and the other historical. The former concerns the victim's humanity, the latter inhumanity to which the victim was reduced. As long as the Stolpersteine state *hier wohnte* [here lived] along with the name of the victim, the former part is fulfilled. The challenge does not concern its ethical or humanitarian insistence or quality regarding the victims. The problem is to be found in the latter, and historical, part, that is, the description of the victim's fate. One might wonder whether the historical part of the Stolpersteine description is simply too vague and underestimates the horror that was committed? Could one not argue that something *far worse than murder* happened to Stein and Frank and all the other victims of National Socialism? Whether the event does not go far beyond being a mere illegal and immoral act?

Nonetheless, the framing of Third Reich exterminations and its victims in juridical and ethical vocabulary appears to be a quite common practice in both public and popular jargon, as well as in scholarly literature in the field, and it can also be found in monuments with, probably, the Memorial to the Murdered Jews of Europe in Berlin as its best-known example. However, colloquial language or actual usage of terms does not in itself provide sufficient reason or precision for such usage. It is not impossible that this kind of framing could run the risk of underestimating the event and, perhaps, even to misrepresent and misjudge its nature, and the victim as well. If this is the case, it is not guaranteed that a monument such as the Stolpersteine, which in its nature wishes to commemorate, and therefore honour, the victims of the Third Reich, will succeed in the proclaimed goal to base that commemoration upon history – despite its unquestionably good intentions.

CHAPTER 2

The Muselmann, or Eliminating Subjectivity

Sacer esto

The purpose of this chapter is to discuss the potential problem underlying the fact that the Stolpersteine describe the victim they commemorate in juridical and ethical conceptualizations. The present chapter will first present a discussion of the form of victimhood in the Third Reich and then, in the last section, discuss it in relation to the Stolpersteine, so that it may be possible to analyse further the connection between history and memory in these monuments.

In his 1995 *Homo sacer*, Agamben describes a strange figure from Roman law: the *homo sacer* [sacred man]. In the third century BC, the Roman grammarian Festus describes this figure in his twenty-volume abridgement to the now lost work of another Roman grammarian: Flaccus' *On the Meaning of Words*:

> The sacred man [*homo sacer*] is he whom the people have convicted for a felony [*maleficium*]; and it is not licit to sacrifice [*immolari*] him, yet he who kills him [*occidit*] will not be condemned for homicide [*parricidi non damnatur*]. In fact, in the first tribunitian law it is noted that 'if someone kills he who is sacred according to the plebiscite, it will not be considered as a homicide'. This is why a bad [*malus*] or impure [*improbus*] man is usually called sacred. (Festus in Agamben 2005a: 79)

The killing of a *homo sacer* did not constitute homicide, and the act itself was even withdrawn from the realms of religion, leaving him beyond both *ius humanum* and *ius divinum*, beyond profane and sacred law: 'This violence, that is, the unsanctionable killing that, in his case, anyone may commit', Agamben explains, 'is not classifiable as sacrifice, as homicide, as the execution of death penalty, or as a sacrilege' (2005a: 91f.).

The previous chapter in the present book concluded that the description on the Stolperstein, as a rule, stated that the victim in question was murdered [*ermordet*]. If, then, it can be shown that the victim of the NS era constitutes a modern case of *homo sacer*, it would appear that at least regarding the historical aspects of such commemoration the Stolpersteine do not reflect a conception of history in the sense of *wie es gewesen* [how it really was] but as something else, which consequently is in need of explanation.

It is important to reflect a little on the Latin terminology in the quotation above, attention to which Agamben insists. It is made explicit by Festus that killing [*occidit*] does not imply murdering [*parricidi*]. Lewis and Short note in their lexicon that *parricidi* is neuter genitive case, meaning 'the murder of a free citizen' (1879: II. Transf., B). It would, naturally, make no sense to say that a murder was not a murder – which would be a *contradictio in terminis* – whereas it makes perfect sense to say that killing is not necessarily a murder. Modern examples will be familiar to a contemporary reader, as in the cases of soldiers at war, abortion, euthanasia, car accidents, or even in cases where the police shoot civilians. These are all instances where, if certain criteria are fulfilled, killing is not murdering. At the same time, it is clear that these examples are all highly disputed, as are the different criteria, which is why they perhaps are not so clear after all.

A sacred man, Agamben explains, is abandoned through the sacrament of language: *sacer esto* [be sacred]. This *sacer esto* is the formulation of a 'political malediction' (Agamben 2008: 52), a curse that collapses the difference between fact and law, legality and illegality, within the law and outside the law, permitting the killing of a citizen without it constituting murder, and without his death being inscribed in any kind of rituality. *Sacer esto*, which leads to the establishment of the *homo sacer*, Agamben writes, 'is not a formula of religious malediction, which sanctions an *unheimlich* character, that is, both the august as well as vile character of something: the formula is instead the original political formulation of the imposition of the sovereign bond' (2005a: 94f.). '*Sovereign is the sphere*', Agamben stresses, '*in which one can kill without committing homicide and without celebrating a sacrifice, and sacred life – that is, life that can be killed, but not sacrificed – is the life that has been caught in this sphere*' (2005a: 92).

In any case, it is true that in the Third Reich, being Jewish was suddenly something more than biological heredity or belonging to a religious community; it could also simply be proclaimed, as in the 1935 *Law on Reich Citizenship*: a *Mischling* [Jewish half-caste] was a full Jew if born after either 15 September 1935 (if his parents were married) or after 13 July 1936 (if they were not married). Jewish-ness was not simply and not only something one *was*. Just as the *homo sacer* was produced as sacred in the linguistic sacrament of the utterance *sacer esto*, one could literally be proclaimed to be a Jew – and, in fact, also a communist or a political opponent, etc.

From the German writer and philosopher Walter Benjamin and his concept of *das bloße Leben* [bare life] from his 1921 *Critique of Violence*, Agamben develops the idea of a secularized version of *homo sacer*: naked life [*nuda vita*] (Agamben 2005a: 74.f.):

> What is caught in the sovereign ban is a human life that can be killed, but not sacrificed: the *homo sacer*. If we give the name naked life or sacred life to the life that constitutes the first content of sovereign power, we are also predisposed to a principled answer to the Benjaminian question concerning 'the origin of the dogma of the sacredness of life'. Sacred – that is, life which can be killed but not sacrificed – is originally the life which is caught in the sovereign ban and the production of naked life is, in this sense, the originary performance of sovereignty. (Agamben 2005a: 92f.)

The term 'naked life' then is a gloss on Festus' *homo sacer*. Nonetheless, its explanatory force and method are by way of a poetic metaphor, although Agamben insists, nonetheless, that it functions as a technical term. By a similar use of a poetical, or at least metaphorical, formulation it could be said that naked life is that of the human being who has been stripped of juridical clothes and left naked. Naked life becomes Agamben's 'translation' or modern comment (gloss) on Festus' *homo sacer*.

When Agamben writes that the 'meaning of the term *sacred* in our culture continues the semantic history of *homo sacer* and not that of the sacrifice' (2005a: 126), he means that the term does not concern the isolated spheres of rituality or religion, but rather a mixture where together they constitute the political. In other words, the term *homo sacer* designates a human being caught in the sovereign bond, like the bond in which, for instance, God held Job. Sacred, as in this example, does not point in the direction of religiousness (it is not, as Agamben wrote, something *unheimlich*) but, instead, to the absoluteness and the totalitarian aspect of power. This kind of metaphorical tension in Agamben's concept of naked life has, nonetheless, a significant conceptual content, and is seen when he reflects on the meaning of the ban (cf. the Latin *bannire*), that is, in ultimate analysis, of banning a person from law: 'The life of the bandit', Agamben echoes the English seventeenth-century political philosopher Thomas Hobbes and his comparisons between cities and gods, men and wolves, 'like the one of the sacred man, is not a piece of animal nature without any relation to the law and the city; it is rather a threshold of indifference and of passage between animal and man, *physis* and *nómos*, exclusion and inclusion: *loup garou*, the werewolf precisely. *Neither man nor wolf* paradoxically living between the two worlds without belonging to either' (2005a: 117).

Agamben establishes a link between myth and reality: the myths of the werewolves become the myths of the Jews, both with real juridical content. The zones between cities and forests where the werewolves resided become the ghettos and camps where the Jews resided. As the *homini sacri* [sacred men], those who the Third Reich exterminated in the camp were not permitted to enter the ritual sphere of burial, but were simply disposed of, dumped as human waste; their deaths did not constitute either murder or homicide. The Third Reich did not convict the detainees of any felony – rather, it institutionalized the deprivation of such a right into extermination.

It is worth mentioning that Festus defined the *homo sacer* as one who is directly sentenced by the people [*populus iudicavit*]. A sort of criticism of democracy is therefore inherent in Agamben's development of the term naked life – not least when considering the fact that Hitler was appointed Kanzler by Reichspräsident Hindenburg according to the constitution of the democratic Weimar Republic. With the centrality of *Volk* [people] in the Third Reich, Agamben likewise, although indirectly and discretely, indicates a link to Festus' democratic principle.

In the corpus of witness literature that Agamben examines in his book on perhaps the most notorious camp, Auschwitz, the 1998 *Remnants of Auschwitz*, he underlines the way in which the Muselmann is described. The term Muselmänner refers to those victims in the Third Reich camps who were so physically and psychologically destroyed that they appeared to have left the sphere and world of the living and to have lost the capacity to care for anything, whether themselves or others. The Muselmänner feel neither joy nor sorrow, neither shame nor regret: they simply are. The French author Jean Améry calls the Muselmänner 'walking corpses'; the Italian painter Aldo Carpi, as 'living dead'; finally, one of the most famous Auschwitz survivors and writers of witness literature, Primo Levi, writes that 'one hesitates to call them living' (cit. in Agamben 1998: 49). 'They live', Agamben concludes, '"on the limit between life and death", like the title says on the work that Ryn and Kłodziński have devoted to the Muselmann still today the only monograph on the subject' (1998: 50).

Agamben refers to Ryn and Kłodziński's 1994 *An der Grenze zwischen Leben und Tod. Eine Studie über die Erscheinung des 'Muselmanns' im Konzentrationslager* [*On the Limit Between Life and Death: a Study on the Appearance of the 'Muselmann' in the Concentration Camp*]. Agamben's claim that there does not seem to be any interest in asking such questions as Ryn's and Kłodziński's – and, hence, Agamben's own – is to some extent proven by the 2010 *Concentration Camps in Germany* containing no trace of these questions, despite the fact that this 'collection of essays offers the first overview in English of recent scholarly research – the "new histories" – on the Nazi concentration camps'; and that, secondly, Falk Pingel's essay is meant to deal with the inmates' life' (Caplan and Wachsmann 2010: 1; 7. Cf. 58–60).

In a 1964 interview on German television, Hannah Arendt said that what was so terrifying about the exterminations was not the killing itself, but the way in which it was done: 'I mean the method, the fabrication of corpses [...]' (Arendt 1964c: 14). Agamben stresses Arendt's point even further; the horror of the method is found even before this 'fabrication of corpses' – in the production of naked life, or in Levi's terminology, of the Muselmann. The final stage of naked life, where life and death, even in relation to themselves, seem to have lost all value and meaning (Agamben 1998: 75f.). Although it is true that governments have killed people for centuries in more or less the same way as the Third Reich did in the eastern parts of Europe in trying to create their *Lebensraum* [living space], the Third Reich is the only form of government that constructed facilities for the sole purpose of disposing of and ultimately exterminating, via a process of total dehumanization and delegalization, those they did not want in their Reich.

What makes Auschwitz unique in the history of humanitarian catastrophes is the extent of such fabrication and systematization of turning those who were exterminated into naked life, a zone between human and non-human, before they were eliminated. The horror of the camp is not only that millions were exterminated, but in particular the state towards which the camp potentially moved all victims before they were eliminated. This is what together makes Auschwitz and the Muselmänner paradigms of the Third Reich. The goal was not simply to kill the detainees, pure and simple. They were detained, day after day, week after week, month after month, year after year. Life itself became part of the process of extermination. Nor were the detainees in the camp slaves, in the sense these are known from, for example, the United States during the nineteenth century or from antiquity, where Aristotle defines them as living tools. It was, Levi explains, as if his work was part of the detainee's own dehumanization (1989a: chapter VI). It was as if his death began every day before he really died. It was as if his life ended every day before it really did. Life and death became meaningless, because there was no actual difference between them. It was this zone that Agamben called the sovereign sphere (2005a: 92).

The Muselmänner were something completely new, and to Levi they are the backbone of the camp. In his *If This Is a Man*, Levi describes the Muselmänner as 'an anonymous mass, continuously renewed and always identical to non-men who march and labour in silence, the divine spark dead within them already too empty to really suffer' (1989a: 150). To produce as many Muselmänner as possible seems to Levi to be, if not the purpose of the camp, then at least so in reality and consequence. The gas chamber was simply the last step in the process of total dehumanization and delegalization in the final production of naked life. 'Death is, at this point, a mere epiphenomenon' (Agamben 1998: 80). It is therefore necessary, so it would seem, to have an even closer look at the Muselmann's form of life (or lack of such one), and see whether it is possible to establish a more precise analysis of him in trying to define Third Reich victimhood.

Auschwitz: Between Life and Death

The paradigm for Third Reich extermination is, without a doubt, the death and concentration camps. Throughout this chapter, and by emphasizing Agamben's interpretations from the *homo sacer* project, the main character in this event is the Muselmann. To what extent could this particular form of life be said to constitute the paradigm for commemoration of Third Reich victimhood to which the Stolpersteine are devoted? That is, how far do the five fates correspond with what is known of victimhood in the camp, paradigmatically represented by the Muselmann? The concerns here are not primarily historical, however. The inquiry does not intend to bring forward anything historically or factually new about the victims, or about what Agamben simply defines as the camp. The Third Reich's exterminations as an historical event have been, as Agamben writes, 'sufficiently clarified', and although further historical surveys may shed new light on the subject, 'the framework can as a whole be considered as accomplished' (1998: 7). The same cannot be said, Agamben continues, 'regarding the ethical and political signification of the extermination or even of the human comprehension of what happened, that is, in the end its actuality' (1998: 7). By following this line of thought, the scope of the coming discussion is to investigate the nature of the relation between history and commemoration, fact and construction, so that it may be clear how the Stolpersteine, to use Agamben's words, actualize the camp.

In his book *Bloodlands* (2010) as well as in lectures, Timothy Snyder has underlined that millions of civilians were exterminated outside the specific facilities of the death and concentration camps. In fact, the number of civilians exterminated by the SS *Einsatzgruppen* in the cities and countryside in Eastern Europe and the Soviet Union far exceeds the number exterminated in the camps. Adding an Agambian light to Snyder's historical investigations, it would thus seem that the countryside of Eastern Europe is no more or less a camp than Auschwitz. However, the reasons for Agamben, in his book on Auschwitz, making this particular camp (which was both a death camp and a concentration camp) into a paradigm, are not historical as such but rather based on Auschwitz constituting the most extreme '*conditio inhumana* ever given upon earth' (2005a: 185). Whatever the horrors of the Eastern European countryside were, it is as if these were somehow accumulated and concentrated in Auschwitz. When considering Auschwitz as a paradigm in such a philosophical manner, the intention is to focus less on the factual circumstances concerning this particular camp and more on the human–ethical aspects of this paradigm. In such consideration, the Muselmann constitutes a privileged track.

One group more than any other was subjected to the measures and decrees of the Third Reich, the Jews. In the NSDAP's *25-Point Programme*, presented in the early 1920s, the Jews are the only ones who must leave Germany. In *Mein Kampf*, Hitler's anti-Semitism is one of the few systematic strategies in evidence. Last, the Nuremberg Laws were likewise designed particularly to solve what the National Socialists called 'the Jewish problem'. This, of course, does not alter the fact that once a person became a detainee in the camp, the individual differences between Jews, homosexuals, communists and other detainees lost their relevance. Whatever the differences were between the different groups of victims, these were all cancelled once a detainee was in the NS-camp.

Looking closer at the terminology, to constitute the camp as a philosophical concept and technical term respects the referentiality of the Stolpersteine: they refer without distinction to both death camps and concentration camps, as well as to all other spaces and facilities in which civilians were exterminated. The Stolpersteine refer, again without distinction, to Jews, homosexuals, communists, etc. – in short, to whoever fell into the hands of the Third Reich; that is, the monuments refer to the *Opfer des Nationalsozialismus* [victims of National Socialism] (Demnig 2015: 3). In the pages to come, the central question therefore is to what extent the Muselmann's victimhood is compatible with the kind of victimhood the Stolpersteine are suggesting and commemorating. In other words, what is the relation between history and memory, between the victims of the camp, who according to Levi and Agamben were all potentially Muselmänner, and the victims the Stolpersteine commemorate?

In 1946 Victor Klemperer published his now classic book on *The Language of the Third Reich*. Klemperer had written it while he lived, and even survived, in the Third Reich, thanks to NS-legislation that in fact protected him from being sent off to the camp because his wife, Eva, was 'Aryan'. In the book, the Romance philologist wrote of one of the clearest signs of National Socialism: *der Stern*, that is, the yellow Star of David, which all Jews were forced to wear on their clothing as a means of identification – governmentally as well as socially (Klemperer 1975: chapter XXV).

The policy was not new, though: already in the Middle Ages, Jews had on various occasions been forced to wear identification marks. However, the Third Reich had a range of classification systems developed to suit each category it considered 'un-German':

> The colors' and their [the triangles'] meaning were: *Red*, German political prisoner (generally communists); *Yellow*, Jew (actually a six pointed star produced by overlapping two triangles); *Violet*, Jehovah's Witness; *Blue*, Emigrant; *Green*, Common criminal; *Black*, Asocial; *Brown*, Gypsy; *Pink*, Homosexual. Within these categories, a number of special sub-categories also existed, further defining the prisoners. For example, Jewish criminals wore a six-pointed star that was half yellow and half green. The same was true for Jewish political detainees (in this case, yellow and red). (Edelheit and Edelheit 1994: 448)

The classification system for the Jews was the only one to be applied also outside the specific camp facilities, in towns and cities, in the countryside and in the urban areas (Edelheit and Edelheit 1994: 262f.). This was an effect of the decree of 1 September 1941: *Polizeiverordnung über die Kennzeichnung der Juden* [*Police Regulation Concerning the Marks of Jews*] (RGBL, 5 September 1941, 547, cit. in ALEX). The Third Reich had already issued similar decrees regarding Jews in occupied Poland, and this foreign policy could now be inferred domestically as well. In the eyes of the Third Reich, the Jews were simply among the most dangerous 'un-German' elements, and thus had to be marked so that they could always be identified.

Klemperer's thoughts on the star are clear: with the Star of David, he was no longer a citizen. He was a human being who had lost all humanity and dignity; not least because, Klemperer explains, 'every Star-Jew bore his ghetto with him like a snail his house' (1975: 180). The question, naturally, stands out: who – or worse, what – was Klemperer? What is this reduction, this stripping of humanity, which leaves him naked – ethically, humanly and legally?

In her 1951 *The Origins of Totalitarianism*, Hannah Arendt gives an accurate description of the kind of life one could find in the camp, dwelling on such a threshold between life and death, human and non-human. Arendt refers to David Rousset, himself a survivor of the Buchenwald camp, and to his 1947 *Les Jours de Notre Mort* [*The Days of our Death*] and writes:

> The real horror of the concentration and extermination camps lies in the fact that the inmates, even if they happen to keep alive, are more effectively cut off from the world of the living than if they had died, because terror enforces oblivion. Here, murder is as impersonal as the squashing of a gnat. Someone may die as the result of systematic torture or starvation, or because the camp is overcrowded and superfluous human material must be liquidated. Conversely, it may happen that due to a shortage of new human shipments the danger arises that the camps become depopulated and that the order is now given to reduce the death rate at any price. David Rousset called his report on the period in a German concentration camp 'Les Jours de Notre Mort', and it is indeed as if there were a possibility to give permanence to the process of dying itself and to enforce a condition in which both death and life are obstructed equally effectively. (Arendt 1962: 443)

Some ten years later, in 1961, Hilberg published his account of *The Destruction of the European Jews*. In his memoirs from 1992, the scholar reflects on some of the reasons for his terminological choices: 'My training in the social sciences took place in the 1940s. The methodological literature that I read emphasized objectivity and neutral or value-free words', Hilberg writes, and then concludes: 'To this end I banished accusatory terms such as "murder", as well as such exculpatory words as "executions", which made the victims into delinquents, or "extermination", which likened them to vermin' (Hilberg 1996: 87f.).

This description of human beings who have been politically transformed into a zone between life and non-life appears again in Burleigh and Whipperman's 1991 *The Racial State*, and it is interesting how the two authors describe what can best be called a process towards deportation: 'The Jews were discriminated against; their human rights were abrogated; they were physically isolated from the non-Jewish population, and totally eliminated from economic and professional life. It did not require much more bureaucratic ingenuity to summon, detain in collection points and finally deport, people who had no rights and virtually no money to call their own' (Burleigh and Whipperman 1991: 96).

Hilberg's motives, for refraining from terminology that would in his eyes liken the victims to vermin, seem appealing at first glance. Nonetheless, looking at camp footage and film, of mass graves or of swimming pools filled with victims, men and women of all ages, young and old, it makes one wonder if the Third Reich had not succeeded, after all and just as Hitler had announced, in eliminating these people 'as lice' (Hitler cit. in Agamben 2005a: 127). Hilberg, in other words, solved only part of the problem: in his analysis, he maintained the humanity of the victims, but at the cost of an objective description of what happened to them, which does seem, indeed, far from humanity. The Stolpersteine, as any such monument, must try to solve this challenge of commemorating humanity (the victims) while not forgetting the inhumanity under which they perished (Third Reich); it must somehow be able to represent both humanity and inhumanity in one and the same act of commemoration.

The Muselmann is derived from the Persian word *muselmân*, meaning a Muslim. *Encyclopaedia Judaica* defines this figure as

> death camp slang word for prisoners on the edge of death who have surrendered to their fate, that is, showing the symptoms of the last stages of hunger, disease, mental indifference and physical exhaustion. This term was mostly used at Auschwitz. It seems to have originated from the typical deportment of the sufferers, e.g., to squat with their legs tucked in an Oriental fashion, their faces masklike in stiffness. (Berenbaum and Skolnik 2007: vol. 14, 623)

The Encyclopaedia continues its 'aesthetic' definition of the Muselmann with a citation from Primo Levi, along with the passage from *If This Is a Man* that was quoted above:

> The musselmaner [*sic*], the drowned, form the backbone of the camp, an anonymous mass, continually renewed and always identical, of non-men who march to labor in silence, the divine spark dead within them, already too empty to suffer. One hesitates to call them living; one hesitates to call their death death, in the face of which they have no fear, they are too tired to understand ... If I could enclose all the evil of our time in one image, I would choose this image, which is familiar to me: An emancipated man with head dropped and shoulders curved, on which face and in whose eyes not a trace of thought is to be seen. (Berenbaum and Skolnik (eds) 2007: vol. 14, 623. Cf. Levi 1989a: 149f.)

'The ethics of Auschwitz', Agamben writes, 'begins precisely in the point in which the Muselmann, the 'integral witness', for ever had abandoned every possibility of distinguishing between man and no-man – also this is ironically contained in the rhetoric title *If This Is a Man*' (1998: 42). Ironically, Agamben explains the question posed in this title, that one awaits 'either an affirmation or a negation', something that never happens (1998: 52). The humanity of the Muselmann, to follow Agamben's reading of Levi, is neither affirmed nor disproved in the camp, but remains on the threshold between the two, that is, neither human nor non-human. How is one to characterize this threshold that these authors – from Arendt and Hilberg, Burleigh and Whipperman, to Levi and Agamben – seem to place the detainees of the camp? What is this suspension of humanity that defines Auschwitz, and what is the ethical nature of the Muselmann?

Se questo è un uomo [*If This Is a Man*]: *Se* [*if*] in Italian requires the imperfect subjunctive, and so one might have expected Levi's title to be *Se questo fosse un uomo*. However, this form is only used when the 'if' really is hypothetical or unknown – when it really is not the case, or when one wishes to express that the factuality of what is being stated is very doubtful. For instance: *se Copenhagen* fosse *la capitale dell'Italia, i danesi* sarebbero *felici* [If Copenhagen *were* the capital of Italy, the Danes *would be* thrilled. On the other hand, when the condition is less hypothetical, and expressing something about the future that is likely to take place, the indicative is used: *se* telefoni vengo *subito* [If you *call* me I *will* come at once].

Regarding Levi's book, it is important to remember that due to the *se* [if], the very core of Levi's title, the difference does not regard what is certain and what not. Rather, the difference instead concerns degrees of uncertainty and of the hypothetical or potential. It is precisely this rather complex, linguistic, poetical play that Levi here uses to express what in the end is at stake in the connection between camp and human being: not a difference between what is certain and what is not, that is, not between humanity and non-humanity, but rather a zone in which the fact of humanity is reduced to degrees of the hypothetical. Humanity, one could say in an Agambian tone, is neither affirmed nor negated, but suspended. To Levi, this is the fate of the Muselmann and the backbone of the camp.

In the history of philosophy such an idea of the hypothetical has been used at least once before. Thomas Hobbes, who was mentioned briefly above, also made use of such poetic play when he wrote about the state of nature in his 1642 *The Citizen*. It was in this connection that Hobbes in his foreword made use of an aphorism about the werewolf, in whose very name the hypotheticality indicated above is recognized – the 'were' in the name werewolf. Nine years later Hobbes would use the aphorism again, this time in his grand œuvre from 1651, *Leviathan*. The aphorism appears rather neglected in the history of philosophy and ideas, and only emerges, the Italian historian Carlo Ginzburg points out, much later in Sigmund Freud's writings. The psychoanalyst is reporting the dream of a young Russian about a werewolf, which is probably the reason why Freud labelled the dream as an *Urszene*, thus hinting to the world of myths (Ginzburg 2000: 239–51).

Hobbes's aphorism about the werewolf reads as follows: '[…] that *man to man is a kind of God*; and that *man to man is an arrant wolfe*. The first is true, if we compare citizens among themselves; and the second, if we compare cities' (Hobbes 1998: 89). Hobbes is, of course, not saying that during a state of nature men suddenly transform into Gods, or that cities take on the form of werewolves. Instead, Hobbes explains, this is the result of a situation where the city is to be considered *tanquam dissoluta*, that is, dissolved or, in other words, when the normality of the state of law is suspended. The cities then act as if they *were* werewolves, and men as if they *were* Gods. This is the reason why, Agamben writes in *State of Exception*, the state of exception 'must be considered as a mythologeme corresponding to the state of nature' (2004: 15). What occurs, Agamben wrote some years before, is 'a threshold of indifference and of passage between animal and man, *physis* and *nómos*, exclusion and inclusion: *loup garou*, the werewolf, neither man nor wolf who lives paradoxically between the two worlds without belonging to neither' (2005a: 117).

Levi pushes the Hobbesian paradigm to the extreme. What is at stake is the question of or, rather, the limit between, human and non-human, as witnessed personally by Levi in Auschwitz, where he experienced the Muselmänner, and is perfectly captured in the both hypothetical (cf. *Se questo* [*If This*]) and the confirming phrases (è un uomo [*Is A Man*]) in the book's title. Thus, since the title does not, as one might expect, end with a question mark, this further strengthens the paradox: first the hypothetical is stated via the *Se* [if] followed by, not a human being but, actually, a 'something' [*questo*], only to end in the ascertainment that the statement about this something, this hypothetical *questo* [this] is in fact a human being (*è un uomo* [*Is A Man*]). Moreover, the title is a fractured sentence: it lacks a main clause, that is, the consequence following the if-clause, the hypothetical. Hence, the question Levi really asks is: if this is a man, then what? This is the central challenge Levi has so elegantly hidden in his title's if-clause: if this man actually is a man, then what is he?

The lacking main clause actually appears already in the poem on the book's first page. Levi keeps in line with the divine dimension of the threshold between affirmation and negation that was originally located in Hobbes, and paraphrases the Book of Deuteronomy (6, 6ff.) which functions as an answer to the question: if this is a man, consider that Auschwitz has happened:

> Consider *if this is a man*
> Who works in the mud
> Who does not know peace
> Who fights for a lump of bread
> Who dies of a yes or of a no
> Consider if this is a woman,
> Without hair and *without name*
> Without any strength of memory
> Her eyes empty and her womb cold
> Like a frog in winter.
> *Meditate that this has happened*:
> I command these words to you.
> Engrave them on your hearts.
> While staying or leaving the house,
> When you go to bed when you rise;
> Repeat these words to your children.
> Or else may your house shatter,
> Disease shall paralyze you,
> Your offspring turn their faces away from you. (Levi 1989a: 2, italics added)

Taking the present book's object into account, the following parallels are interesting and of significance to the Stolpersteine: the detainees, to Levi, lack a name – this had arguably been taken away from them and substituted by a number tattooed on their forearms. The melancholy and sorrow with which the poem opens ends with a threat ('Or else ...') that Levi expresses via the Book of Deuteronomy and its focus on the importance of the home. Those who receive this divinely inspired command of remembrance, and who must meditate on the fact of Third Reich extermination, must do so while staying and leaving their house and dwelling. Perhaps yet an analogy between the poem and the Stolpersteine exists: the repetition of Auschwitz's reality focuses on one's own children, that is, not children in general but yours and mine. The command, like the poem, is highly personal and individually directed. This pedagogical command is even stronger than the former, which was concerned with considerations as to whether this was a man or not. Failing this task, which is commanded in the last phrases of the poem, will result in destruction, sickness and abandonment.

On account of Levi's testimony, in his *Remnants of Auschwitz* Agamben argues that the Muselmann must be considered as a paradigm of the camp, because here is the life that lives on the very threshold of humanity and animality, life and death, question and fact:

> As if there were in Auschwitz something like a Gorgon's head which one could not – nor wanted to – see at any cost, something so inconceivable that one tries to make it comprehensible by bringing it back to the categories which at the same time are the most extreme and familiar: life and death, dignity and indignity. Between these, the true cipher of Auschwitz: the 'core of the camp', he whom 'nobody wants to see', and who in every testimony inscribes a lacuna – fluctuant and without finding a definite position. He is truly the *larva* our memory does not succeed in burying, the unforgettable with whom we have to decide to come to terms. In one case, in fact, he presents himself as the nonliving, like the being whose life is not really life; in another, like him whose death cannot be called death, but only production of corpses. Thus, like the inscription of life in a dead zone, and of death in a living zone. In both cases – since man sees his privileged bond with that which constitutes him as man, that is, the sacredness of death and life, break into pieces – to be called into question, is the very humanity of man. The Muselmann is the nonhuman persistently presenting himself like human, and he is the human which is impossible to tell apart from the inhumane. (Agamben 1998: 75f.)

Precisely on these central points of insistence Agamben has been met with severe criticism. Esther Norma Marion presents a reflection on Agamben's book on Auschwitz, expressing little sympathy for the field Agamben sets out to analyse, that is, Auschwitz as a terrible yet privileged door for examining not only the ethics of the camp personified by the Muselmann but, more generally, the ontology of ethics. 'What is troublesome and potentially insidious', Marion even writes, 'are the political, ethical and historical consequences of an appropriation of the Holocaust with redemptive and *ahistorical* underpinnings that disenfranchise collective and individual memory' (2006: 1014, italics added). Yet Marion does not produce any arguments as to why it is troublesome and potentially insidious to approach Auschwitz philosophically, let alone why the Muselmann – the core of Agamben's argument – is ahistorical.

Nicholas Chare has tried to follow another, though very similar, pathway. In referring to Jay M. Berstein, known for his work on Hannah Arendt, to Holocaust scholar Geoffrey Hartman and to Dominick LaCapra, editor of a book about Agamben, Chare writes that these three scholars all 'emphasize the frames of reference that disappear because of Agamben's choice to focus almost exclusively on the figure of the *Muselmann*' (Chare 2006: 58). Judging these criticisms to be 'all sound', Chare nonetheless continues to write: 'His [Agamben's] understanding of language is one that institutes a gap between *bios* and *zoe*, between speech and silence, between possibility and impossibility of saying. He then situates testimony in this gap' (Chare 2006: 59f.). Could Agamben's method be problematic in letting the Muselmänner be the true witnesses of the camp, and does the frame of reference really disappear *because of* such a method that Chare argues?

It is true, in any case, that to Agamben the Muselmann is not empirically historical interesting. However, Agamben's approach is ahistorical only to the same extent to which Levi's texts are considered ahistorical, something which is true only for an inveterate positivist. In the perspective of investigating the Stolpersteine philosophically, these questions are all the more crucial. The Muselmann constitutes a paradigm for the camp, but not as a historical figure *tout court* but instead as the character through which it is possible to learn something about the human and ethical conditions in the Third Reich camp, which indeed are very historical. When the Stolpersteine speak of *Opfer des Nationalsozialismus* [victims of National Socialism] they refer to this space of the camp (Demnig 2015: 3).

The hostility towards approaches such as Agamben's (but, as a consequence, also Levi's, although indirectly so) that concern dimensions of the Third Reich exterminations, deviating as they do from a strictly empirical–historical approach, is considerable. The argument appears to be that such approaches are deemed to contribute to a general underestimation and neglect of the historical reality. Once the testimony is brought back to or, perhaps, opened up in the sphere of poetics itself, one consequently betrays the reality of Auschwitz, so critics such as Marion, Berstein, Hartman and LaCapra argue. As a consequence, to these authors not only is Agamben's approach irrelevant – and to Marion even dangerous – but also witness literature that concerns aspects other than those of a specific historical nature becomes irrelevant. If this reasoning is followed to its unreasonable end, a book such as *If This Is a Man*, as well as the historical novel that deals with Auschwitz, would be beside the point.

Chare is close to realizing that this is perhaps to take history one step too far, but he then quickly hurries back to take the position of extreme historicity shared by the authors upon whom he based his analysis in the first place. The gap that Chare correctly found to exist between speech and silence, possibility and impossibility of saying always already has a context – a reality – just as Chare reveals in the title of his article, but he is afraid to accept the consequences and take full responsibility for this. The Muselmann of which Levi speaks, and Agamben interprets, is not a poetical construction. Naked life may very well be Agamben's metaphor for interpreting life in the camp, but it refers explicitly to a human life in history that has been stripped naked of its humanity, that is, the Muselmann, and is therefore very much real.

Of course, it is clear that witness and testimony represent other realities than the actual gas chambers at Auschwitz, and therefore another form of evidence and proof. But this is nothing other than what Levi says when he writes that the true witnesses, the Muselmänner, 'do not have a history' (1989a: 150), and in whose place he must therefore now give witness, provide them with such a history and write what they could not (Agamben 1998: 31f.). 'There is', Agamben writes in a spirit that would have pleased Carlo Ginzburg (1991: 83), who dedicated one of his central texts to Levi (Ginzburg 1992: cf. esp. 544), 'a nonjuridical consistency of truth in which *quaestio facti* can never be brought back to *quaestio iuris*. This is precisely the errand of the survivor […]' (Agamben 1998: 15). As for the Stolpersteine, the question is whether these monuments would admit the existence of such an errand in terms of commemoration. This question will be dealt with in the last pages of this chapter.

Shame and Subjectivity

It is possible to get a firmer grip and to describe in greater detail how and why, for Agamben, Auschwitz signals the end and ruin of any ethics of dignity as personified by the Muselmann. Naturally, this possibility is important to the present book's inquiry since the Stolpersteine rigorously advocate an ethical paradigm reaching, perhaps, its culmination in Demnig's own formulation that with the Stolpersteine '*bekommt das Opfer seinen Namen wieder*' [the victim gets his names back] (2002: 13). Or, as Marlis Meckel proclaimed in, perhaps, a variation of this slogan in her 2006 book: *Den Opfern ihre Namen zurückgeben* [Giving the Victims Their Names Back].

In the funeral rites of the European Middle Ages, which Ernst H. Kantorowicz examined in his 1957 *The King's Two Bodies: A Study in Mediaeval Political Theology* (a title referring to both Carl Schmitt's *Political Theology* and to Kantorowicz's own earlier research about the 'mysteries of state'), it is clear that the *dignitas* refers less to the king's body and more to his function as king – that is, to the Crown. Thus, on the king's death an effigy was made of him, the purpose of which was to conserve the king's dignity from death. The effigy was then treated to a gigantic theatrical event with all the pomp and circumstance as if it had been the real king. This bizarre ritual was what allowed the dignity to transfer to the following king, leading to the Latin aphorism *dignitas non moritur* [dignity does not die] (Kantarowicz 1997: 419–37).

What is of interest here is not the suggestion of some kind of similarity between the deaths of mediaeval kings and those of the victims of the Third Reich. Instead, what is essential is that the whole ritual of royal funerals is made possible because the effigy is treated *as if* it were the real king (*funus imaginarium*) relating to the body of the king. Dignity signifies that one is recognized – ritually or otherwise – as having such dignity. Dignity is the clothing we dress each other in, the gift we give in order to recognize the other as one of us. In fact, Agamben writes, dignity is 'something autonomous regarding the existence of its carrier, sc. an interior model or an external image with which he must adapt and which must be preserved at any cost' (1998: 63).

In the extreme case, like that of the camp, the distinction between the human being and his dignity collapses:

> Also for this reason Auschwitz signals the end and ruin of every ethics of dignity and of adaption to a norm. The naked life to which man has been reduced, neither demands nor adapts to anything: naked life itself is the only norm and absolutely immanent. And 'the ultimate sentiment of belonging to the species' can under no circumstances be a kind of dignity. (Agamben 1998: 63)

Auschwitz is the zone where self-respect and dignity are meaningless and hence 'they cannot be genuine ethical concepts, since no ethics can insist on excluding a part of humanity, however unpleasant and difficult to see' (Agamben 1998: 58).

The naked life of the Muselmann does not only lie beyond the spheres of human and sacred law; he resides ethically in a no-man's land too: 'in referring to the juridical condition of the Jews after the racial laws, also the Nazis made use of a term that implied the dignity: *Entwürdigen*. The Jew who has been deprived of every *Würde*, of every dignity: he is simply a man – and, precisely therefore, no-man' (Agamben 1998: 62).

The focus of Agamben's *Remnants of Auschwitz* is to examine the problem of ethics in regard to Auschwitz but not, in Leland de la Durantaye's words in his excellent introduction, 'on how the *space* of the camp is a figure for the "biopolitical" spaces of modern city, as it was in [the first] *homo sacer*, but instead on bearing witness to the life lived there' (Durantaye 2009: 248). To Agamben, this does not mean trying to develop a new theory of ethics based on the testimonies of the surviving witnesses; the idea, instead, is to ask what it takes for something like ethics to arise. Therefore, de la Durantaye writes, 'what we should note is that Agamben examines shame as an extending beyond the empirical coordinates of any specific act or omission' (2009: 278). How and why can it be said that ethics is something akin to an 'ontological happening'? If ethics is not to be understood, as discussed above, in terms of either dignity or norm, then how can it be understood?

'The ethics of the twentieth century opens with Nietzsche's overcoming of resentment', Agamben writes (1998: 92), because, the philosopher continues, it is hardly likely that an Auschwitz survivor would want his sufferings endlessly repeated over and over again, as Nietzsche's *ewige Wiederkehr* [eternal return] from *The Gay Science* would imply (cf. Nietzsche 1999: vol. 3, 570 §341). Modern ethics, therefore, falls short of understanding Auschwitz, Agamben concludes – after all, to imagine that for instance Levi would want to relive his time in Auschwitz does seem unreasonable. However, the question is whether not Agamben misreads Nietzsche's text on this crucial point. The Nietzschean memory neither wants to justify the past nor to repeat it over and over again. In common with his peculiar, metaphorical style, Nietzsche is polemic and cannot be read as literally as Agamben's strange and rather forced conclusion suggests.

What Nietzsche stresses is that to overcome resentment one must accept the pastness of the past – not in order to forget the memory of it (and hopefully Auschwitz will never be forgotten), but to create the needed critical distance between past and present. Nietzsche's text addresses the contemporary human being of any era, asking him to accept the past to such a degree *as if* the past could be repeated again and again. Nietzsche is fully aware that a total acceptance of the past is impossible; the resentment can never be completely overcome. Indeed, if it were completely overcome, the past would be forgotten. The window to the past would be shut. To Nietzsche, this impossibility is what makes man a historical being. The extent to which man accepts the past designates, at the same time, the extent to which he is able to overcome resentment and to define history as critical. Not to forget but to overcome, to work through the past designates the Nietzschean ethics of history (Nietzsche 1999: vol. 1, §§1–3, 248–71). Paradoxically, Agamben himself refers to this very same conception of history, which he nonetheless has just refuted: 'One cannot want Auschwitz to return in all eternity, because, truthfully, its arrival has never stopped, it is always already repeating itself' (Agamben 1998: 93). To Nietzsche, this is precisely what designates the eternal return of an event: it has never stopped being present.

As a matter of fact, this Nietzschean conception of history even appears in Levi's work. In one of his dreams (which is later repeated in its poetic form in *At an Uncertain Hour* (1984: 16)), Levi either sits together with friends, family, or at work, or finds himself in the green countryside – all in all, in peaceful and pleasant surroundings. All of a sudden, everything collapses around him, the table, the people, everything, 'and now I *know* what this means, and I also know to have always known it: I am in the Lager again' (Levi 1989b: 218f.). But there is another argument, perhaps even more decisive, demonstrating the eternal return. By way of his writings Levi each time accepts the present reliving of a part of Auschwitz's past. Levi's writings – as well as the dream he describes via his poem – *is* the eternal return of Auschwitz, without which he would not have become an author; without which Levi could not have become a witness. The eternal return is the survival strategy *in nuce* to Levi.

To Agamben, what defines ethics lies within the possibility of shame to take place. Shame reveals itself on the threshold of subjectification and desubjectification. Shame is examined as an ontological existential, as the gate to ethics as such, because it marks the moment when the human being comes into being; in other words, the moment in which humanity is constituted, not once and for all but over and over, again and again. With shame, the issue of sadomasochism is to Agamben, perhaps rather surprising, enlightening: if the sadist and the masochist were discovered in the heat of their lust, shame would not belong to either one of them. The shame would blush scarlet on their cheeks, but derive from neither one of them: subjectification/desubjectification, Agamben writes in his book on Auschwitz, 'circulates incessantly between the two poles without really belonging to anyone' (1998: 100). They mutually dress and redress each other in dignity and if their shame should be revealed, it would involve them both equally.

Opposite to the sadomasochist incident is the situation existing between the SS and the detainee in the camp. The continuous subjectification – or creation – of *the* German Aryan has its desubjectification, its counterpart, precisely in *the* detainee. They need each other in the same sense, it would seem, as the sadist and the masochist need each other. Yet, unlike the sadomasochist orgy, the SS and the detainee never change poles – it does seem rather unlikely that the detainee would desire the SS in the way that the masochist desires and, in fact, needs his sadistic 'better half'. Instead, the two poles remain absolute and with a single origin.

To prove his point and to show the extent of what admittedly does appear as an extraordinary comparison, Agamben presents an example. In 1945, with the war at its end and the Allied troops approaching, the SS began transferring the Buchenwald detainees to the facilities at Dachau. Sometimes, if a detainee was not sufficiently fast, the SS killed him. At other times, and without any apparent reason, the SS would randomly choose someone – anyone – to kill. In the French author Robert Antelme's 1947 *The Human Race*, Agamben finds a witness account where this is described in all its irrationality and meaningless evil. This time it involves a young Italian student from Bologna:

> An SS calls out again. '*Du komme hier!*' [You come here!]. Another Italian steps forward. It is a student from Bologna. I know him, and I look at him noticing that his face has turned pink. I looked at him closely, and I still have that astonishing blush before my eyes. He is ashamed, and does not know what to do with his hands .... He turned pink right after that SS said to him, '*Du komme hier!*' He looked around himself before blushing, but it really was him they wanted and, at the moment when he no longer doubted, he turned pink. (Antelme cit. in Agamben 1998: 95)

Agamben asks why this young Italian student felt ashamed. He was simply chosen, and that is all. Nothing else happened. He had not done anything. He simply stood there like any other detainee. Yet he blushed, he felt ashamed. He knew he was going to die. But what, in the personal history of this young man, could be so shameful in those few seconds? In what sense could shame, rather than fear of death, be more telling about the nature of victimhood and the kind of ethics that the detainees were deprived of in Auschwitz and in the camp?

In order to approach these questions, Agamben brings into the analysis the French philosopher Emmanuel Levinas. Shame does not arrive, Agamben explains, 'like in the moralist doctrine, from the conscience of an imperfect or lacking being' (1998: 96). Shame, Agamben is taught by Levinas, is instead that from which one cannot escape. It is when reflecting on Levinas' analysis of shame alongside the example of the young Italian student that the example of nudity appears: 'If nudity results in us being ashamed, it is because we cannot hide that which we would prefer to hide from the glance of the eye. Because, the unrestrainable impulse of escaping from oneself is encountered by an equally certain impossibility of evasion' (Agamben 1998: 96).

Agamben further supports his interpretation by following his insight from Levinas back to Levinas' master, Martin Heidegger. In the heat of the war, between 1942 and 1943, Heidegger gave a course at Freiburg University on two pre-Socratic philosophers, Parmenides and Heraclitus, and elaborates on the relation between nudity, truth and the human being. In this investigation shame, surprisingly, plays a decisive role. Following the intuition from his *Hauptwerk* from 1927, *Being and Time*, Heidegger seeks the deeper relation between truth [*ἀλήθεια*] and *Dasein* [being-there], the latter of which is Heidegger's term for the form-of-life that can ask, in particular, the question of truth. Heidegger defines truth as *Entdecktheit* [discoveredness] and explains: 'Being [*Das Seiende*] gets the hiddenness torn away. Discoveredness is always also a *robbery*.' Is it a coincidence, Heidegger rhetorically continues, 'that the Greeks always expressed themselves in a privative (*ἀλήθεια*) statement concerning the essence of truth [*das Wesen der Wahrheit*]?' (2001: 222, §44b).

In the course on Parmenides, the idea that deprivation and discoveredness are crucial for understanding being is recognized and so truth is developed through the concept of shame [*αἰδώς*], which according to Heidegger constitutes 'the basic word' in 'true Hellenism' (Heidegger 1982: 110, cit. in Agamben 1998: 98. Cf. Heidegger 2001: 44f., §9). The reason is that just as *Dasein* carries truth (i.e. *ἀλήθεια* [revelation]) with it, so too does it carry shame as the revelation of man's hiddenness and what defines *Dasein* as human. Interpreting shame [*αἰδώς*] as shyness, Heidegger writes the following:

> What is clear through the opposition to *λάθα* (concealing) is that shyness determines *ἀλήθεια*, what is unhidden according to its unhiddenness, in which the whole essence of the human being stands with all its ability [*Vermögen*]. (Heidegger 1982: 110)

Shame, then, is not a feeling in man, Heidegger continues, but instead what 'determines his essence, that is, Being's connection [*Bezug*] to human beings' (1982: 110). The relation between *Dasein* and shame is in every sense fundamental: 'Being itself carries shyness, namely to be' (Heidegger 1982: 111, cit. in Agamben 1998: 98). What constitutes *Dasein*, according to Heidegger, is that because *Dasein* potentially and always already carries shame with it, *Dasein* can always be revealed, and in the 'revelation', being is unfolded and presents itself.

In Heidegger's analysis (at least in its Agambian conception), shame is that moment in time when the subject becomes aware of the fact that it is subject(–ed); the historical flash in which the subject realizes that he is revealed as such in a world, to the other. Shame is the historical point when a subject becomes aware not only that he sees, but also that he is seen. *Dasein* is the individual who has become aware that its being is constituted in the world between itself and the other in a constant process of subjectification and desubjectification, in the process of constant *λάθα* [concealing] and *ἀλήθεια* [revelation]. The event when the individual renders an account of this exposition of itself and world is what constitutes it as a shameful being and therefore as a human being, that is, as *Dasein*.

'The blushing', Agamben writes in referring to the Italian student with whom the discussion of shame began above, 'is that remnant which in every subjectification betrays a desubjectification and which in every desubjectification bears witness of a subject' (1998: 104). Shame is therefore not a state but instead an event and something that comes into being – it is something that is produced. In shame, the subject has no content other than his own desubjectification; he has become witness of his own disorder, his own fall as subject: 'One can also express this', Agamben explains, 'by saying that *the subject of testimony is he who bears witness to a desubjectification* [...]' (1998: 112). This double movement, both subjectification/desubjectification, is that to which shame testifies, according to Agamben.

Some relevant conclusions can be reached when comparing the analyses of shame above with the example of the Italian student. Clearly, the dialectics of subjectification/desubjectification has stopped. Whenever there is sovereign power controlling shame and stopping the process of subjectification/desubjectification – that which makes humanity human – that is the time at which naked life is produced. The dialectics that operated in the sadomasochist scene allowing, in the end, dignity to flow between the two poles in a mutual scene of attributing recognition and dignity, does not exist here. Shame turns into nudity, the *I* into sovereign (the SS), and the other into naked life (the Italian student). Not to recognize the shame in another human being is to produce oneself as sovereign and the other as naked life; in the most extreme case of Auschwitz, this is a life that may be killed but not sacrificed, a life beyond the worlds both of men and gods, politics and law, rights and dignity.

The example of the Italian student obtains its true meaning in a comparison with the Muselmann. For the naked life to which the Italian student was undressed still bears the possibility of becoming a witness, just as Levi. When the Italian student blushed, he regarded himself as a human being and shame opened up to be witnessed by him. As for the Muselmann, not only is this model of shame reduced, it is completely absent. In the Muselmann, shame can no longer take place. The Muselmann is the naked life beyond the process subjectification/desubjectification. The Muselmann is the figure who has touched the bottom, the personification of a human being who has been produced beyond the borders of humanity while still alive. Neither he nor the other detainees see his humanity any more. He is the one who can only live *as if* he were a human being. That which made him human has been taken away from him.

Overcoming the Threshold between History and Memory

Throughout this chapter, the purpose has been to search for the form of victimhood that could be said to constitute the paradigm for commemoration of Third Reich victims to which the Stolpersteine are devoted. Agamben's insistence on the centrality of naked life and the Muselmann has been made clear in this regard – hence forming the two sides of what could be called a secularization of *homo sacer*, the figure from ancient law who was beyond the realms of law and traditional ethics. It has been argued that a philosophical view that focuses on the Muselmann's ethical dimension is not simply a construction without historical bearing or reference, hence contrary to the positions of Berstein, Hartman and LaCapra, according to Chare (2006), who also seem to share in that opinion.

It is now possible, therefore, to discuss how these preceding analyses and interpretations correspond to the way in which the Stolpersteine frame the victims of the NS-era via the five fates, which was argued above to constitute the core of the monument: dead [*tot*], murdered [*ermordet*], ???, escaped in death [*Flucht in den Tod*] and escaped [*Flucht*] (Demnig 2015: 4). It is clear, in any case, that these five descriptions of fate from which potential sponsors of the Stolpersteine may choose (most frequently at least) seem to function as that which gives witness to the life and death of the victim (humanity) and to Auschwitz, to the camp (inhumanity). The five fates in Demnig's Stolpersteine could be said to constitute what naked life and Muselmann do to Levi and Agamben: the attempt at a conceptual, and sometimes even a poetical, description of Third Reich victimhood.

To what extent, then, are the Stolpersteine bound by history as monuments for commemoration? Naturally, there is a significant difference between the description of victimhood represented by the Stolpersteine and that discussed by Levi and Agamben, for instance. The former deals with commemoration, and such memory has a much looser obligation to facts. The latter, on the other hand, is obligated by historical facts and concerns giving witness and producing scholarship bound by certain principles of research (Levi and Agamben). The Berlin Memorial to the Murdered Jews of Europe, for instance, is far less specific in its historical appeal, and the name of the monument is only displayed once in the gigantic 19,000 m^2 memory landscape of huge square and rectangular stone blocks, which stand without any inscription or mark in a desert of anonymity. When wandering around in that stone desert, a feeling of loneliness, confusion and despair is probably stronger than the reflection on specific historical circumstances. Different monuments appeal to different aspects of the event: the Memorial to the Murdered Jews of Europe anticipates a sort of pre-knowledge about the Third Reich and its actions upon which the monument founds its act of commemoration. The Stolpersteine, on the other hand, establish and insist much more on a certain conception of history which is then repeated over and over again on each and every single stone by indicating specific dates and specific victims that perished at a certain point in history; each even explains how each individual victim was annihilated.

What is so interesting about the Stolpersteine is, in this regard, that when they very carefully and specifically define victimhood by a certain historical period (1933–45) they indicate one specific victim's dates of birth and death and then state something about the facts concerning the victim's annihilation. Nothing universal seems to be stated about Third Reich victimization, contrary to, for instance, the Memorial to the Murdered Jews of Europe, which states that Jews were murdered. According to their principle of individualization, the Stolpersteine specify in detail, again and again, the *historicity* of each particular victim: this specific victim lived here, this victim was born in this year, this victim perished in that year. The Stolpersteine therefore constitute a monument whose main concern is to place a specific victim in a specific place and time in history, by presenting a range of pieces of information.

Nonetheless, some kind of formalization is found in the Stolpersteine – despite the fact that they present rather personal details about each victim. The reason that led to the particular victim in question being deported, and probably annihilated, is not given. For example, Stein was annihilated because she was Jewish, not because she was a Doctor of Philosophy. Stein was annihilated because of *who* she was, not *what* she was. The same goes for, such as, Dr Julius Bier, Dr Walter Blank and Dr Richard Cahen, as well as any other of the more than fifty doctors from Cologne who the Third Reich exterminated. Of course, in Germany, such a title becomes part of one's civil name, but the question is really why this is relevant when commemorating Stein or any other victim who had obtained a doctorate. In comparison to victims with no title, the consequence is that the Stolpersteine reproduce the same social, political and other hierarchical differences that existed between the victims when they were alive, as if they aim to commemorate these facts rather than the fact that each victim was deported and usually annihilated irrespective of his or her place and role in society. Even in death, the hierarchy of life therefore seems to follow the victims. The Memorial to the Murdered Jews of Europe has, as the name reflects, chosen quite another strategy.

This appears to be the price Demnig's monument must pay when not identifying the victims by any kind of group (racial, political, sexual, or other) and thus to insist on 'one human being – one stone – one fate' (2015: 3). A group is made up of individuals, and does not exist in its own right. A group does not have a civil name and does not live in a house. Rather than to represent the event symbolically, the decisive historicity and individualization in terms of time and place, as a means to both describe and commemorate what happened to the victims of extermination via, in particular, the five fates, is what constitutes the basis for the Stolpersteine upon which they must therefore be discussed. When the Stolpersteine, as a monument, try to represent the humanity of the victims in the midst of the inhumanity in which they found themselves, such a task is therefore not first and foremost artistic – an aspect that would seem to apply merely to the craftsmanship, the formation and the structure of the stone and of its brass plate – but historical.

On the premises of the Stolpersteine, that is, to establish a commemorative monument explicitly upon the historical condition of a victim's annihilation, the sponsors are supposed to possess a certain knowledge about this when deciding to indicate the specific nature of the victim's death – although, in the end, this is ultimately decided by Demnig. The contents of the five fates must somehow correspond to or be compatible with what Agamben called naked life or Muselmann, because these concepts, as analysed above, describe what happened to victims of the Third Reich.

Two of the five fates suggest that the victim in question was able to make a decision regarding his life and death, respectively: escaped in death [*Flucht in den Tod*] and escaped [*Flucht*] (Demnig 2015: 4). Others do not: dead [*tot*], murdered [*ermordet*], ??? (Demnig 2015: 4). Also, this *caesura* in the realms of victimhood testifies to the hierarchy within annihilation itself. In Levi's book *The Truce*, he presents a Muselmann for whom any decision was impossible: the three-year-old child, Hurbinek, who was probably one of the most terrible examples of a victim's fate in the camp. The child was 'an Auschwitz-child', without parents or relatives, paralysed from the waist down, thin and with 'terribly alive eyes' (Levi 1989b: 14). Hurbinek was not his real name. In fact, he probably did not have a name and the detainees of Auschwitz simply called him Hurbinek. He was also mute; he lacked language. Hurbinek only made one sound, which 'Levi doubtfully transcribes as *mass-klo* or *matisklo*', Agamben comments (Agamben 1998: 35; cf. Levi 1989b: 14). 'Hurbinek, the nameless, whose tiny forearm – even his – had been signed with the tattoo of Auschwitz. Hurbinek died in the first days of March 1945, free though not redeemed. Nothing remains of him: he bears witness through these words of mine' (Levi 1989b: 15; cf. Agamben 1998: 35).

Considering Levi's example and then trying to identify Hurbinek's death in terms of one of the five fates suggested by the Stolpersteine is anything but easy. If it is at least admitted that what happened to Hurbinek is not unknown, and that he did not make any kind of choice, one small step has been taken in the direction of an answer. However, rather than Hurbinek as a victim who did not decide on his life or death, is it not the case that this possibility never existed for him? As has been argued above, neither Levi nor Agamben believe that there exists any possibility of decision with regard to anything for the Muselmann. If this is true, then it seems that the Stolpersteine operate with at least two fates – 'escaped' and 'escaped in death' – which presupposes a form of victimhood that is far from the reality in the camp, that is, a condition that does not acknowledge the state of the Muselmann to which, for instance, Hurbinek belongs.

This leaves two applicable fates for Hurbinek: dead [*tot*] and murdered [*ermordet*]. While it is true that Levi wrote that Hurbinek died, this does not mean that his death constituted a proper death. Hurbinek's life just ended. Levi wrote, as discussed above, that one hesitates to describe the Muselmänner as living, but neither were they dead. They were in a much more horrible place, like the one in which Hurbinek was, between life and death. If one were to ascribe Hurbinek's fate as dead [*tot*] this would be an extreme and inappropriate understatement. This leaves us then with the Stolpersteine's clearest (juridical) fate: murdered [*ermordet*].

It is quite significant that Levi does not identify Hurbinek's assassin. In fact, no one in particular murdered or annihilated him. Just as was Anne Frank, so too was Hurbinek a victim of an unknown and unidentified perpetrator. Most of all, his killer was Auschwitz, which of course does not make any juridical sense. A condition such as Auschwitz, or a form of government such as the one conducted by National Socialism, cannot be brought to trial – only subjects of the law can. After all, this juridical impossibility was the reason behind inventing completely new juridical concepts for the Nuremberg Trials, such as, for instance, crime against humanity or even the term genocide, invented for the purpose by the Polish lawyer Raphael Lemkin towards the end of the war. Regardless of the success of such inventions of *post festum* law, it unquestionably testifies to the fact that Third Reich extermination has been recognized long since to exceed common law and law in general. The Stolpersteine evidently do not share that opinion. The point can therefore be made even stronger: none of the five fates of the Stolpersteine acknowledges the state of the Muselmann.

The Stolpersteine insist that what happened to the victims of the Third Reich is, in fact, *not* far worse than murder or maltreatment. The Stolpersteine state that the reality of the exterminations can be captured in juridical terminology or in traditional ethics. It is precisely on this *historical* ground that the Stolpersteine face their most severe challenge. For Stein and Frank to be murdered, as the inscription reads on their stones, a state of law would have had to exist; they would have had to be considered subjects of that law and, moreover, the possibility for a potential perpetrator would have had to exist. Not only had the Nuremberg Laws of 1935, and a range of other decrees, long since deprived Stein and Frank of their status as subjects of law as well as of their German citizenship, leaving them stateless; further, the exterminations were conducted by the National Socialist government and therefore by the German state, making the recognition of a perpetrator impossible or, at least, juridically dubious. To be added to this is that the term murder applies only in civil law and not constitutional law, which is the matter here.

Perhaps just as problematic, the Stolpersteine present the idea that the historical evil of Third Reich exterminations can be reduced to, or at least captured by, a corresponding juridical term. It was argued via Agamben above that to reduce history to law is very problematic. Law has no concept of evil, nor of right or wrong. Law is a system that follows formal rules of application. Law has no consciousness and no ethics. These circumstances taken into consideration, it is remarkable that the desire to describe the exterminations in terms of law continues to be so strong, to which not only the Stolpersteine but also the Memorial to the Murdered Jews of Europe testify.

The praiseworthy idea of the Stolpersteine to not place the exterminations and the victims in the veil of the group, and therefore to bring the victim forward, or even back from an otherwise anonymous mass, is thus replaced by an equally unfortunate placement in the veil of law and ethics. Such a one makes believe that the exterminations are crimes, which can be embraced in the ordinary terminology of jurisprudence. But there was nothing normal or ordinary about the exterminations. Naked life in the Third Reich was subject to the most extreme degree of *Entwürdigung*; that is, to a production into a zone were life had been stripped of the clothes of law and ethics. The mass graves and gassings were not a result of faulty ethics or even of execution. Both were the result of extermination, of a gigantic production of naked life swept away like trash, as though it were not human. This event took place long before the lives of the victims were finally brutally taken from them. *Something far worse than humiliation, faulty ethics or murder happened to the victims of the Third Reich.*

It is far from true that all the victims suffered such extreme fates as Hurbinek or the other Muselmänner. However, as Arendt explained, the historical horror of the exterminations lies not in the act of extermination itself but in the state towards which potentially *all* victims were produced before they were eliminated. The Stolpersteine, however, maintain that the exterminations simply represent another branch of crime, somehow leaving the normality of the state of law intact and proclaim, hence, that *ermordet* [murdered] simply designates the killing of a human being – adding to this, of course, that no universal definition of murder exists, any more than does a universal law. Setting aside the particular fate indicating that a given victim survived (escaped), the engravings (dead, murdered, ???, escaped in death) all stem from the realms of law and ethics, thus running the risk of turning the Third Reich into something far more juridically and ethically sound than it ever was – or than it ever wanted to be. Whatever a more suitable inscription of fate on the Stolpersteine might be, it must somehow acknowledge this fact: victims of the NS-era suffered something *far worse than murder and faulty ethics.*

The question thus presents itself: why, then, the wish on the part of the Stolpersteine to place the victims within the sphere of law and ethics, when this seems so impossibly far from the facts and realities of the camps, and the circumstances under which the victims perished?

It was mentioned above that one of Demnig's central ideas is that with the Stolpersteine 'the victim gets its name back' (2002: 13). Although millions and millions of people were deported and exterminated, the Stolpersteine insist that they can make it up to these victims, that they can give them their names back: a Stolperstein, Demnig said in an interview, 'symbolically restores dignity to every victim' (Katzman and Paulix 2005: 17). The dignity that is given back is presumably, and most importantly, to be found in the juridical and ethical concepts of the Stolpersteine's five fates – dead [*tot*], murdered [*ermordet*], ???, escaped in death [*Flucht in den Tod*] and escaped [*Flucht*] – by which the monument tries to describe what happened to the victims.

However, rather than a proper description, the fates must somehow be understood by way of Demnig's utterance quoted above: via the fate the victim receives what he or she lost. The fates are not merely intended as historical descriptions, but also as contemporary and commemorative gifts to the victim. Of course, name and dates of birth and death are factual, in a rather straight forward manner, but the five fates testify to something more. It is therefore clear that the Stolpersteine advocate a very special use of history, rather than insist on a historical description *tout court*. To the Stolpersteine, the kind of factuality they advocate could be more precisely described as formative or constitutive, as when Demnig wants to give the victim back what he or she has lost. The fate is intended to redress the victim in terms of the dignity that he or she lost, by suspending the difference between history and memory and thus creating a peculiar third zone. But how is one to understand this strange kind of factuality and use of history?

The answer can be found by turning to Jan Assmann, the founding father of modern cultural memory research. Whatever a more precise definition of cultural memory scholarship would entail, it seems safe to say that its field of research is neither simply the past, something that would otherwise make it too akin to the discipline of history, nor the ways in which the past has been scientifically represented, something that would otherwise make it too akin to the discipline of epistemology, that is, the history of science. Instead, cultural memory scholarship concerns the manner in which both history, as well as the past, have been and perhaps continue to be remembered and represented with some contemporary purpose or intention.

In his *Das kulturelle Gedächtnis* (1992), Assmann defines cultural memory as follows:

> For cultural memory what counts is not actual history but only remembered history. One could also say that in cultural memory actual history becomes transformed into remembered history and, thus, into myth. Myth is a foundational history, a story that is told in order to enlighten a contemporary time of its origin. Completely independent from the question of its historicity, the Exodus is the foundational myth of Israel: As such it is celebrated in the Pesach celebrations, and as such it belongs to the cultural memory of the people. Through memory history becomes myth. Without being unreal, history, on the contrary, first becomes reality [*Wirklichkeit*] in the sense of an ongoing normative and formative power. (Assmann 2007: 52)

What Assmann presents here is the difference between events as remembered myths (e.g. the celebration of the Pesach, as Assmann suggests), and events as remembered reality (e.g. the commemoration of victims of the Third Reich). The Stolpersteine, so it seems, find themselves between these two possibilities, which is why some remarks concerning this discussion must be made.

In *Cultural Memory*, Assmann refers to Maurice Halbwachs, the founding father of cultural memory scholarship via his posthumous *The Collective Memory* (1950) written during the 1930s. Assmann's interest in Halbwachs – who graduated in philosophy under none other than the great Émile Durkheim, whose nephew was the equally famous Marcel Mauss who wrote the ground-breaking *The Gift* (1923–4) – concerns the French researcher's distinction between history and memory. Halbwachs, Assmann writes, conceives history (*die Geschichte*) as the counter-concept of collective memory, although he sometimes mentions history as tradition, as opposed to memory. In any case, via the citation from Assmann above, it is clear that Assmann's focus is directed against such a distinction between fact or tradition on one side and memory on the other: 'The transition between "mémoire" and "tradition" may be so fluid that it here appears rather less than meaningful to impose sharper *conceptual* differentiations.

Therefore, we use the concept of (collective) memory as a meta-concept in which we distinguish between "communicative" and "cultural" memory' (Assmann 2007: 45, italics added).

Assmann's conclusion to his presentation of Halbwachs therefore reads, not surprisingly, as follows: 'The past [*Vergangenheit*] does not stand unaffected, it is a *cultural construction*' (Assmann 2007: 48, italics added). As such, it could be added: whether the past is communicated orally, culturally or whether the past concerns the Pesach or the Third Reich exterminations. In thinking of Assmann's inspiration, Halbwachs, and of his mentor, Durkheim, some biographical details of the two French scholars do strike one as particularly odd when Assmann refuses to ascribe the difference between myth and fact any importance. Shortly after writing *The Collective Memory*, Halbwachs was deported to Buchenwald concentration camp, and died there in 1945. If Durkheim, also Jewish, had lived to see the German forces invade France in 1940, he too, eventually, would probably have suffered a similar fate. To Assmann, the evidently different ontological status between the instances of the ancient, and most likely mythological, Hebrews and what happened to the Jews during the Third Reich exterminations does not provide any difference in terms of commemoration or, more problematically, conceptualization.

Based on these comments, if one were to ask whether the Stolpersteine *describe* a fact or whether they *commemorate* a fact, the results up until this point of the present book suggest that the Stolpersteine do both and neither: following Assmann's idea of cultural memory, the Stolpersteine constitute a normative and formative power that is partly independent of, and partly dependent on, the event's historicity. The monument describes the particular victim via each stone's heading of *hier wohnte* [here lived], name, home etc., while at the same time establishing a cultural construction of history, that is, of the victim's fate and what happened to the victim in question. This act is what constitutes the means to redistribute a gift of an ethical and juridical nature back to the victim, in the shape of the victims' lost dignity.

It has been demonstrated above that, in the words of Assmann, 'what counts is not actual history but only remembered history', and that through memory 'history becomes myth', so that, finally: 'Without being unreal history, on the contrary, first becomes real in the sense of an ongoing normative and formative power' (2007: 52). The decisive problem for Assmann is, hence, that his theory is unable to allow a theoretical distinction between history and memory – a distinction that to Assmann therefore becomes more and more irrelevant. The theoretical difference is rejected in Assmann because these conceptual pairs are given equal status. Assmann leaves no room for a critical evaluation of the sources and their accounts and proclaimed facts. All sources are simply expressions of memory – be they true or false, representing myth, memory, or factual history. The Bible and Levi's testimony have the same ontological status. To Assmann, in terms of commemoration, it would not matter whether the Stolpersteine commemorated actual victims of National Socialism or not. Memory fulfils a function in a given community, in constituting a formative power irrespective of its link to reality.

What is so serious – and, indeed, problematic – in Assmann's theory of cultural memory scholarship is not, in fact, his quite realistic account of how history can be mythologized by memory. This diagnosis is unquestionably true, something to which both the myths in the Third Reich about the Jews as well as about the German *Volk* testify. Instead, the problem in Assmann is that when it comes to cultural memory, he views it as *theoretically* irrelevant to distinguish between history and memory, fact and construction. The difference, Assmann wrote, 'may be so fluid that it here appears rather less than meaningful to impose sharper conceptual differentiations' (2007: 45). It is as if Assmann forgets that just because the difference between memory and actual history may be and, perhaps, even actually is quite fluid, this does not imply that reality does not matter. Where memory and history really are fluid, this should strengthen, not weaken, the need for conceptual differentiations, since they are so much more crucial for estimating whether or not one is dealing with history or memory (cf. Assmann 2007: 45f.). Without this distinction monuments such as the Stolpersteine, which are intended to commemorate the victims of Third Reich extermination, run the risk of being reduced to a mytho-historical memory. The analyses that have been conducted in this chapter show that the Stolpersteine place themselves in such a mytho-historical sphere, in a zone that begins with the 'here lived' and the name of the victim, but ends in a fate that understates the historical reality.

In this book, the central thought is that because the Stolpersteine necessarily refer to a reality, it is possible to discuss whether or not the act of commemoration respects this reality, and whether or not these monuments help, or perhaps even block, commemoration of the victims and the historical and ethical task of not forgetting Auschwitz. Carlo Ginzburg's warning from his 1991 *Checking the Evidence: The Judge and the Historian* shares Agamben's point and therefore expands not only to Assmann but also to the Stolpersteine that manifest such an explicit example of Assmannian cultural memory: 'The fashionable injunction to study reality as a text should be supplemented by the awareness that no text can be understood without a reference to extratextual realities' (Ginzburg 1991: 84). This is, in the end, the advice that this book has followed all along, and will continue to follow. Because this principle is absent from Assmann and from the Stolpersteine, for both memory rather than reality structures the use of history. This might work well for religions, but when it comes to the commemoration of victims of the Third Reich's exterminations, this is a very unfortunate consequence – theoretically as well as politically and ethically. Auschwitz refers to an extra-textual reality. 'How can one, without reality', Ginzburg asks in *Unus testis* (dedicated to Levi) by way of a citation from the French historian Pierre Vidal-Naquet, whose mother was annihilated at Auschwitz, 'distinguish between the novel and the historical account?' (Vidal-Naquet, cit. in Ginzburg 1992: 534).

CHAPTER 3

The State of Exception as Paradigm for the Third Reich

A Key to the Third Reich

By now the fact that the Stolpersteine use juridical and ethical vocabulary as the language of reference for describing the historical circumstances concerning the victims' fate has been discussed several times in this book, and it has been suggested that the exterminations greatly exceed the spheres of law and ethics. While the extreme personification of naked life – the figure of the Muselmann – was used to show why a traditional ethics of dignity was inadequate for describing the form of life and death in the Third Reich camp, the actual nature of government in the Third Reich still needs to be investigated. Is it possible to come even closer in describing why a juridical conception of National Socialist victimhood, such as the fate *ermordet* [murdered] stated on the Stolpersteine, is inadequate and even inappropriate as it would seem to underestimate the true horror of the event? This question, along with all its dilemmas and pitfalls, structures the present chapter and can be read as a continuation of the questions and interpretations that concluded the previous chapter. In this regard, the term 'state of exception' will play a key role.

The status of the German *Rechtsordnung* [legal order] during the Third Reich is one of the toughest questions in modern European scholarship, and spans history, jurisprudence, sociology and philosophy. And, as with anything else regarding the Third Reich – setting aside philosophical themes – the literature in the field is overwhelming, and grows by the day. However, whereas few scholars have asked whether the Third Reich can at all be said to constitute a juridical form of government, many have tried to place it in yet another variant of 'dictatorship', and therefore in some kind of constitutionalism, however undemocratic.

By way of their engravings, the Stolpersteine reflect such a constitutionalist perspective. The Third Reich is conceived, hence, as a state of law in which legal principles – whether dictatorial or not – were left to rule the state – however terrible. As the engravings on the Stolpersteine display: the victims were murdered. Naturally, if the structure of the Third Reich in the end was neither legal nor constitutional, this would complicate matters: for if the victims of the Third Reich deportations and exterminations were eliminated beyond the limits of law, what happened to them? If the previous analyses are correct, and naked life does not constitute a case of murder, how is one to describe the form of government under which the victims of the Third Reich were exterminated and to which the Stolpersteine wish to call attention?

In investigating such matters, the works of Carl Schmitt are crucial. His thinking simply is, as Reinhard Mehring has suggested, a '*geistesgeschichtliche* [intellectual–historical] key to National Socialism' (2005: 39). Yet, Schmitt's authorship is a paradox. First, with *The Custodian of the Constitution* (1931), Schmitt strived to secure the constitutional character of the German democratic Weimar Republic. However, when two years later Schmitt became a member of the *Nationalsozialistische Deutsche Arbeiterpartei* [National Socialist German Workers' Party], which quickly established itself as a form of government, Schmitt similarly tried, nonetheless, to outline what he judged to be an anti-constitutional state's juridical ground. Schmitt did this despite, in an article in the 19 July 1932 issue of the *Tägliche Rundschau*, having warned against parties with anti-constitutional leanings, that is, against both the communists and the National Socialists (Blasius 2001: 46). Circumstances like these make Schmitt one of the most difficult *Zeitzeuge* [contemporary witnesses] from the Weimar Republic, through its decline and fall in the winter of 1933, to the Third Reich.

However, rather than depicting Schmitt as a 'fallen intellectual', beyond any wish to provoke or insult, he is selected here because, as Hannah Arendt pointed out some years after the war, he is absolutely central in trying to understand the Third Reich from within (Arendt 1962: 332, n.66). However, reference to Schmitt is not always appreciated, and, even if Agamben's predilection for Schmitt is substantial, naturally this cannot of itself serve to qualify my use of him in the following analyses. Before arguing for the relevance of Schmitt, it may be beneficial to look briefly at some of the challenges others have experienced in this regard, and in particular at how they tried to solve potential problems.

To place Schmitt at the centre of an analysis in which the goal is to attempt to understand his texts rather than to judge him has always been difficult, and remains so. In 1955, when Theodor Adorno and his wife, Gretel Adorno, edited the collected works of the great German philosopher Walter Benjamin, they 'omitted those footnotes in which Benjamin acknowledged the importance of Schmitt's ideas', as Joseph W. Bendersky writes in his 1983 book on Carl Schmitt (1983: 277). This was not to be Adorno's last misrepresentation concerning Schmitt's influence on European thought. On 9 November 1930, after he had completed his 1928 *The Origin of German Tragic Drama*, Benjamin wrote a letter to Schmitt expressing his appreciation:

> Most honourable Professor! One of these days you will receive my book *The Origin of German Tragic Drama* from the publisher. [...] You will very quickly notice how much the book is indebted to you in its presentation of the doctrine of sovereignty in the seventeenth century. (cit. in Noack 1993: 111)

Yet in 1966, when Adorno and his associate, Gershom Scholem (also a close and dear friend of Benjamin), sat down to edit Benjamin's letters, they omitted this letter from the corpus. The intellectual and professional affinity between a Jew and a National Socialist theorist was to be eliminated by all possible means. This was done to such an extent that one could speak, as Bendersky does, of 'an attempt at intellectual disassociation' (1983: 276). Or, in the even stronger words of Sam Weber, it is as though 'the acknowledgement of a debt amounted to a general identification and thus, in view of later developments, to a moral contamination of Benjamin by Schmitt' (1992: 6).

Thus, in the coming pages Agamben's advice will be followed in order to 'turn the scandal around' (2004: 69):

> The correct question regarding the horrors committed in the camps is not, in particular, the one hypocritically asking how it was possible to commit so atrocious crimes against human beings. More honest and certainly more useful would be to attentively investigate through which juridical procedures and political dispositives human beings could have been so deprived of their rights and prerogatives until the point where committing whatever action against them would not appear any longer as a crime (at this point, in fact, everything had truly become possible). (Agamben 2005a: 191)

Verordnung zum Schutz von Volk und Staat

This section briefly mentions the most important political circumstances leading to the state of exception. On this subject, the Weimar Constitution's Art. 48 is central. In fact, Agamben writes in his *State of Exception*, the

> history of Article 48 of the Weimar Constitution is so tightly woven into the history of Germany between the two wars so that one cannot understand Hitler's rise to power without first analysing the uses and abuses of this article in the years between 1919 and 1933. (2004: 24א.[1] Cf. Agamben 2005a: 186f.)

While the Germans prefer the term *Ausnahmezustand* [state of exception], although *Notstand* [state of emergency] is also used, the Italians and French prefer instead to speak about emergency decree and state of siege, while the Anglo-American world refers to martial law and emergency powers. The usage of 'state of exception' in this book is not to be understood as applying to any special form of law, such as that which might apply during war or revolution. Instead, following Agamben, the state of exception is to be understood as a philosophical concept concerning the 'suspension of the juridical order itself; it defines the threshold or the limit concept' (2004: 13).

The Weimar Constitution's Art. 48, sec. 2 reads:

1 When the Hebrew alphabet's aleph (א) appears in Agamben's texts it is also reproduced in the quotations.

> In case public safety is seriously threatened or disturbed, the Reichspräsident *can* [*kann*] take necessary measures [*nötigen Maßnahmen*] to re-establish safety and order [*Sicherheit und Ordnung*], if necessary using armed force. In the pursuit of this aim he *may* [*darf*] suspend [*außer Kraft setzen*] the civil rights described in articles 114, 115, 117, 118, 123, 124 and 154, partially or entirely. (Trans. in PSM-Data Geschichte, trans. modified, italics added)

Reichspräsident Hindenburg, who held the office from 12 May 1925 till his death on 2 August 1934, had more than once to deal with the wishes of different governments to ensure public security and order through such use of Art. 48.

In fact, what ought to have been an exceptional use became almost the rule in the young Weimar Republic. 'The *Ausnahmezustand*', Bendersky writes, 'had become a common recurrence' (1983: 38). Agamben reaches the same conclusion:

> The governments of the Republic, beginning with Brüning's, made continuously use of art. 48 – with a relative pause between 1925 and 1929 – to proclaim a state of exception issuing decrees of necessity on more than 250 occasions. They made use of these, amongst other things, to imprison thousands of communist militants, and to establish special courts with the ability to proclaim capital punishment. (Agamben 2004: 258)

The last years of the Weimar Republic have for this reason been called a presidential dictatorship, as in Brüning's 'presidential system of government', that is, a technocratic government having only obtained the confidence from Hindenburg, and not from the Weimarian Reichstag (Broszat 1969: 24–32).

On 16 July 1930, when Chancellor Brüning suffered a defeat in the Reichstag and his own government was voted out, Hindenburg first dissolved the parliament using Art. 48 and then called new elections. It is significant that Hindenburg did not choose to call the elections straight away. It is true, nonetheless, that by using Art. 48 Hindenburg gained sixty days, the time limit in which a new parliament had to be reconstituted according to the constitution. On 5 June 1931, Hindenburg issued the *Notverordnung zur 'Sicherung von Wirtschaft und Finanzen'* [The Emergency Ordinance for 'The Safeguard of Economy and Finance'], pointing in the direction of the contemporary practice of proclaiming the state of exception because of economic and financial challenges; this was again made possible by recourse to Art. 48. It is noteworthy that Hindenburg's decision was nonetheless supported by a majority of the Reichstag (Vogt 1987: 151).

In the parliamentary elections of 6 November 1932, Hitler and the NSDAP were democratically elected to parliament, receiving 33.5 per cent of the vote and making it the largest party in the Reichstag (Vogt 1987: 153–5). Via special requirements in the electoral law, the National Socialists increased their number of seats in the Reichstag from 230 to 608 out of 661 and in this way constituted 92 per cent of the parliament (Funke 1987: 515). The conservative containment of Hitler, as the attempt to keep Hitler and the NSDAP from power had been called, once again showed itself to be helpless against the party's democratic success (Thamer 1994: 223).

It was no great surprise, then, that on 30 January 1933, Hindenburg appointed Hitler Reichskanzler. 'Only the appointment of Hitler to Kanzler', Thamer writes, 'would resolve the deadlock and lead to a constitutional formation of majority' (1994: 224). All sides, Thamer continues, had moreover whispered to Hindenburg that 'the National Socialists are just really idealistic young people with whom one would soon be through' (1994: 224). Hindenburg's reasons for appointing Hitler were democratic and, for once, in harmony with the spirit of the Weimar Constitution. Had Hindenburg appointed Kurt von Schleicher to form a government, this would have required the continued use of Art. 48, in which the state of exception would then again have continued to be the rule rather than the exception. Schleicher needed Art. 48 in order to form a government; Hitler did not:

> After almost three years of unsuccessful state of exception [*Ausnahmezustand*] Hindenburg appeared weakened due to the conflict with Prussia about the Reich executive. As he was worried about a possible complaint on breach of the constitution in case of prolongations of the emergency decrees [*Notverordnungen*] that would benefit Schleicher, Hindenburg finally appeared to be moving back to parliamentary grounds. (Funke 1987: 518)

In order to understand the period between 1933 and 1945 in which the deportations and exterminations of millions of people took place, whose victims the Stolpersteine are aimed at commemorating, it is imperative not to forget that Hitler and the NSDAP did not *take* power. To speak of a *Machtergreifung* [seizure of power] due to a confused, senile, old president – or, like Nikolaus Wachsmann, to speak of 'the *capture* of power in 1933' (Caplan and Wachsmann (eds) 2010: 18, italics added) – does seem to be rather out of touch with a reality that was, in fact, far more problematic, but nonetheless democratic. 'Regarding many phases and aspects', Horst Dreier writes, 'it is probably more correct to speak of a "handover of power" [*Machtübergabe*]' (2001: 10, n.3).

The NSDAP were part of a democratically elected parliament in which they formed a government – something no one else was able to do. The paradox is, of course, that Hindenburg's decision to end the *Notverordnungspolitik* [politics of emergency decree] and the use of the state of exception by appointing Hitler rather than Schleicher turned out to be the end of the very democracy he intended to preserve, and would shortly be the beginning of a form of government whose brutal consequences would exceed by far those of the previous era.

On 28 February 1933, shortly after Hitler had taken office, he requested that Hindenburg accept the demand from his new Kanzler to issue a decree for the *Verordnung zum Schutz von Volk und Staat* [Decree for The Protection of People and State]. Using the Constitution's Art. 48, Hindenburg, as so many times before, employed the necessary measures invested in him by the constitution and accepted Hitler's request (Drobische and Wieland 1993: 26). The decree reads:

> Based on art. 48, sec. 2 of the constitution of the Reich the following is decreed for the prevention of communist anti-state acts of violence:
>
> §1
>
> The articles 114, 115, 117, 118, 123, 124 and 153 of the Constitution of the German Reich are suspended [*außer Kraft gesetzt*] until further notice. The articles concern restrictions of personal freedom, the right of freedom of expression including restrictions on freedom of the press, freedom of association and assembly, interruption of secrecy of letter, postal, telegraph and telephone, directives on house searches and confiscation as well as restrictions of property also beyond what here otherwise is permitted by law. (RGBL, 28 February 1933, no. 17: 83, cit. in ALEX)

Considering the German Reichstag had been burned almost to the ground the night before, Hindenburg's acceptance was not surprising.

This particular circumstance has also lead to the decree being called the *Reichstagsbrandverordnung* [Reichstag Fire Decree]. The decree was never annulled during the life of the Third Reich, something that has led researchers to state that 'on 28 February 1933 the duration of twelve years of German juridical Bartholomew's Night were rung in [...]' (Drobische and Wieland 1993: 26). The Decree for The Protection of People and State, Agamben writes in his 1995 *Homo sacer*, stating the decree

> was implicitly rooted in article 48 of the constitution which was still in force, and amounted without a doubt to a declaration of the state of exception ('articles 114, 115, 117, 118, 123, 124, and 153 of the constitution of the German Reich [...] are suspended until further notice'). (2005a: 187)

The National Socialists did not use the term *Ausnahmezustand* [state of exception] in their request to Hindenburg. Instead, they used the formulation *Schutz von Volk und Staat* [Protection of People and State]. The choice of words or technical terms was not a coincidence. In their motion, the National Socialists used terminology and references to civil rights well known to the Weimar Republic. The difference in words between protecting people and state on the one hand – as the National Socialists proclaimed to do – and guaranteeing security and order on the other hand – as the Weimar Constitution guaranteed – was not great. In fact, as Rudolf Echterhölter writes, the first legislative acts of the Hitler government differed 'not fundamentally from those of their authoritarian predecessor' (1970: 15).

Although for lawyers such as Reinhard Neubert, Werner Spohr, Martin Boehr and Klaus Lauer, the law consisted of little else than Hitler himself, they nonetheless continued to use rather standard juridical vocabulary. However, this vocabulary was given a push in a direction that slowly and step-by-step left the sphere of normality while still giving the impression of belonging to it. Spohr, in his 1937 *Schutzhaft und ordentliches Gericht* [Protective Custody and Proper Court], so Drobische and Wieland argue, is paradigmatic in this regard in speaking of a '*gewollten Ausnahmezustand* [wanted state of exception] for the implementation of the National Socialist state' (Drobische and Wieland 1993: 28, italics added. Cf. Agamben 2004: 11f.).

It is rather surprising that the decree on Protection of People and State appears to be neglected in the research on the Third Reich. At least one example of such neglect is found when consulting the mammoth 2008 work *Die Verfolgung und Ermordung der europäischen Juden durch das nationalsozialistische Deutschland 1933–1945* [The Persecution and Murder of the European Jews in National Socialist Germany 1933–1945], which over a ten-year period and a total of sixteen volumes constitutes 'a thematic comprehensive [and] scientific founded selection of sources', the editor Wolf Gruner writes in the preface to the first volume (2008: 7). The documents include everything from state papers between the *Schutzstaffel* (SS) and the Third Reich, to decrees, articles from both Jewish and National Socialist journals and newspapers, diary entries, etc. Yet, what can only be described as a significant document in this matter – the Decree on Protection of People and State of 28 February 1933 – has found no place in the collection.

With the *Ermächtigungsgesetz* [Enabling Act] of 24 March 1933, Hitler obtained plenary powers. The actual name of the law was: *Gesetz zur Behebung der Not von Volk und Reich* [Law for the Remediation of Need of People and the State], which does bear an unmistakable similarity to the already existing *Verordnung zum Schutz von Volk und Staat* [Decree for the Protection of People and the State]. A common strategy in the research literature is to focus almost exclusively on this latter decree hence, as mentioned, ignoring the decree from the previous year. As early as in his 1936 *Law in the Third Reich*, Karl Loewenstein – a lecturer on constitutional law who, in 1933, had been forced to leave Germany due to the banning of his subject being taught by so-called non-Aryans – commented on this law: 'The legal basis for government by decree is the '*Gesetz zur Behebung der Not von Volk und Reich*' of March 24 1933, RGBL. I, 141' (1936: 787f., n. 20).

With plenary powers, Loewenstein argues, Hitler became a kind of pseudo-president, leaving the real president as a mere stooge. Hitler's government could now pass laws autonomously, bypassing the Reichstag and allowing the government to leave the separation of powers behind. One of the immediate effects that the Enabling Act had was that, through the *Gesetz gegen die Neubildung von Parteien* [Law Against the Establishment of Parties] of 14 July 1933, all political parties besides the NSDAP were made illegal (cf. Bendersky 1983: 196f.).

One could argue for the centrality of the Enabling Act based precisely on these matters. However, Thamer comments on a peculiar phenomenon followed by the death of Hindenburg on 2 August 1934 – an event that cleared the way for Hitler to declare himself *Führer und Reichkanzler* – and this problematizes such an argument:

> Already the day before, a presentation was passed in the cabinet according to which Hitler would take over. The office of the Reichspräsident would be dissolved and together with the office of the Reichkanzler it would be united in the appointment of 'Führer and Reichskanzler'. Nobody observed that this would also *violate* the Enabling Act. (Thamer 2005: 6, italics added)

Since the 'office' of *Führer und Reichkanzler* does not exist within the realms of the Weimar Constitution, the Enabling Act – which is a constitutional decree – is *causa sui* violated by this 'office'. Therefore, the Enabling Act can have no juridical application once the 'office' of *Führer und Reichkanzler* is a reality. Instead the Enabling Act mostly appears to have been necessitated by the fact that Hindenburg was still alive. With the death of Hindenburg, Hitler was in no need to make any juridical contortions and could now, as Führer, tie in with a constitution that had already been suspended more than a year.

The legality or otherwise of Hitler's title is therefore difficult to assess. No such title had ever existed before in Germany. The title remains in a juridical grey zone, just as its entire juridical status, having been effectuated by Hitler's self-proclamation and not by the Reichspräsident (since both he and his office were dead), which would normally have been the case. Not only did the state of exception seem to be in perfect harmony with a form of government that wanted to place all power in the hands of one man, and contrary to the Enabling Act, it contained a juridical vacuum (hence not only a questionable democratic rule of law) in that the state of exception ultimately was placed in the hands of the Führer rather than in the constitution.

It is important to not forget that what was so dangerous with the National Socialist form of government developing in this period was less the confusion of powers (which the Enabling Act contains), but the fact that it let the Weimar Constitution exist alongside its suspension (which Art. 48 contains) in what the German lawyer Ernst Fraenkel described at the beginning of the war as *The Dual State* (1969). At the same time as some citizens were convicted for felonies in courtrooms and given fines in a society conducting business as usual, other citizens were being rounded up, detained in camps and ultimately exterminated in order to protect people and state. It is significant, Agamben writes, 'that the camps appeared together with the new laws on citizenship and denationalization of citizens [...]' (2005a: 196).

Rescuing or Creating the Constitution

Carl Schmitt has written two central books on the state of exception: *Dictatorship* from 1921 and *Political Theology* from the year after. These two books will help in determining whether Schmitt's theory is capable of explaining the form of government in the Third Reich to which the Stolpersteine refer. Two aspects are interesting in this regard:

A) The state of exception, as compared to the two forms of dictatorship Schmitt identifies, that is, commissionary and sovereign.
B) Necessary measures as an essential element in the state of exception.

Schmitt's first analysis of the state of exception is elaborated via dictatorship, which he assesses to be 'a central concept in political science and constitutional theory' (Schmitt 1994a: xiii). When he sets out to develop his theory of dictatorship, Schmitt's goal is not only to explain the state of exception juridically but also to ground the state of exception constitutionally, that is, in the realm of state law. Schmitt's general challenge is how to explain the applicability of the law – which, of course, as norm, can only be general upon a situation that can only be particular that is, the exception. Schmitt's logical dilemma is how to make the exception (the situation, what is singular) fit in with the rule (the norm, the law).

'The dictator', Schmitt writes, in reference to his beloved Roman Empire, 'has the task of eliminating the dangerous situation, which is the reason for his appointment, that is either to wage war [*dictatura rei gerendae*] or to suppress a domestic riot [*dictatura seditionis sedandae*] [...]' (1994a: 1). The dictator is, he continues, 'a sort of king with unlimited power [*Gewalt*] over life and death' (Schmitt 1994a: 2). The lawful nature of this form of government, to Schmitt, lies in the fact that the dictator was answerable to a constitution – however little this was of significance when it came to practical politics. In the end, the dictatorship represents a *Rechtsordnung* [legal order] because it will eventually either save the existing constitution or establish a new one, depending on the outcome of the previously mentioned dangerous situation. In Schmitt's book on dictatorship, this constitutes the difference between 'commissionary and sovereign dictatorship', constituting 'the fundamental decision' (1994a: 3).

Whether or not the dictatorship is commissionary or sovereign depends on the status of the constitution, that is, on its reinforcement or rejection. In the commissionary dictatorship it is reinforced:

> The commissionary dictatorship overrules [*hebt auf*] the constitution *in concreto* in order to protect the same constitution in its concrete existence. [...] if the existence of the constitution is threatened, then it needs to be guaranteed through a temporary suspension [*Suspension*] of the constitution. The dictatorship protects a certain constitution against an attack that threatens to overrule the constitution. (Schmitt 1994a: 133)

The constitution can be suspended [*suspendiert*], Schmitt continues on the following page, 'without ceasing to be valid because the suspension [*Suspension*] only concerns a *concrete exception*' (1994a: 134). This last phrase is repeated with little variation the following year in *Political Theology*, where the state of exception is said to concern 'a concrete case' (Schmitt 1994b: 20). In his book on the state of exception, Agamben can therefore conclude that the commissionary dictatorship, 'represents, thus, a state of law where the law does not apply but rests in vigour' (2004: 49).

If, on the other hand, the constitution is unlimitedly suspended both temporally and locally, then the dictatorship is sovereign, because the old constitution is *not* given back its old legality, and a new constitution is inferred as obtaining a new form of legality. Schmitt explains:

> In the whole current order [*Ordnung*] of things the sovereign dictatorship only sees the condition that it wants to remediate through its action. The sovereign dictatorship does not *suspend* an existing order [*Ordnung*] by what is founded in this order, that is, a constitutional right. Instead, the sovereign dictatorship tries to create a condition where it can make possible a constitution that it regards as the true constitution. (Schmitt 1994a: 134)

In the sovereign dictatorship, Agamben concludes once again, 'where the old constitution no longer exists and the new is present in the "minimum" form of constituting power, a state of law is represented where the law applies but it is not formally in vigour' (2004: 49).

To Schmitt, the state of exception is juridically explicable and constitutional because it resides in either constituted power in the form of commissionary dictatorship, or it resides in constituting power in the form of sovereign dictatorship. Nonetheless, Schmitt's attempt to secure the existing or future life of the constitution is paradoxical because, Agamben writes, 'what should be inscribed in the law is something essential exterior to it, that is, nothing less than the suspension of the same juridical order [...]' (2004: 45).

Whereas in 1921's *Dictatorship*, the discussion of the state of exception was placed in the form of dictatorship, the year after, in *Political Theology*, it appears slightly changed. Now the state of exception is developed in the form of sovereign, the 'highest not derived dominance' [*Herrschaft*], Schmitt writes (1994b: 13). Where Schmitt first anchored the state of exception in the juridical sphere and in the dialectic between constituting and constituted power, he later anchors the state of exception in 'the two fundamental elements of law: the norm (*Norm*), and the decision (*Entscheidung, Dezision* [...])' (Agamben 2004: 47).

In *Political Theology*, Schmitt's solution to the paradox of how to anchor the exception in the rule now simply consists of identifying the sovereign with this very paradoxical nature of the state of exception itself. The sovereign, Schmitt writes, 'stands outside the normal existing legal order [*der normal geltende Rechtsordnung*] and belongs to it nonetheless, because he is responsible for the decision whether the constitution can be suspended in toto' (1994b: 14). It is on this account that Schmitt conceives his perhaps most famous aphorism: the 'sovereign is whoever decides on the state of exception' (1994b: 13). The state of exception defines the sovereign, and not the other way around. In the state of exception, Schmitt continues, 'the decision separates itself from the legal norm [*Rechtsnorm*] and the authority proves (paradoxically) that in order to create law he does not need to have it' (1994b: 19).

The situation created in the exception, Agamben explains, is therefore, from a juridical perspective, rather complicated, because, it

> is not a fact, because it is created solely by the suspension of the norm; but for the same reason, it is not even a juridical fact, even if it opens up for the possibility of the law's vigour. This is the ultimate meaning of the paradox Schmitt formulated, when he wrote that the sovereign decision 'demonstrates to not be in need of law in order to create law'. Rather than the sovereign decision concerns the control or neutralization of the excess, it concerns especially the creation and definition of the space itself in which the juridico-political order can obtain value. (Agamben 2005a: 23)

Even though Schmitt places the state of exception more solidly in the state (the sovereign) rather than in the law (the constitution), it remains constitutional nonetheless. At this point in Schmitt's thought, there is no law beyond the constitution. André Doremus and Hugo Ball express this almost aphoristically: 'No law exists beyond the state, and no state exists beyond the law' (Doremus and Ball 2004: 67). The exception still concerns an evocation of the constitution – old or new:

> If this condition [the state of exception] is realized then it is clear that the state remains while the law [*Recht*] steps back. Because the state of exception is always something other than anarchy and chaos, in the legal sense an order [*Ordnung*] still remains although not a legal order. [...] In the exception the state suspends [*suspendiert*] the law [*das Recht*] due to the law of self-preservation, as they say. Here, the two elements of the concept 'legal order' [*Rechts-ordnung*] face one another, proving their conceptual independence. (Schmitt 1994b: 18f.)

Almost prophesying the state of affairs in Hinderburg's last years in office, Schmitt writes that the sovereign is the only one keeping the state alive in the lacuna of the state of exception, whether commissionary or sovereign. The sovereign simply becomes the one guaranteeing law's relation with reality, that is, 'the very possibility of its application', so that the state of exception may create 'a zone where the application is suspended but the law remains, as such, in vigour' (Agamben 2004: 43):

> The exception does not subtract itself from the rule; rather, the rule suspends itself, gives room for the exception and only because it maintains itself in relation to the exception, does it constitutes itself as a rule. The particular 'vigour' of law consists

> in this capacity of law to maintain itself in relation with an exteriority [...]. The state of exception is not, thus, the chaos which precedes order, but the situation resulting from the suspension of order. (Agamben 2005a: 22)

In the exception, the norm applies to the exception by no longer applying, instead withdrawing from it. The exception is therefore not simply an exclusion, but rather an *inclusive exclusion*, which serves to include what is at the same time excluded (Agamben 2005a: 26–7).

In the appendix to his book *Dictatorship*, added a couple of years after the first printing, Schmitt continues a series of clarifications that seem to have arisen in the wake of his two books on the state of exception. The appendix is interesting in the context of the present book, because Schmitt discusses the Weimar Constitution's Art. 48, which is of such immense importance in understanding the Third Reich, the state of exception, and the following 'legal' ground for the deportations and exterminations that the Stolpersteine with to commemorate.

The full title of the appendix is *Die Diktatur des Reichspräsidenten nach Artikel 48 der Weimarer Verfassung* [The Dictatorship of the Reichpräsident according to Article 48 of the Weimar Constitution]. In the appendix, Schmitt specifically addresses the problem of presidential power, and in particular the problem of defining the space where the state of exception as a juridico-political order can obtain value, which is precisely what Schmitt's first chapter intends to clarify: 'the practical implementation of the state of exception' (Schmitt 1994a: 214).

Schmitt's preoccupation with Art. 48 was, however, no new concern. In *Political Theology* Schmitt had mentioned the Weimar Constitution in connection with the state of exception: 'In the current German constitution of 1919, the state of exception [*Ausnahmezustand*] is proclaimed by the Reichspräsident [...] under the control of the Parliament, which at any time can demand that it be overruled' (Schmitt 1994b: 17). Nevertheless, Schmitt emphasizes that, despite such parliamentary control, the decision to employ Art. 48 contained no restrictions at all. As a consequence, the Weimar Reichspräsident formed a constitutional backdoor that could very probably lead to nothing other than 'a limitless absolute power [*Machtvollkommenheit*]' (Schmitt 1994b: 18).

It is advantageous to read the Weimar Constitution's Art. 48, sec. 2 again: 'In case public safety is seriously threatened or disturbed, the Reichspräsident *can* [*kann*] take necessary measures [*nötigen Maßnahmen*] to re-establish safety and order [*Sicherheit und Ordnung*], if necessary using armed force. In the pursuit of this aim he *may* [*darf*] suspend [*außer Kraft setzen*] the civil rights described in articles 114, 115, 117, 118, 123, 124 and 154, partially or entirely' (trans. in PSM-Data Geschichte, trans. modified, italics added). Schmitt comments on the absurdities of these formulations as follows:

> If the Reichspräsident in this way *disposes over death and life* the inferred barrier from sentence 2 then becomes an empty formality and, as a matter of fact, meaningless. If he *vi armata* shoots all editors, typesetters and print workers of a newspaper and levels the printing house to the ground, one does not really need to calm him down by saying that he *may* [*darf*] forbid the newspaper. [...] The authority to take all necessary measures does not readily include the second authority, that is, to suspend fundamental rights. (Schmitt 1994a: 221, italics added)

Schmitt underlines that since the first sentence in this way declares that the Reichspräsident can, in fact, do whatever he wants (take any kind of necessary measures), the second sentence neither limits nor restricts the meaning of the previously mentioned necessary measures and the power of the Reichspräsident.

Just as importantly, what Schmitt has made evident is that the state of exception implies the most crucial of all legal, political and ethical referentialities: the life of the citizen. 'The sovereign', Agamben writes, 'does not decide on the licit and illicit, but on the original implication of the living in the sphere of law' (2005a: 31). Life is, in other words, that to which the exception refers. 'The life, which is thus obligated', Agamben continues, 'can in the last instance only be implicated in the sphere of law through the presupposition of its inclusive exclusion, only in an *exceptio*' (2005a: 32).

Thinking back on Schmitt's attempts to juridically define the state of exception in the Weimar Republic, it is clear that the Hitler government's use of Art. 48 points in another direction. The state of exception as such was not regarded as exceptional: 'Because the state of exception', Agamben writes in regard to the National Socialist government, 'is, in fact, "wanted", it inaugurates a new juridico-political paradigm where the norm becomes indistinguishable from the exception' (2005a: 190). In fact, in the decree of 28 February 1933, the suspension is not limited, either territorially or temporally, but simply in a state lasting *bis auf weiteres* [until further notice] (RGBL, 28 February 1933, no. 17, 83, cit. in ALEX).

It is interesting to note that while Schmitt's primary preoccupation with the state of exception is to secure and explain it juridically, Agamben appears to address more specifically its problematic political consequences. In particular, he addresses the question of the nature of laws issued during a state of exception:

> [...] the specific performance in the state of exception is less the confusion of powers, upon which too much insistence has occurred, and more the isolation of the 'force-of-law' from the law. It defines a 'state of law' where, on the one hand, the norm is in vigour but does not apply (it has no 'force'); and, on the other hand, actions which have no value as law obtain its 'force'. [...]. The state of exception is an anomic space, where what is at stake is a force-of-law without law (which should really be written: force-of-~~law~~). (Agamben 2004: 52)

In contrast to Schmitt, Agamben questions the state of exception, not only as a juridical category lacking the form of law, but also as a dispositive that releases state violence without a firm constitutional anchoring, only having the force-of-law – problems Schmitt prefers to mention *en passant*.

It is now possible to draw two general and central conclusions regarding the juridical nature of the Third Reich: Schmitt's theory of the state of exception cannot work if met by either one of two possible scenarios:

A) if the constitution is suspended *without* being given back its former legality, or;
B) if the constitution is suspended *without* a new one taking its place.

If the nature of the state of exception, according to Schmitt, is that it resides on the threshold between law and fact, between the juridical and the political (in the person, or persons, of the sovereign) before it either gives life to the old or to a new constitution, then it must likewise be clear that, whatever the nature of a situation that exists on this very threshold itself, this cannot be captured in the realms of the law.

If the state of exception does not correspond to either (a) a commissionary dictatorship or (b) to a sovereign dictatorship, then the state of exception simply develops into a *bellum omnium contra omnes* in an eternal Hobbesian state of nature (Hobbes 1966: chapter XIV), which was precisely the situation in the Third Reich. At this time in Schmitt's authorship, the desired state of exception, of which National Socialist lawyers would later speak, is meaningless. This is exactly why Schmitt faced such severe challenges after the state of exception was declared on 28 February 1933.

Thorough reflection on Schmitt's thoughts on the state of exception therefore reveals that the Third Reich and the exterminations must be something quite other and far more extreme than what a juridical and constitutional understanding would allow to be conceived. The fact of 'the physical elimination not only of political adversaries, but of entire categories of citizens who at the end, for one reason or the other, could not be integrated into the political system', testifies that the event is beyond ordinary law and politics, Agamben writes (2004: 11). Annihilation, not murder or execution, is the event that structured Auschwitz and the Third Reich.

This naturally leads to a very delicate question: under what terms can a situation such as that of the Third Reich be described, when it consists of a twelve-year-long threshold that developed into a state – a *continuous* state – of exception, neither rejecting the old constitution nor creating a new one? In other words, what was the specific juridico-political nature of the Third Reich that led to the elimination of millions of victims? In any case, if the reality to which the Stolpersteine refer is to be understood, it is clear that Schmitt's theory of the state of exception is inadequate.

Biopolitics: Foucault and the Third Reich

Earlier in this book, the Muselmann was discussed as forming the backbone or paradigm of Third Reich victimhood, and it was argued that the Stolpersteine had difficulties in acknowledging such victimhood. An attempt to understand the specific juridico-political structure of the Third

Reich would thus naturally follow this intuition and look closer at the location where the Muselmann was detained: the camp. However, instead of 'deducing the definition of the camp from the events that took place in it', as Agamben writes in *Homo Sacer*, 'we ask instead: what is a camp, what is its juridico-political structure and why could similar events have taken place here?' (2005a: 185).

In this section, an analysis of the term biopolitics will take up the thread from the preceding section and attempt to see if it is possible to come closer to describe the reality in which the *Opfer des Nationalsozialismus* [victims of National Socialism] (Demnig 2015: 3) found themselves. Again, the fundamental concern is not only whether the Stolpersteine do justice to the victims they wish to commemorate, but also whether the Stolpersteine effort to describe the Third Reich, as a state of law in which a victim of annihilation was a murder victim or suffered some other fate, could reasonably be made using the terminology of jurisprudence and ethics.

Biopolitics and biopower were developed in the last and most interesting phase of Michel Foucault's authorship. At that time, Foucault had decided to take his research one step further: 'It is necessary to build an analytics of power [*pouvoir*] that no longer takes law [*le droit*] as model and code', Foucault writes in the last chapter of *The Will to Knowledge*, the first and most famous volume of *L'Histoire de la sexualité* [*The History of Sexuality*] (2001: 119). Foucault explains the reason for this in one of the most prominent aphorisms in the book: 'One could say that the old right to *make* die [*faire* mourir] or to *let* live [*laisser* vivre] has been substituted with a power to *make* live [*faire* vivre] or to reject it into death' (Foucault 2001: 181). To Foucault, this transformation is radical: 'For millennia man has remained what he was to Aristotle: a living animal with the additional capacity for political existence. Modern man is an animal whose politics questions his existence as a living being' (Foucault 2001: 188).

Until around 1976, Foucault had been performing an archaeology of the different *dispositifs* of power regarding the mental institution, the hospital and the prison in his books *Folie et déraison* (1961) [*Madness and Civilization*], *Naissance de la clinique* (1963) [*The Birth of the Clinic*] and *Surveiller et punir* (1975) [*Discipline and Punish*]. After these books, Foucault directed his investigations, Agamben explains, towards 'the growing inclusion of man's natural life in the mechanisms and calculations of power' (Agamben 2005a: 131), which is why the character of Foucault's interests slowly changes. And it is in this central *Kehre* [turn] that Foucault elaborates the notions of biopolitics and biopower.

What becomes evident when reading Foucault's 1976 Collège de France course, *Society Must Be Defended*, is that biopolitics and biopower are uniquely and closely connected to democracy – a theme Foucault had already touched upon earlier that year in *The Will to Knowledge*. The course seems to have given Foucault the opportunity to elaborate further on his ideas of governmentality, which he will define as *l'art de gouverner* [the art of governing] the following year in *Security, Territory, Population* – also a course at Collège de France (2004: 98). In a biopolitical form of government, life as such is more closely tied to state administration than in any other form, such as for instance monarchy. Under the *ancien régime*, for instance, who or what the citizens were was almost irrelevant from a political point of view. Neither life nor living presented themselves as political problems that necessitated new conceptualizations of government.

Since life in all its aspects – from demographic statistics, infant mortality rates, to national health and sickness levels and crime statistics, etc. – begins, at a certain point in history (located by Foucault in Modernity), to become increasingly at the centre of politics, for Foucault a new form of government correspondingly begins to manifest itself increasingly although still retaining its democratic foundation. Since democracy, in the end, builds its force on a splintering of power in the realms of general decentralization (and not only in a tripartition of power) in hospitals, prisons, *cliniques*, etc. as Foucault had shown in his earlier works, it is only natural that an investigation of these manifestations will go beyond the traditional borders of politics.

Hence, Foucault says, the biopolitical methodology

> does not concern itself with the analysis of the regulated and legitimate central forms of power and what could be their general mechanisms or set of effects. Instead, it is concerned with grasping power at its extremities and ultimate lineaments where it becomes capillary. This means taking hold of power in its most regional and local forms and institutions, in particular where this power – in submerging the rules of law [*règles de droit*] that organise and delimit power –thus extends beyond these rules, invests itself in institutions, takes the shape of techniques and provides itself

> with instruments of material intervention – eventually even violence. [...] Rather than search for the knowledge of where and how the power to punish is rooted in sovereignty – such as is presented by philosophy in either monarchic or democratic law – I have tried to look at how, in the end, punishment and the power to punish have taken shape in a certain number of local, regional [and] material institutions – whether as torture or as imprisonment – in a world that is both institutional, physical, regulated and violent by effective apparatuses of punishment [*appareils effectifs de la punition*]. (Foucault 1997: 25)

Commenting on racism as an example of this new form of bio-power and biopolitics, Foucault explained the following to his students on 17 March 1976:

> Unlike discipline, which is addressed to bodies [*corps*], this new and non-disciplinary power is applied to the living man or, if you prefer, it does not address only man-as-body [*homme-corps*] but the living human, the human living being, that is, in the end, if you prefer, man-as-species [*homme-espèce*], [...] something which is no longer anatomo-politics of the human body, but which I call a 'biopolitics' of the human species. (Foucault 1997: 216)

Of interest here is that Foucault considers this new human-species to be the population: 'Biopolitics concerns', he explains, 'the population and the population as a political problem, that is, as a problem that is at once scientific and political, as a biological problem and as power's problem [...]' (Foucault 1997: 218f.).

However, only three years later Foucault devoted another course at Collège de France to liberalism – that is, to the greater impact of political individualism than had been seen before its apparition in the eighteenth century – and Foucault still maintains the absolute centrality of biopolitics as, in the end, a politics founded upon the mass or, in other words, on the population rather than on the individual. Such a politics, Foucault explains:

> is not at all about looking in details at the individual but, instead, via global mechanisms, to act in such a way as to obtain some global conditions of equilibration and regulation. In short, to take life into account along with the biological processes of the human species and to insure upon these not a discipline but a *regularization*. (Foucault 1997: 219f., italics added)

Not only does the wording of the 1935 Nuremberg Laws (whose popular name is racial laws) and their intention of securing the 'true' Germans against 'Ungerman' elements (of which the Jews are paradigmatic) seem to support the relevance of such a Foucauldian approach. As well, the National Socialist idea of a general governing or regulation of the entire population and the very life itself of the citizen suggests that Foucault's ideas would be revealing concerning the Third Reich. Germany in the period from 1933 to 1945 seems, indeed, to have established itself as the perfect Foucauldian and biopolitical laboratory.

However, in his course *Society Must Be Defended* – as in Foucault's authorship, in general – there are hardly any thoughts given on the Third Reich and the exterminations. Apart from Foucault mentioning the Final Solution and Hitler (and this only five times) leading him to rather hastily define the Third Reich as a biopolitical form of government, he is silent on the matter (1997: 49; 72; 232–4). Foucault does not even mention the death camps or concentration camps. All this is quite strange, since the camps really ought to have constituted a perfect paradigm for an investigation of local and regional manifestations of power.

When, finally, Foucault does at last speak about the Third Reich, this remains on a very general level, and only in the last lesson in *Society Must Be Defended* does he address the Third Reich directly, though occupying no more than ten pages in the 200-page book containing his lecture. Even if it could be said that Foucault really does what he promised – that is, stop the analysis at the beginning of the twentieth century – some theoretical and methodological restrictions in Foucault even necessitates such an omission. It is not impossible to suggest that perhaps Foucault himself already knew of these restrictions, something that could explain why he refrains from a more thorough interpretation of the Third Reich, the camp and the exterminations.

The theoretical challenge in Foucault's biopolitical interpretation, that is, his art of governing, when confronted with the Third Reich, is that it has as its basic presupposition the functionality and existence of the state of law and, along with this, clearly marked limits between friend and foe, domestic and foreign, legitimate and illegitimate, private and public. While it is quite true that to Foucault and the biopolitical analysis, law incorporates still larger spheres of private life into the state calculus and bureaucracy, becoming in the end omnipresent, these changes, nonetheless, still occur within the sphere of law.

The prison and the convicted felon represent (however potentially unjust, horrible and evil) a space of confinement in the realms of the state of law. In the Third Reich, on the contrary, it is not the law that incorporates still larger parts and spheres of the citizen and his world but, on the contrary as was shown above, the exception. Everyone is, in principle, a foe, just as everyone is, in principle, a friend, and the difference between public and private, citizen and man is suspended. Art. 48 in the Weimar Constitution that was examined above makes this very clear: private life is the business of the state, which is expressed via the suspension of

> freedom of expression including restrictions on freedom of the press, freedom of association and assembly, interruption of secrecy of letter, postal, telegraph and telephone, directives on house searches and confiscation as well as restrictions of property, also beyond what is here otherwise permitted by law. (RGBL, 28 February 1933, no. 17: 83, cit. in ALEX)

The state of exception effectively breaks down the boundaries of the state of law upon which Foucault's methodology and theory are constructed. The camp and the detainee (the Muselmann) may very well constitute a biopolitical space, but they are located in the realms of the state of exception, not law.

Agamben underlines these restrictions in Foucault's biopolitics the following way:

> This is the reason why it is not possible to inscribe the analysis of the camp in the trail opened by Foucault's works – from *Histoire de la folie à l'âge classique* [*Madness and Civilization*] and *Surveiller et punir* [*Discipline and Punish*]. Being the absolute space of exception, the camp is topologically different from a simple space of confinement. This space of exception, in which the link between localization and ordering is definitively broken, is what has determined the crisis of the old 'nomos of the earth'. (Agamben 2005a: 24א)

Instead of a Foucauldian conception of biopolitics in the sense of the law's almost indefinite expansion into the human *bios*, the Agambian conception of biopolitics in the sense of the state of exception maintains the suspension of the law in the creation and production of naked life. This is what leads to the 'immediate biopolitical meaning of the state of exception as the original structure in which law through its own suspension includes the living in it [...]' (Agamben 2004: 12; cf. Snoek 2010: 48). The living (human life) thus captured in Foucault is a subject of law; in Agamben, it is naked life.

Albeit Foucault's paradigms might change and even push their individual meanings to the very extreme, it is a fact no less that the paradigms operate within the normality of the state, however excessive and brutal. If anything, Foucault is interested in the change of norm and normalcy – juridically, politically, institutionally, etc. – while Agamben is concerned with the suspension of norm and normalcy.

For this reason, Agamben can describe the events of the camp in terms which would have been impossible for Foucault to accept (and nor can they be understood in any notion of the state of exception in Schmitt's sense). A constitutive link simply exists between exception and camp:

> What happened in the camps indeed exceeds the juridical concept of crime to the extent that often one has simply omitted to consider the specific juridico-political structure in which these events were produced. The camp is merely the place where the most absolute *conditio inhumana* ever given upon earth was realized: in the last analysis this is what counts for the victims as well as for those who come after. (Agamben 2005a: 185)

The exterminations of the Third Reich, therefore, did not constitute a mad or insane action, according to Agamben, but were part of a technically skilled form of what Agamben defines as a new biopolitical government that goes beyond the notion of Foucault (and also Schmitt) and that of the law.

Agamben explains it the following way:

> The Jew during Nazism is the privileged negative referent of the new biopolitical sovereignty and is, as such, a flagrant case of the *homo sacer* in the sense of a life that can be killed, but not sacrificed. Thus, his killing constitutes [...] neither capital punishment nor a sacrifice, but simply the actualization of a mere '*capacity to be killed*', inherent in the condition of the Jew as such. The truth – which is difficult for these victims to face, but which we must have the courage to not cover with sacrificial

> veils – is that the Jews were not exterminated in a mad and giant holocaust but, literally, like Hitler had announced, 'as lice', which is to say: as naked life. The dimension in which the extermination took place is neither religion nor law, but biopolitics. (Agamben 2005a: 126f.)

Being the space of a continuous state of exception, the camp forms the paradigm for the Third Reich in constituting a clash between fact and law, because the existence of the law becomes indistinguishable from its application or use. Since the law is suspended, thus lacking the form of law, it comes to light in a constant manifestation of law's infinite withdrawal from reality, resulting in a constant exception or, in other words, in a pure force-of-law lacking law. When law's only normality is its exception, the exception no longer proves the rule, but has become norm itself.

Agamben teaches: 'For this reason on closer view, in the camp the *quaestio iuris* is no longer absolutely distinguishable from the *quaestio facti* and, in this sense, any question concerning the legality or illegality of that which happened in the camp is simply meaningless' (Agamben 2005a: 190). The space in which the naked life of modernity's *homo sacer* lived – the Muselmann – is the biopolitical space of the durative state of exception: the camp.

Führer and Führertum

In all probability, Schmitt (as, perhaps, Foucault after him) was aware that the Third Reich was something far more extreme than any conception of which the law, constitutionalism and their individual transformations could ever conceive. When Schmitt sets out to describe the theoretical outlines of the Third Reich in his 1933 *State Movement People*, his aim in the forty-six pages of this short book is to develop a set of new concepts for a way in which this new form of government could be grasped (cf. Bendersky 1983: 208f.).

Redefining law in the most extreme way in his attempt, Agamben, quoting from the book, describes Schmitt's efforts the following way:

> No one has expressed with more clarity than Schmitt this peculiar nature of the new fundamental biopolitical categories. In his essay *Staat, Bewegung, Volk* [*State, Movement, People*] he approximates the concept of race – without which 'the National Socialist state could not exist, and without which its juridical life would not be possible' – to the 'general and indeterminate clauses' that had ever more profoundly penetrated twentieth century's German and European legislation. (Agamben 2005a: 192)

Schmitt states clearly at the end of his book that the only people who are juridically relevant are those having 'an affiliation to people and race [*Volks- und Rassenzugehörigkeit*]' (1933: 45). Thus, Agamben writes in *The Kingdom and the Glory*, that 'racism becomes the dispositive through which sovereign power – which to Foucault coincided with the power over life and death and to Schmitt with the decision on the exception – is reinscribed in biopower' (2007: 91א).

Agamben had once before touched upon the problem of racism in National Socialism, in his first book in the *homo sacer* project:

> A concept such as race in National Socialism (or, in the words of Schmitt, of 'equality of descent' [*uguaglianza di stirpe*] functions like a general clause (analogous to 'state of danger' or 'good morals'), which does not refer, however, to an external factual situation, but realizes an immediate coincidence between fact and law [*diritto*]. The judge, the civil servant, or whoever else, had to reckon with the concept of race and no longer orient themselves according to a norm or a factual situation. Instead, exclusively binding their own community of race with the German people and with the *Führer*, they move in a zone in which the distinction between life and politics, between questions of fact and questions of law, literally has no meaning any longer. (Agamben 2005a: 193)

It is true that the political concept of *Volk* [people] seems to constitute the basis for racism, as Agamben suggests. However, at the beginning of his book Schmitt nonetheless writes that *Volk* signifies 'an apolitical aspect' (1933: 12), whereby the political concept reaches a biological conceptualization.

In reading Schmitt's book, it becomes clear that over the pages his general ambition concerns transforming *Rasse* [race] into *Artgleichheit* [similarity of species], that is, to transform a biological term into a semi-political term that nonetheless includes the former. In this way Schmitt makes *Artgleichheit* into a principle of *Führung* [leading] and thereby the one and only principle of government in the new NS government. Similarity of species, Schmitt therefore writes, partly anticipating Foucault's later investigations of racism, 'of the one and only German people is, hence, for the purposes of leading the German people politically, the inevitable premise and foundation' (Schmitt 1933: 42).

In his preference for focusing on *Artgleichheit* [similarity of species] rather than the perhaps more obvious *Rasse* [race], Schmitt's attempts may be described as a 'juridicalization' of Third Reich terminology. In any case, it is important to remember that the similarity of species somehow also contains a racial element. In the end, Schmitt's attempts appear to be a mixture of partly biological, partly political terms and conceptualizations, which are then pulled away from their natural and immediate semantic sphere in order to be placed in a new sphere without, however, losing their former meaning.

Agamben has tried to give the following explanation for this peculiar mention of race in National Socialism:

> One cannot understand the peculiarity of the National Socialist conception of race – and, at the same time, the strange vagueness and inconsistency that characterizes it – if one forgets the *biopolitical body* constituting the new fundamental and political subject: it is neither a *quaestio facti* (for instance, the identification with a certain biological body) nor a *quaestio iuris* (the identification of a certain norm of application), but the site for a sovereign political decision that operates in the absolute indifference between fact and law. [...]. A concept such as race in National Socialism (or, in Schmitt's words, of 'similarity of species') [...] realises an immediate coincidence between fact and law. (Agamben 2005a: 193)

What ultimately constitutes the true act of *Führung* [leading] is the sovereign decision on who belongs to the National Socialist race. It therefore comes as no great surprise that the last sentence of *State, Movement, People* manifests just how central the similarity of species is to National Socialism in its Schmittian interpretation: 'Similarity of species' [*Artgleichheit*], Schmitt writes, is that without which, 'a total *Führerstaat* [a state based upon leading] cannot last one day' (1933: 46). However, if the nature of

Führung [leading] is similarity of species [*Artgleichheit*] one might wonder what, then, is the nature of the Führer?

A comparison between the Führer and Italy's *il Duce* [leader] is quite illustrative when describing the former. From a juridical point of view, Hitler was something very different from – and far more dangerous than – a dictator. The Third Reich was likewise something far more lethal than simply a dictatorship. Hitler was Führer and as such was the principle of government in the Third Reich. As mentioned, this was a title never used previously in constitutional German law or elsewhere, just as also *il Duce* was new to the Italian mentality. *Il Duce*, however, was not Benito Mussolini's formal title. Mussolini was *Capo di governo* [Leader of Government], which was a new formal title, nonetheless; it had never been used before and replaced the former *Capo dello Stato* [Leader of State] (Gentile 2012: 112). Mussolini was also *Capo del Partito* [Party Leader] and the 'new office referred to Mussolini's person' (Gentile 2012: 112).

Despite their mutual and radical changes to the two countries' juridical conceptualizations of power and forms of government, it is important to not forget that the Italian state under the National Fascist Party government never formally ceased to be a state of law – despite the almost constant proclamations of state of exception. Mussolini continued to act – at least formally – under the constitution, which was never suspended *in toto* as in the Third Reich. From a juridical point of view, Hitler was above the law, to such a degree that he *was* the law. The Führer did not stand in any kind of relation to the constitution like Mussolini did (however loosely), but to its suspension. Not the state, but the state of exception, was the Führer's bond with Germany. Not only did the law not relate to Hitler as a legal person, the law did not even relate to Hitler through an office. Law, in National Socialist Germany, related to Hitler's *physical* person.

The principled distinction and difference between the Führer and *il Duce* becomes evident when considering the specific terminology of their two respective titles. *Duce* is a term of European nobility, going back to the Romans, and thus having also inherited its special military connotation. As such, it is recognized in the English duke, in the French *duc* and in the Venetian *doge*, all having the Latin root *dux* in common. The lexicons inform that its principal meaning is that of a conductor, in which its

Latin root is recognize once again, or of a guide (Gaffiot 1936). Julius Caesar, for instance, uses *dux* in his *Gallic Wars* when explaining who Divico is by defining the Gallic king of the Helvetii as commander of the Helvetii: '*dux Helvetiorum fuerat*' (Caes., *Gal.*, 1.13:2). A little further in Caesar's text, *dux* is used again, but this time around to explain how he, before presenting his plan, ordered his lieutenant 'to ascend to the highest ridge of the mountain with two legions, and using those who had examined the road as guides [*cum duabus legionibus et iis ducibus*]' (Caes., *Gal.*, 1.21:2). And Cicero, in his *On Duties* (although the Latin *officium* can also mean 'office') in referring to both Plato and the Stoics, explains that men must live in accordance not only with each other, but also with nature, the word *dux* is used even in this regard: 'and as men too are born for the sake of men, that they may be able mutually to help one another; in this direction we ought to follow nature as our guide [*in hoc naturam debemus ducem sequi*]' (Cic., *De off.*, 1:22).

Although one could argue that *dux* is similar to the military meaning of general (its second meaning, according to the lexicons), it is more important in this investigation to determine that *dux* refers not only to a military code but also to a moral code of conduct and, in consequence, to something that is ruled by a given order: either a military order, as in Caesar, or a moral order, on whose *officium* [office] Cicero elaborates. The new office in which Mussolini placed himself as duke, as well as the militarism seen in the National Fascist Party, testifies to both these meanings.

To some extent also the Führer had a paradigm in antiquity. However, rather than to the Roman Empire, Hitler's status relates to the Greek antique formula of the *basileus nomos empsychos* (sovereign [is] living law). The formula, Agamben teaches in his *State of Exception*, is found in Diotogenes' treatise on sovereignty, and whose importance for the origin of the modern theory of sovereignty, 'should not be underestimated' (Agamben: 2004: 89). Agamben had previously treated this formula and demonstrated its relevance to the Third Reich (2005a: 36–45; 194). Thus, when commenting on Diotogenes' treatise, it is not strange that Agamben – almost paraphrasing his earlier book – writes that the meaning of *nomos empsychos* in relation to the law can only be that the sovereign 'is not obligated by the law, so that the life of the law coincides with him in an integral anomia'

(Agamben 2004: 89). 'The *nomos empsychos*', Agamben concludes in a wording important in every sense to the current investigation, 'is the original form of the nexus that the state of exception establishes between the law's outside and inside and, in this sense, it constitutes the archetype of the modern theory of sovereignty' (2004: 90).

Even when reading Ian Kershaw's famous ideas on *Working Towards the Führer* in his discussion of Hitler's Führertum [leadership], where Kershaw refers to the Weberian terminology of charismatic authority, it strikes one just how much Kershaw's thoughts coincide with the ancient formula of the *nomos empsychon* (Kershaw 1993: esp. 111–13). To describe Mussolini in terms such as these would be unthinkable. The ideology of the National Fascist Party, despite other evident problems, is neither anti-constitutional nor biopolitical. National Socialism *is* anti-constitutional, biopolitical and something far more dangerous and lethal as it is founded upon the state of exception and the very threshold of fact and law, outside and inside of the juridical system where the only existing 'law' is Hitler.

The fundamental relation between such a law and Hitler was later expressed paradigmatically in Adolph Eichmann's famous aphoristic utterance, to which Hannah Arendt brought attention in her book on the Eichmann trial in Jerusalem: *Führerworte haben Gesetzeskraft* [Führer-words have the force of law] (cit. in Arendt 1964a: 148). Schmitt had in fact already testified to what can only be called the biopolitical nature of the Führer and the Third Reich, when in 1934 Schmitt tried to justify the assassination of SA leader Ernst Röhm:

> The Führer protects the law from the worst abuse, when he in a moment of danger via his leadership [*Führertum*] as the highest court man [*Gerichtsherr*] creates immediate law [*Recht*]. 'In that hour I was responsible for the fate [*Schicksal*] of the German nation and thereby *the German people's court man*.' The true leader is always also judge. The office of the judge [*Richertum*] flows from the leadership. He who separates the two from one another or even wants to oppose them, either turns the judge [*Richter*] into a counter-leader [*Gegenführer*] or into the instrument of a counter-leader and seeks to unhinge the state with the aid of justice [*Justiz*]. (Schmitt 1934: 946f.)

Röhm, Schmitt argues, had in fact already given both his life and his death to the Führer.

Agamben comments as follows on the legality of Führer-words:

> Just like the word of the *Führer* is not a factual situation that gradually transforms into a norm but is, rather, itself a norm insofar as it is living voice, in this manner the biopolitical body (in its twofold feature of Jewish body and German body, of life unworthy of being lived and as full life) is not an inert biological presupposition to which the rule refers, but is at the same time norm and criterion of its own application, that is, *a norm that decides the fact that decides its application*. (Agamben 2005a: 193)

Thus, behind Schmitt's argument on the state of exception lies a *Rechtsordnung* [legal order] containing its own internal dichotomy or conflict, thus necessitating the sovereign decision in order to save the juridical order. As was underlined above, in the state of exception 'the two elements of the concept "legal order" [*Rechtsordnung*] face one another, proving their conceptual independence' (Schmitt 1994b: 18f.). Yet, in the Third Reich, when the exception has become the rule, the former separation between legality and order is now replaced by the two terms *Richtertum* [the office of the judge] and *Führertum* [leadership], which are inseparable in the most ultimate sense:

> To a community [*Gemeinwesen*], however, that in such a way is organized and ordered in state, movement, people also belongs its own *inner* law [*innere* Recht] of every state carrying life- and community regulations [*Gemeinschaftsordnungen*]. In a special way these are founded on the sworn oath of loyalty to the Führer [*Treue zum Führer*]. (Schmitt 1934: 949)

When killing Röhm, Hitler, as Führer, simply exercised the inner law by which the *Volk* [People] had constituted him in the form of the oath. Hitler's actions are always already legal, which is why he can say that he acted as the German people's court man.

Schmitt's argument – and what makes it biopolitical – is that not only was Hitler's action justified in regard to Röhm. As Führer, Hitler had even acted as the protector of German life and the guarantor of the people's right to life, which Röhm, according to Schmitt, thereby endangered. The Führer now provides the security and protection that the Weimar Constitution had formerly provided, and he decides solely on its means and needs.

It has been shown that the five fates – dead [*tot*], murdered [*ermordet*], ???, escaped in death [*Flucht in den Tod*] and escaped [*Flucht*] (Demnig 2015: 4) – must indicate that the Stolpersteine commemorate the victims as subjects of law and therefore gives the impression that the Third Reich was a constitutional state. However, via Schmitt's two terms of dictatorship – commissionary and constitutional – that have been examined in this chapter, it becomes clear that the Third Reich cannot be conceived as either of these. Neither the existing nor the future constitution is at the centre in National Socialism and the Third Reich.

Agamben has successfully demonstrated that the form of government in the Third Reich, which Fraenkel called a dual state – where the Weimar Constitution was suspended (it had the form of law, but no force) and the state of exception effectuated (not having the form of law but having its force) – represents a biopolitical state of exception. Such a biopolitics is beyond Foucault's conception, because the exception rather than the law is what produces the naked life via an inclusive exclusion. Actions performed during the Third Reich can, by necessity, not be described in the normal vocabulary of politics or law, since both presume the existence of a state of law, in which the Third Reich does not qualify. The Führer does not constitute a constitutional figure, and his Führertum is not a constitutional office.

It is in this regard that the problematic nature of the forms of victimhood in the Stolpersteine present themselves. A state that does not operate within the fundamental and constitutional distinction between legal and illegal, fact and law, cannot be described in terms of the conceptual pairing of perpetrator and murder victim by any ordinary meaning of these words – especially not when the murder victim was, in fact, subjected to state organized annihilation and to state policy while other branches of penal law functioned as always. Since the reality of the Third Reich breaks down the familiar and ordinary categories of jurisprudence and politology, new figures of interpretation need to be at centre. The paradigm for the National Socialist form of government is not the dignified subject of law but the naked life and the Muselmann, both beyond law and dignity in the face of delegalization and dehumanization.

While it is to be appreciated that a monument wishes to reflect who each of the victims were as citizens before they came under National Socialist government and to commemorate this fact, it is to be regretted that the Stolpersteine make pretence that the camp somehow continued to treat them as subjects of law, when in fact they were ultimately and rather simply exterminated by a constitutional state. The crucial question that demands an answer, therefore, is: if it is so obvious that the Third Reich was not a state of law and the victims were beyond any ethics, why do the Stolpersteine persist with these aspects? In other words, what are the Stolpersteine really doing in terms of use of history and as commemorative markers?

Before these questions can be answered, it is necessary to investigate another historical reference that rather paradoxically does not seem to testify to a particular use of history at all – on the contrary, the reference appears to be very factual: the *hier wohnte* [here lived] on the Stolpersteine, indicating where the victim lived. Is it not the case that, just as with the five fates, the bald fact of the victim's dwelling-place gives little room for expressing or giving witness to the extreme separation of the law and the exception, the home and the camp? Or, in short, is it the case that the mere placement of a Stolperstein in itself represents a case of biopolitics, in that it refers to a private home and residence while installed in public space and, in this way, gives witness to the brutality of the Third Reich?

An important cipher in this matter is Demnig's statement that with the Stolperstein 'the victim will get its name back' [*bekommt das Opfer seinen Namen wieder*] (2002: 13), and that a Stolperstein 'symbolically restores dignity to every victim' (Katzman and Paulix 2005: 17). Together, these two utterances will structure the last chapters of the present book, reaching a hopeful culmination in a discussion of the Stolpersteine as to what could be called commemorative performatives in Chapter 6.

CHAPTER 4

Home and Being: Memory between Cartography and Ruin

The Dissolution of the Home

Having discussed the victim and the form of government under which the victim was annihilated in the previous chapters, it is now possible to analyse the meaning and consequences of the first engraving one reads on the Stolpersteine: the *hier wohnte* [here lived]. In many respects, this is what – to state the hypothesis – forms Demnig's idea of giving the victims their names back as well as restoring their dignity. The *Wohnort* [place of residence] is a crucial referential and historical mark of victimhood. After having dealt with the five fates and the place of residence, it will then be possible in the final chapters of this book to analyse the Stolpersteine in their commemorative entirety, in order to further tighten and continue the discussion from the earlier chapters concerning history as problem, that is, the challenge between history and memory, fact and commemoration.

This chapter begins by inquiring into the nature of the intimacy between private and public, house and square, which for millennia have been key distinctions in the West, but which the Stolpersteine now seem to have been set in motion – or perhaps even compromised – by being installed themselves in the public pavement while using, nonetheless, the private homes of contemporary citizens as the primary identificatory mark. Having set out to analyse the meaning of house, home and dwelling, Martin Heidegger's reflections on *Wohnen* [dwelling] will henceforth play a key role. On this basis, the chapter ends with a discussion of how the Stolpersteine stand in regard to Heidegger's thinking on dwelling.

Aside from the principle of *Blut und Boden* [blood and soil], house and home are two other major fields of intensity in National Socialism and the Third Reich. In a state of law, today or in the days of the Weimar Republic, few features are more fundamental than law and private ownership. In the previous chapters, it has been made clear that one of the basic components of the Stolpersteine was that victims were not only deported from their homes and residences, but that they were deported in the ultimate sense, that is *unto* death or *from* life. When the Stolpersteine establish dwelling [*Wohnen*] as the key term for commemoration of the victims of the NS-era, a central feature must therefore be recognized: the Stolpersteine consider that to live in a home and to bear a name are so fundamental to every human and to every victim that these two circumstances cannot simply be reduced to mere factual circumstance. In other words, on the Stolpersteine, even though Jews, starting from 1939, were given the names Israel (for men) and Sarah (for women) by the German state, these were not proper names. Likewise, even though Jews lived in what National Socialist terminology determined as a *Judenhaus* [Jewish house], this was not a home as such. The meaning of deportation to the Stolpersteine expands to these ontological issues of being and dwelling, the intimacy between a human being and his or her name. Precisely in this regard, Heidegger's thinking is interesting.

The extraordinary fact that the Stolpersteine aim to represent each and every single victim with a monument has already been commented on. The importance ascribed to the victim's home (although the victim's work place could also be commemorated) is just as extraordinary, because this is also commemorated. Never before in German commemoration have victims of extermination been tied so closely and so intimately to their individual homes or, in their professional capacity, of occupying an office or a trade.

The architecture normally associated with monuments for victims of the Third Reich is undermined by the Stolpersteine. The earlier bombastic art – paradigmatically represented in the Berlin Memorial to the Murdered Jews of Europe – is unknown to the Stolpersteine; their expression is, at least in this perspective, much humbler, much simpler and seems to be more in harmony with individuality than with totality. The Great Evil is now turned upside down; its parole does not shout but, on the contrary, presents each victim's name, again and again, in a kind of endless whisper in front of a home, rather than once and for all in a public square. It is not unlikely that the exterminations really do appear far more violent and drastic by this monument in miniature via the repetition of a victim's deportation and annihilation, one after the other. It is as if the Stolpersteine are intended to represent the performance of the National Socialist government, whose general politics of deportation in each case meant that one and then another were forced to leave their homes. There is a kind a repetition in the Stolpersteine that, here at least, reflects each individual's history of dwelling and deportation in the totality of the event at large.

Despite the use of other headlines ('here learned or here taught; here worked; here practised [...] and here resided [*hier lebte*]' (Demnig 2015: 4)), and even though stones without any heading are also possible, it is clear that the focus every time is the same: a Stolperstein refers in each and every case to a given and individual activity – dwelling, working, teaching, etc. – that took place in a home or in a particular building at a particular time, which then was forced to stop. For instance, as mentioned above (cf. Chapter 1), the philosopher Edmund Husserl has a Stolperstein installed in front of Freiburg University where he was professor from 1916 to 1928 (see Figure 3). In 1933, it all ended with his *Berufsverbot* [disbarment], and Husserl, at sixty-nine years of age, gave the chair to his assistant Martin Heidegger.

Michael Imort is therefore too imprecise when, in his 2010 *Stumbling Blocks: A Decentralized Memorial to Holocaust Victims*, he writes of 'handcrafted cobblestones set flush into the public pavement in front of private house entrances' (2010: 234). Not only before private houses but, as pointed out, also apartments and workplaces, in front of every kind of building where a victim formerly undertook some kind of activity, a Stolperstein can be installed. Likewise, Monika Richarz in *Stumbling Stones: Marks of Holocaust Memory on German Streets* is imprecise in seeming to believe that the Stolpersteine only exist 'on German streets' and only in front of 'buildings in Germany' (2008: 325). Richarz mentions no other country, although her essay supposedly 'examines the *origin*, the motivation, the *meaning*, and the *political signification* of the memorial stones' (2008: 326, italics added), all factors that address the European dimension of the

Stolpersteine project, whereby victims in a range of countries can have a Stolperstein installed in their memory.

Without underestimating these other activities and locations commemorated by the Stolpersteine, it is as if these historical facts culminate in the most used headline of *hier wohnte* [here lived]. It is therefore crucial to recognize the fundamental meaning of the German term *Wohnort* [place of residence]: dwelling [*Wohnen*] and location [*Ort*] together constitute the location for victimhood representation by the Stolpersteine.

'A Stolperstein', Demnig writes, 'carries most often the heading: *hier wohnte* [here lived]' (2015: 4), which illustrates just how far the Third Reich went in 'purifying' itself of citizens judged unfit to live in the Reich: National Socialism penetrated life in its entirety, and the Stolpersteine are aimed at representing this in terms of commemorating life down to its most private details, while remaining in the public sphere. In *Stumbling Stones: Holocaust Memorials, National Identity, and Democratic Inclusion in Berlin*, Kirsten Harjes has tried to describe this strategy:

> The Stumbling Stones have to strike a difficult balance between being a public monument, i.e., a public, official piece of collective memory standing for the dead and for the city's wish to commemorate the dead, and being located in the semi-private space right in front of people's doorways. As these doorways are usually the entry to an apartment house with several occupants, and as the sponsors of the stones most often do not live in that house, the tenants will at first have no connection to such a memorial stone. Forcing people of various ages and ethnicities to integrate the memory of the Holocaust into their daily lives – or to actively ignore it – does not necessarily have positive effects [...]. The possibility of negative reactions to Stumbling Stones underlines not only the importance of a well-grounded general education in German history, but also the important role of more ritualised forms of collective memory that provide an interpretative context for the Stolpersteine. (Harjes 2005: 147)

In the light of this citation, it is interesting to read what Salomon Korn, the chairman of *Jüdische Gemeinde* [Jewish Communities] *Frankfurt am Main* and Vice President of the *Zentralrat der Juden in Deutschland* [Central Council of Jews in Germany], wrote in 1996 in *Frankfurter Allgemeine Zeitung* concerning the Memorial to the Murdered Jews of Europe, which at that time had become a heavily debated topic in the German public realm.

In the context of investigating the Stolpersteine, Korn's article constitutes a key text: he shares Harjes' final point concerning a ritualized form of memory, and the Stolpersteine could in that sense be said to be an attempt to solve problems in German memorial culture as these are identified by Korn.

> If it is not religiously supported, then Friedrich Nietzsche's conclusion for commemoration stands: 'Only that which does not stop hurting continues to be remembered.' However, since no pain lasts forever, every tormenting memory will disappear over time – and will be gone after generations. What then remains at best is an aesthetically appealing memorial [*Denkmal*] in which the commemorating event [*Ereignis*] is kept 'neutral to the senses' [*gefühlsneutral*] – corresponding to a historical date in the memory of the contemporaries [*in Gedächtnis der Zeitgenossen*]. And should we hitherto have learned the lessons of the past, the inevitable fact [*Tatsache*] would be even more tolerable, that is, that every memorial in the end becomes the memorial of its own perishability. (Korn 1999: 60)

Korn identifies three important aspects:

A) If a monument is not supported by some kind of rituality, then Nietzsche is right and the monument disappears as an architecture of memory reduced to a *Gefühlsneutralität*.
B) Since no pain lasts forever, not even that of one of the most horrific events (such as the Third Reich exterminations) will last, which means that:
C) Every monument, in the end, must recognize and give witness to its own perishability.

These three points can be analysed further, so that it may be possible to draw some more specific parallels to the Stolpersteine.

A) With the installation of a monument outside the front door of a private residence or workplace, it is clear that any coming and going becomes part of the commemorative act. 'He who does not stumble, does not walk', as one researcher put it (Rönnerper (ed.) in ibid. 2010: 7). Immediately, in front of what could be called 'a Stolperstein home', quite ordinary and rather dull activities, such as sweeping the pavement of leaves, sand or dirt, shovelling snow – actions that are simply part of the maintenance of any property – become part of the commemorative practice. The installation seems to suggest a form of ritualization that consists of a metaphorical stumbling and walking on the victims of extermination, but which nonetheless takes the practical form of home cultivation and ownership responsibility.

B) In the previous chapter, the unfortunate use (or misuse) of juridical and ethical vocabulary on the Stolpersteine was discussed at considerable length. In the current discussion, this critique can be supplemented, in that the Stolpersteine aim to represent pain using vocabulary from that same sphere. Evidently, although not *per se* but at least in relation to their context, the five fates – '*tot* [dead] or *ermordet* [murdered]; for unclear cases: *Schicksal unbekannt* [fate unknown: ???] [...] *Flucht in den Tod* [escaped in death] [...] *Flucht* [escaped]' (Demnig 2015: 4) – express in themselves the pain of the deportation and extermination of millions of civilians. If such engravings were to be read on a large-scale monument, such as the Memorial to the Murdered Jews of Europe, the meaning, naturally, would not alter. However, it is not unlikely that the pain and sadness that the reader experiences would, if not disappear, then at least be shared and perhaps even minimized simply by the presence of others who had also stood by and read. And if the sadness and pain became too great for the reader, he could walk away. He could even choose whether or not he wanted to read of such pain, evil and catastrophe in the first place.

The fact that the Stolperstein engravings are to be read on a monument installed just outside the front door of a random citizen reduces and contracts such a reading to a single reader or a small group of readers, namely, those who live in the house or apartment and have to pass the stone every day in order to enter the front door, as Harjes wrote. The resident cannot escape this commemorative act, because it first and foremost cannot be separated from the resident's dwelling and his more-or-less ordinary non-commemorative comings and goings. It depends firstly on he who dwells there to actualize the memory of the victim who once lived in this particular home. Even though a random pedestrian might stumble upon the victim of deportation, this stumbling refers nonetheless to a home where, in most cases, someone lives:

hier wohnte [here lived], meaning precisely here and not next door. In this home, a victim of annihilation once lived, and now you live here. Not there on the other side of the street, but right here, in this house, at this address. The pedestrian can walk away. The resident can only stay. This very special relation between the former and current residents of a Stolperstein house is also reflected in the grammatical construction of the verb in the headline: *hier wohnte* [here lived]. *Wohnte* [lived] is *imperfectum*, that is, past tense or, in German, *Imperfekt*. The past tense means that the action described is not terminated but, rather, continues into contemporaneity leaving it unfinished and incomplete (Bussmann 1990). Is this not what the Stolpersteine – or in fact any monument – really do in terms of commemoration, in that the past reaches into the unfinished historical process of contemporaneity? In the case of the Stolpersteine, this kind of process or continuation is carried out by the current resident – despite the fact that the relationship between these two residents, the former and current, most probably does not exist, as Harjes pointed out, potentially running the risk of leaving the monument to be ignored or forgotten.

In contrast to Korn's idea of the monument, the Stolpersteine seek to eternalize the commemoration of the victim by letting the current resident reach back in time and commemorate. This is the logical consequence of the Stolpersteine's grammatical construction: the victim's *Wohnen* [dwelling] is left uncompleted, but in the hands of a present *Wohnen* that, nevertheless, can if not complete then at least continue it towards completion. Demnig himself expresses this radical historicism in the following way: 'the victim', Demnig says, 'will get its name back' [*bekommt das Opfer seinen Namen wieder*] (2002: 13), so that a Stolperstein 'symbolically restores dignity to every victim' (Katzman and Paulix 2005: 17).

C) This peculiar historical motor of the grammatical construction is what ultimately acts contrary to Korn's idea that the monument is a carrier of its own perishability. The *hier* [here] means, in fact, here in this home; which was where the victim lived [*wohnte*] and which constituted a dwelling that was then taken away from the victim, preventing it from ending. Or, in the words of Hannah Arendt used earlier, the

> victim in question lived a life but his proper death was taken from him and permanence was given 'to the process of dying itself' where 'both death and life are obstructed equally effectively' (Arendt 1962: 443). It appears therefore that the resident in a Stolpersteine home first and foremost is the person with the capacity of activating that to which the inscriptions testify. In the public realm of pavements and sidewalks, the random resident is the one who becomes the principled vehicle for the commemorative responsibility towards the Stolperstein home – both regarding the former and 'historical' home of the victim, as well as towards the state on whose territory the monument is installed. Although this strategy is not entirely unproblematic, as Harjes underlined, Demnig appears to define it as one of the core strategies for the Stolpersteine. The breaking down of boundaries between state and citizen, private and public is simply central to Demnig's monument: 'To me, a central aspect is over and over again to test boundaries, to cross boundaries. In the end, more than you think is possible. It is feasible' (Demnig 2002: 9).

The reference to, and use of, history in the shape of the private home, domain and ownership on the one side, and the 'gift' [*Paten*] to the state in the public sphere on the other, is important to the Stolpersteine. This is the boundary upon which the monument places itself: from the past to the present, from the public sphere to the private, from the street to the home. All the time, this represents the crossing of a boundary and the eternal carrier of the victim in question is the present resident, and the one after him, and so on. Nevertheless, the difference and, indeed, fundamental boundary between private and public is not simply overthrown by the Stolpersteine. Rather, when the Stolpersteine place themselves on the threshold and boundary itself, what characterizes the monument is a continuous flux of crossing and returning, rather than a static state.

Together function and grammar in this use of history try to escape Korn's conclusion that every monument, in the end, gives witness to its own perishability, to its own existence in history. For although the dwelling that the victim himself could not end is meant to be continued, this happens not solely through the present resident but, in the end, also through the residents who come after. The commemorative function and act are bound by a specific location and home in the past, not by a specific resident in the present. This kind of functionality is repeated, again and again, in an attempt to give back the victim's name and *Wohnen* [dwelling], so that what was once taken away from the victim can now be eternally and continuously offered as the ultimate gift. Contrary to Korn, the Stolpersteine aim to eternalize the commemoration of the exterminations by reducing (or expanding) it to the functionality of the community and, specifically, to the resident in a Stolperstein home. Commemoration will only end when the community no longer exists.

The fact that the resident is the sole carrier of this commemorative act has at least one counter argument: where any difference in cartography is registered – where the past home does not correspond to a present one, there is no resident to take this task upon his shoulders. The caducity of the Stolperstein then presents itself, as there is no present home or *Wohnen* [dwelling] to eternalize it. To some extent the monument ceases to exist as a commemorative operator and lingers in oblivion – at least to a greater extent than would be the case were a present home to stand behind the Stolperstein. The Stolpersteine for Konrad Brzezek and Max Schmidt, at the corner of Holzmarktstraße and Lichtenstraße, a very busy intersection in the Berlin periphery, far from any residence, are examples of such lonely or abandoned Stolpersteine. Their *Wohnort* [place of residence] once existed, but is now only 'present' in terms of these monuments. In this case, the community as a whole, or rather any pedestrian who passes by, rather than an individual resident, carries the task of commemoration.

Thus, solely considering their location, the lonely Stolpersteine are, perhaps, the most interesting and even perhaps the most successful – however paradoxical it might seem. These Stolpersteine tend to refer more explicitly to the catastrophe of Third Reich annihilation and of its exterminations, to destruction and deportation, to oblivion and ruin. Here, the victims' names exist as a kind of individualized cry from the totality of victimhood, insisting on standing out from oblivion and continuing to be part of contemporaneity and of present history, to be part of the lives of those who live today. They testify to the existence of a home that continues to dwell in the past, and only those who pay attention, only those who stumble upon such a Stolperstein in this commemorative landscape, can commemorate and constitute it as a *Denkmal* [memory plate] in the etymological sense of the term, that is, as a thinking [*denken*] of the past. Stefanie Endlich attempts to capture this feature in her formulation that the Stolpersteine constitute a 'mosaic of a comprehensive memory landscape [*Erinnerungslandschaft*], which only becomes recognisable in its totality of the historical event' (2002: 31).

Regarding such a discussion concerning not only where and when to install Stolpersteine but, perhaps more important, also whether present politics should be overturned by present recollection of the past, the position of Jefferson Chase in the Boston Globe is remarkable – although it is doubtful whether his analysis advances finding a solution: 'Where the memorial stones are laid is determined not by governmental committees, but by history itself, as researched by Demnig, schoolchildren, or patrons' (Chase 2004). History *itself*?

Two examples are of interest in illustrating that matters are somewhat more complicated than Chase would seem to admit. The first concerns two Stolpersteine, laid for Ernst Friedrich Beurer and Marta Schmid, respectively, both from Stuttgart and both annihilated in the Third Reich Euthanasia Programme. Beurer suffered from a disease of the cornea that left him blind and quite aggressive, to the extent that his family could not keep him at home (they had initially tried to tie him up in the living room using a chain). He was sent to Anstalt Stetten (today the Diakonie Stetten), and in 1931 to Stetten's Wohnheim Rommelhausen. On 10 September 1940, Beurer was deported to Grafeneck and gassed on the same day – an annihilation method later to be institutionalized throughout the death camps and concentration camps in the Reich. Schmid was epileptic from birth and was sent to Anstalt Stetten before the age of five in 1924. On 5 November 1940, she too was sent to Grafeneck and annihilated. In the newspaper *Stuttgarter Nachrichten*, where these stories are found, the following is the conclusion of a short article:

> In front of *the former residential buildings* the community core – together with the working group Commemoration of the Deaconry Stetten, the association Allmende [litt. common land] and the initiator of the pan-European Stolperstein-campaign – Gunter Demnig will lay three so-called Stolpersteine [because a third Stolperstein

beyond the two mentioned was installed on the same day] for Nazi victims on Thursday October 7. Meeting place is at 12 p.m. on the corner of Lange Straße/ Seitenstraße. (Wolz 2010, italics added)

The second example is also from Stuttgart and concerns one of the city's so-called *Judenhäuser* [Jewish Houses]: as the married couple Max and Mathilde Henle could not continue to live at Hohentwielstraße 146b, because the house owner himself wanted to get married, in March 1939 they had no other choice than to move to Mrs. Henle's sister, Erna Bickert, in Koppentalstraße 3. Ever since *Kristallnacht* in 1938, Jews were precluded from the housing market, and any relocation had to be approved by the Gestapo: 'In this "Jewish House" the Henles lived together with ten Jewish renting parties in the narrowest of rooms!' (Bassler 2013: 66). The couple currently living at Hohentwielstraße 146b, the Erbslöhs, have reacted strongly against the installation of these two Stolpersteine. Their lawyer argued that, in fact, this was not their last self-elected home, and that 'the installed Stolpersteine in the case of a sale would affect the property negatively' (cit. in Bassler 2013: 66). The conflict ended in court. The *Amtsgericht* [Local Court] of Stuttgart did not rule in favour of the homeowners at Hohentwielstraße 146b in the case of Diethard and Helga Erbslöh against the City of Stuttgart, and later neither did the *Landgericht* [Regional Court]. The two Stolpersteine for Max and Mathilde Henle therefore remain in front of the Erbslöh house at Hohentwielstraße 146b (Borgmann 2011).

Quite a few paradoxes emerge from these two examples. Both Beurer and Schmid were sent off long before the National Socialists had come into government, two years before in the case of Beurer and nine years for Schmid. Furthermore, the Stolpersteine are *not* in fact laid at the last self-elected *Wohnort* [place of residence] but, instead, in front of the institution of Anstalt Stetten, to which the Weimar Republic initially sent them in 1931 and 1924, respectively. The Third Reich did not deport Beurer and Schmid from their homes – the Weimar Republic had already done this work for them. The Third Reich simply communicated to Anstalt Stetten that they wished the people in question to be disposed of. As analysed in Chapter 3, the Third Reich merely made use of the institutions already at hand in the Weimar Republic, and gave them a gentle – though nonetheless lethal and terrible – push in the National Socialist direction. Nevertheless, the question presents itself: what in reality were Ernst Friedrich Beurer's and Marta Schmid's last self-elected places of residence? On the premises of the Stolpersteine, a solution could be said to already have been prepared since the heading *hier lebte* [here resided] is preferred in cases 'regarding institutional care' (Demnig 2015: 4), which indeed seems to be the case here. Nevertheless, Beurer and Schmid's Stolpersteine both display: *hier wohnte* [here lived].

Concerning the so-called 'Jewish Houses', naturally the last self-elected place of residence for the Henles is *not* the house from which they were deported in 1942 (because Koppentalstraße 3 was a 'Jewish House') but, instead, the home they had left in 1939: Hohentwielstraße 146b. It is very surprising, therefore, to read the engravings on the two Stolpersteine for the Henles, even if Bassler – who is part of the Stolperstein-Initiative Stuttgart – fails to observe this; because, from the homepage for the Stuttgart Stolpersteine, one learns that the year for the couple's *Zwangsumsiedlung* [forced relocation] is stated as 1942. But 1942 was the year they were sent to Theresienstadt from the 'Jewish House', not the year of their deportation away from their last self-elected *Wohnort* [place of residence] at Hohentwielstraße 146b, which was 1939.

Other facts are surprising as well: 'Attorney Roger Bohn, representing the state, argued', as Bassler quotes from the verdict of the Local Court on 12 February 2011, 'The state has a pavement; there, an artist has laid two plates. Where, ladies and gentlemen, is the violation of ownership?' (cit. in Bassler 2013: 67). Bassler advises that the court based its verdict on §1004 of the German Civil Code. In its English translation, under the headline 'Claim for removal and injunction', the code states the following: '(1) If the ownership is interfered with by means *other* than removal or retention of possession, the owner may require the disturber to remove the interference. If further interferences are to be feared, the owner may seek a prohibitory injunction. (2) The claim is excluded if the owner is obliged to tolerate the interference' (BGB, §1004, italics added).

Naturally, it is not the intention here to go in detail into juridical questions and matters; it is sufficient to mention that the specific paragraph does not state anything concerning damage to property [*Eigentumsverletzung*], which nonetheless appears to structure Bohn's argument. On the contrary, the much more difficult matter concerns whether or not a property is affected 'by means *other* than removal or retention of possession', for instance a decrease in value. The Erbslöhs' lawyer tried to argue along these lines when he argued for the probability of a negative price movement on the particular house in question.

The artist himself, Gunter Demnig, stated the following about the Stolpersteine in front of the Erbslöhs' home after the verdict: 'That's super and wonderful news!', and Demnig continues his interview with *Stuttgarter Zeitung* via a formulation whose significance cannot be underestimated: my Stolpersteine are 'meant to be memorials and commemoration for the victims of the NS-regime – not a reference of guilt [*Schuldverweisung*] to those who owned the houses in question during the time of the Third Reich' (Borgmann 2011). Yet later, concerning the exact location of the Stolpersteine, Demnig on his homepage less enthusiastically advises prospective sponsors that as a rule Stolpersteine are not be to installed 'on a location whereto the victims were forced to move (as for instance in front of the so-called "Jewish Houses" [*Judenhäusern*]' (Demnig 2015: 4).

Demnig, it would appear, is not unaware of the potential problems in his idea of using contemporary private property and dwellings [*Wohnen*] in this way. In answering why current property owners must not be asked whether they wish to have Stolpersteine installed in front of their home or workplace, Demnig gives the following explanation:

> First of all, based on the consideration and sometimes the experience that many house owners would probably prevent such plates [from being installed]. For instance, in Köln-Deutz it occurred that a house owner insisted that the Jewish married couple Grünberg had never lived in his house. As it turned out they actually did live there and the house was Aryanised. If every time I had to obtain the personal consent from the property owner the project could not be realized. (Demnig 2002: 13)

The contemporary citizen, as Demnig states, must be forced to remember and commemorate; must be forced to allow his house and home to become the subject of state commemoration if the Stolpersteine project is not to fail.

These examples help to illustrate Harjes' concern, quoted at the beginning of this chapter: 'Forcing people of various ages and ethnicities to integrate the memory of the Holocaust into their daily lives – or to actively ignore it – does not necessarily have positive effects [...]' (Harjes 2005: 147). Moreover, in the case of Beurer and Schmid, the Stolpersteine inflict too sharp a separation between the Weimar Republic and the Third Reich concerning the treatment of the disabled. A clear-cut transformation from democracy to totalitarianism, from Weimar Republic to Third Reich, is too simplistic and too optimistic. Had the transformation been more abrupt and instantaneous, not only would scholarship about the Third Reich but also commemoration of its victims face problems of a wholly other and less complicated dimension. Unfortunately, this is not the reality. It is not at all impossible that the risk of failing to acknowledge one of the great dangers of National Socialism is substantial, so democracy's self-transformation into totalitarianism is underestimated.

Thus, the coming pages will try to answer the following questions. What is this *Wohnen* [dwelling]? Why is it so crucial, to the extent that the Stolpersteine choose it as their referentiality *par excellence*, that contemporary Germans go to court to fight over it and that Demnig believes that citizens must be forced to let the personal sphere be at the centre of state commemoration?

State and House, *Polis* and *Oikos*

'Martin Heidegger stands as *the* thinker of dwelling [*des Wohnens*]', the first sentence reads in Burkhard Biella's book on 'a philosophy of dwelling' (1998: 9). Over the following pages, the attempt will likewise be to actualize the question Heidegger poses towards the end of his 1951 *Building Dwelling Thinking*, where he ponders the next step in his analysis of dwelling: 'What is the condition of dwelling in our questionable time?' (Heidegger 2000: 163). Having done that, the results of the analysis will then be used to shed new light upon the Stolpersteine.

Already in his 1946 *Letter on 'Humanism'* Heidegger had, in fact, anticipated the later and deeper analysis on home and dwelling: 'Language is the house of Being [*Die Sprache ist das Haus des Seins*]' is one of his aphoristic utterances (Heidegger 1996: 313). At the end of his 'letter', Heidegger even says that he promises to pursue the analysis of dwelling at a later time: 'To speak of the house of Being is not a transfer of the image of "house" to Being [*Sein*]; instead, by the appropriate thinking of the essence of Being, we will one day be able to think what "house" and "dwelling" are' (Heidegger 1996: 358). These are precisely the thoughts that one encounters five years later in *Building Dwelling Thinking*, where the familiarity with earlier themes from the philosopher's 1927 *Being and Time* are quickly recognized, as when Heidegger writes, for instance, that 'dwelling is the manner by which we humans *are* on earth' (2000: 149). To Heidegger, Being [*Sein*] and dwelling [*Wohnen*] are co-extensive for the human being.

In his text, Heidegger inquires into the consequences of the damage and destruction inflicted by the war. His questions are, however, rather unusual. Three times Heidegger addresses what he calls the prevailing housing shortage: once at the beginning of the text – 'In the present housing shortage', Heidegger asks, 'do the houses in themselves ensure that a *dwelling* happens?' (2000: 147); again, later: 'Everywhere and with good reason you hear the talk of housing shortage' (Heidegger 2000: 163); and finally, summarizing the fundamental challenges of the housing shortage in the rhetorical question of whether the human being's *Heimatlosigkeit* [loss of native soil] simply does not consist in the fact 'that the human being still does not think of the *real housing shortage* [*Wohnungsnot*] *as the* need [*Not*]?' (Heidegger 2000: 163). While the war left millions of German citizens without a home, Heidegger's concerns do not regard economic, social or other practical circumstances.

Speaking of the war, Heidegger – at least here – instead relates it to the problem of dwelling in the sense of a fundamental aspect of being human. On the final pages of his text, it becomes clear that the problem holding Heidegger's interest, although undoubtedly moulded by the same war, is actually older than this war itself, and even older than its empirical–historical fact: 'The real housing shortage is also older than the world wars and the destructions [...]' (Heidegger 2000: 163). Why is the housing shortage older – which to Heidegger means more relevant and more interesting – than the one in his contemporary Germany, and what are the consequences of this? By underlining that the war in this way has activated the ancient question concerning Being and dwelling in the direction of a *Not* [need], Heidegger uses the practical housing shortage to make a philosophical claim that in relation to the Stolpersteine is very interesting.

A first and preliminary answer to these questions and peculiarities is given in the opening passages of *Building Dwelling Thinking*: 'This attempted consideration [*Denkversuch*] does not establish construction [*das Bauen*], as such, as a result of architecture and technology, but rather traces building back to those fields where anything what *is* belongs' (Heidegger 2000: 147). Heidegger's *Denkversuch* thus consists of examining precisely how 'what *is*' is *gleichursprünglich* [has the same origin] as building. Apart from its intrinsic philosophical interest, which seems to be a variation of the fundamental ontology of Heidegger's *Being and Time*, its relevance to the present book's analyses of the Stolpersteine is that a key feature of this monument is, as shown in previous chapters, to build a form of historical being (the victim) into the home and dwelling of a present being (the resident) in one way or another. Furthermore, it was also underlined that the question of dwelling that the Stolpersteine in this way set in motion, appears to be divided between the victim on the one side and the resident on the other, the past on the one side and the present on the other, which the Stolpersteine try to eternalize in some way.

Heidegger calls the human being *Dasein* [being-there] and it designates that the creature is capable of constituting its living as dwelling, that is, to have a home. This theme points back to *Being and Time*, where its main character, *Dasein*, was originally introduced; however, whereas, in *Being and Time*, *Dasein* was submitted to the world – or, rather, had fallen to the world – which Heidegger calls a being-in-the-world (Heidegger 2001: §12, 75; cf. id. 1996: 358), in *Building Dwelling Thinking*, *Dasein* cannot be separated from having a home. Hence, as Otto Pöggeler explains, unlike the animal and its cave, *Dasein* has the ability to transform the refuge into a home (1990: 256–8). The key position that the world held before is now supplemented, or perhaps minimized, in the form of dwelling, making this the main stage for the *Dasein*. As Heidegger wants to pursue dwelling genealogically (i.e. as Heidegger proclaimed, to trace an event back 'to those fields where anything what *is* belongs' (2000: 147)) in the realms of philosophy, this points in the direction of a conceptual investigation that, naturally, is closely tied to history. As Heidegger teaches, the 'encouragement about the essence of a case comes to us from language' (2000: 148).

Heidegger presents his genealogical results of *Wohnen* [dwelling] the following way:

> Where the word building [*bauen*] still speaks in its originality, it even says *how far* the essence of dwelling [*das Wesen des Wohnens*] reaches. Building, *buan, bhu, beo* are namely our word '*bin*' [I am] in the phrases: *Ich bin, du bist* [I am, you are], the imperative *bis*, be. What, then, does: I am, you are, mean? The old word building, to which the 'I am' [*bin*] belongs, answers: 'I am, you are' [*Ich bin, du bist*] meaning: I dwell, you dwell [*Ich wohne, du wohnst*]. The manner by which you are and I am, the way according to which we humans *are* on the earth, is *Buan*, dwelling [*das Wohnen*]. To be a human being means: to be on the earth as a mortal, it means: to dwell. (Heidegger 2000: 149)

Being (I am, you are), it appears, fundamentally contains a social aspect; that is, it points in the direction of a community (I live, you live).

Heidegger, whose philology at times can be rather imaginative, is nevertheless in this case confirmed eight years later by Julius Pokorny's Indo-Germanic lexicon. In the Indo-European root **b(e)u–, bh(e)u–*, Pokorny writes, the following meanings are to be found: '"to inflate", "to swell", and from these "to originate, to become and to be", moreover [...] numerous nominal connections with the meanings "the Being, essence, dwelling, residence"' (Pokorny 1959: 146). In pursuing the Indo-European root **bhu*–, Pokorny determines that it can also mean 'earth, world, being [*Erde, Welt, Sein*]' and that it has a parallel to the Greek 'φύσις "nature", φῦλον n. "tribe, gender, species [Art]", φῦλή "community and from it the units of the armed forces", and even to the Latin *fio, fieri*, becoming, originating, being raised' (1959: 147f.). Finally, Pokorny confirms Heidegger's idea of **bhu* meaning 'I am', via the Anglo-Saxon *beo* meaning 'I am [*ich bin*]' (Pokorny 1959: 149). Thus, **bhu*– Heidegger's etymological ground for his terminology of dwelling [*Wohnen*] – contains both something private, as in tribe and gender, as well as something public, as in community and the units of the armed forces.

A decade later, in his major work from 1969, *Indo-European Language and Society*, Émile Benveniste follows Pokorny's etymologies – and therefore indirectly also Heidegger's. A favourite theme in the humanities at the time, probably due to Lévi-Strauss's research on kinship and to the structuralism he and George Dumézil had begun developing, Benveniste writes the following in a chapter in which he deals with 'the formation and suffixation of kinship terms' (Benveniste 1969: 259): 'We have in our possession', the linguist informs us, 'the testimonies of three ancient Doric tribes in a Homeric attributive adjective: Δωριέες τριχαί(ω)ικες "the Dorians (divided) in three *wik–*" (cf. gr. (ω)οῖκος, (ω)οἶκος)' (1969: 259).

Further on in his book, Benveniste confirms once again that, 'the son of **weik–*, of the social unity corresponding to the Latin *uicus* [and the] Greek *(w)oîkos*', means '"the son of the house". The two confirms one another' (1969: 305). Home and house – which in the Romance languages are quite similar in formulations such as *maison*, *casa* [house] and *à la maison, alla casa* [home] – as Benveniste explains, are in fact so intertwined and entangled that they extend beyond the home and the house all the way to the town or city, which is what Benveniste found to be the case in the prefix 'tri'.

Based on the account that the Indo-European **bhu* connects to the Latin prefix 'tri', as Benveniste tried to explain via the source on the Dorian tribes from the example above, the linguist opens with a rather peculiar critique of Aristotle. 'At the beginning of his *Politics*' (Benveniste 1969: 309), Benveniste writes, and probably has in mind the passage 1252a, where Aristotle reflects on the difference between state (*polis*) and household (*oikos*), Aristotle

> poses as the oldest unity that of the *oikos* (the Romans said *domus*). To him, this is the smallest fraction and the first form of society that existed, and he defines it as a community of husband and wife, of master and slave: it is the notion of the Roman *familia*. The *oikos* is constituted by the fact of nourishment and of daily participation in the cult. From here, Aristotle imagines that one passes on to the village, *kôme*, and then to the city, *polis*.
>
> Today, it is not possible to represent matters in such a way. This reconstruction, which divides the social cell and then procedes by successive increments is false. That which existed from the beginning is society, this totality, and not the family, then the clan, then the city. *From the origin*, society is fractioned in units encompassing one

> another. Families are necessarily united within a larger unity and so forth. However, Aristotle turns what his own society had presented him with into a universal status and a philosophical necessity; he turns a historic state into an absolute. (Benveniste 1969: 310)

Benveniste's argument is less convincing: Aristotle's reflections are not historical; they are, so to say, logical, which to him signifies that '[...] the complex must always be divided in the most simple elements or lesser parts of the whole', as Aristotle explains in the very same paragraph from which Benveniste quotes (Aristotle, *Pol.* 1252a). Hence logically, Aristotle is quite right in claiming that one must speak of a smaller part (the private sphere of the *oikos*) before speaking of a larger part (the public sphere of the *polis*). To the same extent, it is true that Aristotle does believe that one can speak of the government of the household as well as of the state. However – and this is most decisive – those who think that these two governments are not different from one another fail to recognize that they represent 'a difference in Being [*οἶον*]' (Aristotle, *Pol.* 1252a).

Unlike his master, Plato, Aristotle imposes a principled difference between *oikos* and *polis*, which he founds not upon a difference in quantity between the few subjected to the government of the household, and the many subjected to the government of the state (which Benveniste seems to believe), but instead on the qualitative and even essential difference between the two governments: the first concerns the private matters of the *oikos*; the second concerns the public affairs of the *polis*. Referring to *Politics* 1261a, where Aristotle once again dwells on this difference, Agamben can therefore determine the following: 'It has been noted that in Plato the distinction between *oikos* and *polis* does not present itself in terms of an opposition like it does in Aristotle. In this sense Aristotle can criticize the Platonic conception of the *polis* and reproach his master for having pushed the unifying character of the city too far, with the risk of transforming it into a household' (Agamben 2007: 35א). To Aristotle, man is always subjected to a form of government, either that of the *oikos* or that of the *polis*.

In Heidegger's *Building Dwelling Thinking*, the Aristotelian difference, as one of quality or even essence between *oikos* and *polis*, is formulated the following way:

> Bridge and hangar, stadium and power plant are buildings, but not dwellings [*Wohnungen*]; railway station and highway, dam and market hall are buildings, but not dwellings. Nevertheless, the buildings mentioned are located in the field of our dwelling. Reaching beyond these buildings, this field, however, cannot be reduced to dwelling. The truck driver feels at home on the highway, but he has not his abode there; the female worker feels at home at the spinning mill, yet this is not her dwelling; the chief engineer feels at home at the power plant, but he does not live there. (Heidegger 2000: 147)

Although these buildings and places in the European *polis* all house people and describe a social character of working and quotidian life, something to which the metaphors in the citation also testify, this does not mean that dwelling takes place. To Heidegger, the fundamental opposition between state and home, public and private, is characterized by the fact that what constitutes dwelling cannot be reduced to some kind of function. What instead characterizes dwelling is a home. Taking this into account, it is important to not forget that the difference to which Heidegger's examples from the citation above testify is not constituted by any kind of essential definition of the human being or who he or she is, but, instead, the other way around: the activity of dwelling, to exist in a home, is what constitutes the human being. Whatever this may be, it remains certain that under no circumstances can dwelling take place in the *polis*.

Given the important difference that Heidegger establishes between home and state, private and public, one could suspect his references in *Building Dwelling Thinking* to be to Aristotle's *Politics*. Heidegger's *Randbemerkungen* [notes in the margin], which are reproduced in the *Gesamtausgabe*, instead show that he had Aristotle's *Physics* in mind. This might not be a coincidence. In any case, this at least hints at the possibility that the difference or, rather, boundary between public and private concerns a specific location. Furthermore, **bhu*, to which Heidegger genealogically traced dwelling, meant to be on the earth (rather than in the city apparently) and Pokorny illustrated this by underlining that dwelling had a parallel in the Greek *φύσις*, nature (Pokorny 1959: 147f.). Heidegger explains:

> A space [*Raum*] is something for which room has been made [*Eingeräumtes*], set free within a boundary – *πέρας* in Greek. The boundary is not that by which something stops but, instead, as the Greeks knew, the boundary is that by which something

> *begins its essence* [*sein Wesen beginnt*]. Thus the concept of *ορισμός*, that is, boundary. A space is in its essence that for which room is made, embedded in its boundary. That for which room is made will each time be permitted and joined accordingly, that is, gathered [*versammelt*] by way of a location [*Ort*], that is, by way of a thing such as the bridge. The spaces, therefore, receive their essence [*Wesen*] from the locations [*Orten*] and not from 'the' space. (Heidegger 2000: 156)

Having Aristotle's *Physics* in mind, one could perhaps argue, hence, that if Heidegger does not think anything strictly political in this regard, it is because his whole conception of dwelling [*Wohnen*] has this boundary [*ορισμός, Grenze*] as its premise, thus permitting something like the political to take place at all on one side and dwelling on the other, and thereby indicating the process that divides the earth and the world into home and state, what is political and therefore public, and what is not and therefore private.

Heidegger's definition of the boundary allows it to be that which separates the *polis* (bridges and hangars, stadiums and power plants) from the *oikoi* (dwellings). But a boundary can also function as a gathering, just as the bridge, for instance, (Heidegger's favourite example) unites two shores that would otherwise be apart (cf. Heidegger 2000: 155). The boundary is a place, a location [*Ort*] because it is that which has been made to exist here (inside) in contrast to that which is there (outside): it is that for which room is made, as Heidegger wrote when contemplating the etymology of the room. A bridge can be considered as a splintering of frontiers in uniting two shores; a house can be considered a delineation, in as far as building a home separates or, rather, produces one (private) space particular and distinct from another (public) space.

Mention of the boundary, therefore, concerns a specific place inside which something exists, and is created in distinction and in contrast to any other place outside. Only by drawing such a line separating the fixed location of the bridge from the less suitable places on the shore or home from state, can the places in question be determined *as* these places and locations, that is, *as* bridge and *as* home. Hence, the location [*Ort*] does not only exist; it has the constitutional character of a creative force.

'Let us once more listen to the encouragement of language', Heidegger urges, in his attempt to decipher yet another philological detail from his genealogy of dwelling (2000: 150):

> The Old Saxon 'wunon', the Gothic 'wunian' means, as the old word to build [*Bauen*], that which remains [*das Bleiben*], the residing [*Sich-Aufhalten*]. However, the Gothic '*wunian*' speaks clearer of how this remaining will be experienced. Wunian means to be at peace [*zufrieden*], to be brought to peace [Frieden], to remain in it. The word peace [*Friede*] means free, the *frye* and *fry* mean saved from damage and threat, saved – from ... that is, spared [...] Dwelling, to be brought to peace, means to remain enclosed [*eingefriedet*] in the frye, that is, in the free that spares any essence. *The foundational tool* [*Grundzeug*] *of dwelling is this sparing* [*schonen*]. (Heidegger 2000: 150f.)

Dwelling [*Wohnen*] is precisely the term in which a clearer parallel to the distinction between *polis* and *oikos*, public and private, exists, but also how the two terms relate to one another, never colliding. For the insight is the same as that reached above: public space is uninhabitable; dwelling is basically private and something taking place on the other side of the doorstep. To be at peace [*zufrieden sein*], which Heidegger traces in his genealogy of dwelling (and later confirmed by Wolfgang Pfeifer's lexicon (1989: 1988)), can therefore only signify the peaceful remaining [*Sich-Aufhalten*] in a home. When the sparing [*Schonen*] in fact points to something public, such as the peace established by the state [*zum Frieden gebracht*] – as peace is, as such, not a term from the private sphere but from the public – this is but a precondition for a dwelling to be a sparing [*Schonen*]. If sparing relates to peace [*Friede*], this is only in the same sense as any boundary must refer to an outside in order to acquire its meaning and constitute itself as the inside.

Privo – from which the English term private is formed – as Lewis and Short's dictionary informs, means: 'Apart from the State, peculiar to one's self, of or belonging to an individual'; even more interesting is the reference under section B: 'Esp. of persons, *not in public or official life, deprived of office*' (Lewis and Short 1879). Even 'building as the construction of buildings' (Heidegger 2000: 149), which is Heidegger's definition of *aedificare*, is found in Lewis and Short as a meaning of *privo*, as when it is said, the two philologists explain: 'Of things: "*aedificia*", isolated, apart from the villages' (Lewis and Short 1879: 103). Reference is made to Cicero's book on old age, in which the philosopher explains that Sophocles wrote tragedies even when he was quite old, which is why character, rather than age, determines skill. This holds not only for the active statesman, Cicero further explains, but also for those living 'a private life, withdrawn from State affairs (*vita privata et quieta*)' (Cic. *Sen.*7, 22, cit. in Lewis and Short 1879).

To Heidegger, that which constitutes *Dasein* is a dwelling taking place behind a boundary in the private sphere withdrawn from the state and its political activities, such as those of a statesman for instance. As Aristotle, so too Heidegger locates an activity that each time is different in nature depending on its public or private location.

The boundary that Heidegger finds so fundamental for existence does not only determine the location and soil where dwelling and *Dasein* may co-exist. A crucial boundary also exists in *Dasein* itself. Heidegger thus dedicates a whole chapter in *Being and Time* to what at first glance does not appear to have anything to do with location: death (Heidegger 2001: chapter I, sec. 2). In *Being and Time*, death can take place only insofar as it happens continuously, that is, 'in an existential *being towards death*' (Heidegger 2001: §45, 234). The authentic being towards death, Heidegger writes, is the *Dasein* who makes a decision, although not to end its life but rather to take on life's historical condition, that is, to take life's constant ending and finiteness upon its shoulders: 'The fact that *Dasein* actually dies also means that it, in its being towards death [*Sein zum Tode*], has always already decided so, in one way or the other' (Heidegger 2001: §52, 259).

'*Dasein*', Biella suggests, 'is thrown back to its own finiteness through the process of the death of the Other' (1998: 85). Just as dwelling consisted of a community with others as shown above ('"I am, you are" meaning: I dwell, you dwell' (Heidegger 2000: 149)), so too does death. Dwelling, just as death, is something that is known of only by way of a community or the other, which Heidegger calls 'Being with others' [*Mitsein mit Anderen*] (2001: §26, 118). Naturally, the closest one can come is to be near death. No one is ever directly together with it: *Dasein*'s Being with others is with the other, not with death (Heidegger 2001: §47, 237–9). No matter how much a human being is together with another, at the time of death he still dies alone. To *Dasein*, death can be died but not experienced, and when finally experienced they both cease to exist and so 'there is no longer any *there* [*Da: ci*]' (Vattimo 2008: 46). Heidegger stresses the fact that the others nonetheless remain together with the dead: 'Out of it [our world] springs the possibility for those who remain to still be together with him' (Heidegger 2001: §47, 238).

In a way that by now ought to be familiar, in *Being and Time* Heidegger imagines death as a boundary between two shores, between life and death that, however, indicates a community or a social aspect that activates some form of commemoration or memory of the deceased. This is why the boundary between the living and the dead, between past and present, is kept from total separation: the living remember the dead and their world. This is what constitutes those who remain as the bridge that unites the shores of this ultimate boundary between death and life, past and present. To the Heidegger of *Being and Time*, death connotes a social or even ritual activity in time and space as far as a community acknowledges the loss of a member and remembers this life that is now lost.

In *Building Dwelling Thinking*, death plays an equally central role in Heidegger's argument, and it now becomes explicit that it also involves dwelling. In fact, death is what makes dwelling altogether possible:

> To die means to be capable of death *as* death. Only the human being dies – even continuously, as long as he remains on the earth, under the sky, before the heavenly. If we call these the mortals, then we likewise think of the three others [...]. We call this unity of theirs *the fourfold*. The mortals *are* in this fourfold insofar as they *dwell* [*wohnen*] [...]. The mortals dwell insofar as they accompany their own essence [*Wesen*] in the area of this capability, so that they are capable of death as death in order for it to be a good death. (Heidegger 2000: 152)

Remembering the legacy from *Being and Time*, it becomes clear just how crucial is the capability of death, something that Heidegger underlines in this citation by italicizing the *als* – that is, death *as* death and not simply as the cessation of life. In being capable of death lies the potentiality of an epistemic element of historical value and importance. Death as such a boundary is what constitutes *Dasein* as a historical being, stretched out between past and present, itself and others (cf. Heidegger 1996: 337). One could say, Vattimo writes in his introduction, 'that only and simply because we can anticipate the proper death as making possible the possibility, Dasein has history, that is, a whole development beyond a fragmentation and a splintering' (2008: 49).

In 1949, just two years prior to *Building Dwelling Thinking*, Heidegger gave a lecture in Bremen entitled *The Danger*. In a central passage, which will later find repetition in Hannah Arendt's thinking concerning the meaning of life and death in the camp, Heidegger writes the following in a rare paragraph on Third Reich victimhood and on the fabrication of corpses (cf. Chapter 2):

> Hundreds of thousands die in masses. Do they die? They perish [*Sie kommen um*]. They are brought down [*umgelegt*]. Do they die? They are stock elements [*Bestandstücke*] of an inventory in the fabrication of corpses. Do they die? They are discreetly liquidated in extermination camps [...]. To die, however, means to deal with death in its essence. To be able [*können*] to die means to be capable [*vermögen*] of this deal. We are only capable of dying if our essence cares about [*mag*] the essence of death. Yet, in the middle of innumerable deaths the essence of death remains disguised [*verstellt*]. Death is neither the empty nothing, nor merely the transition from one Being to another. [...]. To be capable of death in its essence means to be able to die. Those who are capable of dying are first mortals in the crucial meaning of this word. The massive distress of innumerable, macabre undead deaths is everywhere – and, nevertheless, the essence of death is disguised for human beings. The human being is not yet the mortal. (Heidegger 1994: 56)

Agamben, who first reminds his reader of the central status death has in *Being and Time* ('Being-towards-death', he writes, 'perhaps expresses the ultimate intention of Heidegger's ethics' (Agamben 1998: 68)), notes that Heidegger's NSDAP membership considered, the philosopher was met with some astonishment on delivering this analysis of death. The date of the publication surely added to such astonishment. This was even, the publisher of the *Gesamtausgabe*, Petra Jaeger, writes, 'Heidegger's first public appearance after the Second World War' (cit. in Heidegger 1994: 177).

However distasteful Heidegger's character was – in this and in many other related regards not only concerning the Third Reich and the NSDAP – his analysis of death is precise here, just as it had been so many years earlier. It supports Agamben's conceptions of naked life and of the Muselmann that was discussed above (cf. supra Chapter 2), while also supplementing not only Arendt's points but also Hilberg's, Klemperer's and, especially, the survivors' description of the Muselmänner: 'walking corpses', 'living dead', 'one hesitates to call them living' (Agamben 1998: 49), etc. 'What is certain', Agamben writes in conclusion to these authors (but to Heidegger in particular), 'is that the victims saw the dignity of death so negated; they were condemned to perish in a death that was not dead' (1998: 68).

A fundamental challenge, if Heidegger is correct in his analysis of death (Agamben at least thinks that he is), is how to remember and commemorate a death that is not death. How is it possible to acknowledge and remember victims that long since had been deprived of the possibility of dying and who, as Heidegger wrote, simply perished? This question is extremely important to the commemorative task of the Stolpersteine, to which it is now possible to turn, because if the monument fails to acknowledge that each victim constitutes an undead death one must ask what it is, then, that the Stolpersteine actually commemorate.

Dwelling and Stolpersteine

Having now analysed how Heidegger conceives of *Wohnen* [dwelling] in *Building Dwelling Thinking* and having made some relevant parallels to *Being and Time*, some of the most important results may now be used to reflect on what this means to the form of commemoration that one finds in the Stolpersteine. The present chapter opened by discussing the fact that the cartography according to which the Stolpersteine are installed is that of the past, and it is now possible to comment further on this circumstance.

The new piece of land, inhabited by victims of Third Reich deportations and exterminations via the Stolpersteine, is located on the very threshold and boundary between a previously private home belonging to a citizen and the contemporary public – rather often, as discussed, a current home and a contemporary resident are also affected. Where Heidegger's formula implied something rather straightforward in the realms of a neighbourhood and a community, that is, the mutual presence of citizens (I dwell, you dwell, etc.), the Stolpersteine splinter this conception and replace it with something that is, in fact, of a more direct historical nature. To Heidegger, dwelling concerned the fundamental aspects of any contemporary existence; the Stolpersteine advocate a form of dwelling that also activates a certain and specific past: the Third Reich from 1933 to 1945.

It is clear, in any case, that the location (i.e. their *Ort*) for the Stolpersteine is by no means new or invented as, for instance, a memorial site can be excavated after years of existence in hiding or, as the Memorial to the Murdered Jews of Europe, a monument may be independent of its specific location. The Stolpersteine locations are quite known and rather ordinary: they are driveways, sidewalks and entrance areas. These lands are the first places the citizen meets on his way as he leaves or arrives at his home. Not only between 'I dwell' and 'you dwell', in the words of Heidegger, but also between home and state. Although they take up public ground, the functionality of the Stolpersteine and of their *hier wohnte* [here lived] suggests that they are platforms of communication between the 'I' and the other, between the public and the resident – at least in those cases where the victim's former home corresponds to a present home.

The Stolpersteine identify and underline zones or boundaries that test and ultimately challenge the conception of dwelling. In one direction the zone or threshold upon which the Stolpersteine are installed opens towards the victim's previous home via *hier wohnte* [here lived], in the opposite direction, and at the same time, the Stolpersteine, by way of their specific location on public soil (*Ort* [location]), open towards the present. Thus, although the location contains an ongoing opening and a flux between home and state, the fuel in the historical engine of the Stolpersteine is not the isolated *Ort* [location] itself. Rather, the location needs the resident in order to ignite the spark that activates and sets this particular commemorative idea in motion, hence transforming dwelling into a memory of Third Reich victimhood. This is why the abandoned or lonely Stolpersteine trigger other problems (and even solutions) as discussed above, because no one activates this form of commemoration.

One could ask what aspects of the Third Reich the Stolpersteine, by way of their location [*Ort*], actually symbolize. What is it that a tiny stone in the private–public zone is capable of commemorating, not merely in terms of engravings but rather by the fact of being installed at that specific place in front of that specific former home rather than in a square or in a park?

In Stefanie Endlich's *Ein 'dezentrales Monument'? Anmerkungen zu einem ungewöhnlichen Denkmalskonzept* [*A 'Decentralized Monument'? Comments on an Unusual Memorial Concept*], which was referred to above, some interesting reflections are provided regarding these aspects. In her article, Endlich stresses the violence that the Third Reich inflicted upon the victim and its former home (or workplace), something that is evidently true. Underlining this aspect of the National Socialist government, at the same time – according to Endlich – this also constitutes the central task of the Stolpersteine determining their success:

> The location that is chosen for the 'Stolpersteine' – each time in the sidewalk just outside the front door – leads commemoration back to the boundary [*Grenze*] of the private space, to the threshold between house and street, interior and exterior space, security and persecution, individuality and anonymity. The interference of the private sphere, the exclusion from the neighbouring context, regulations and prohibitions for the obstruction of everyday life, of the freedom of movement and the theft of home [*der Raub der Wohnung*] were the early steps of the ever more aggravating and accelerating measures of persecution. Violence began not in far-away camps [*Lagern*] or behind prison walls, but in the neighbourhood. (Endlich 2002: 31)

The success of the Stolpersteine, according to Endlich, consists in their citation of the Third Reich's actions. The task of the Stolpersteine is therefore to intervene commemoratively in the depths of the private sphere in a way corresponding to the methods of the Third Reich. The destruction of boundaries between inside and outside, public and private, as well as the destruction of dwellings, is all perfectly symbolized by the location that is chosen for the Stolpersteine. The specific *Ort* [location] as the manifestation of the here in *hier wohnte* [here lived] is what testifies to such a politics of persecution. When wanting commemoration to underline that deportation and annihilation started not in camps far away but in the neighbourhood, to Endlich the Stolpersteine are therefore well suited because each and every time they give witness to the boundary that was hence broken. In the terminology suggested in the present book, what Endlich finds so appealing is that the Stolpersteine reproduce the former biopolitics of the Third Reich.

While Endlich underlines what to her is an apparently positive quality in the Stolpersteine monument, she feels no need to draw attention to the problems contained in this form of biopolitical commemoration – however symbolic. But rather than discussing the fact that 'the boundary [*Grenze*] of the private space' is presently broken down by the Stolpersteine, resulting in an 'interference of the private sphere', the citation above simply ends the paragraph in Endlich's text. For the rest of the text, she will compare the Stolpersteine 'with other remarkable memorial art projects' (Endlich 2002: 31).

If Heidegger is right in his argument that a home, a dwelling necessitates something private – *vita privata et quieta* [a private life, withdrawn from State affairs] as it was argued with Cicero above (Cic. *Sen.* 7, 22, cit. in Lewis and Short 1879) – the Stolpersteine may very well succeed in commemorating the victim's home and place in society by such an activation and use of the past, but it is not at all certain that this will not happen at the expense of the potential present resident. Especially not if Endlich's analysis is correct and the Stolpersteine are contemporary biopolitical monuments. All of this, naturally, depending on how much one believes that the Stolpersteine force their entry into the private sphere and lives of current residents. To Endlich, at least, it appears to be rather a felt presence.

'[E]ach time in the sidewalk just outside the front door' (Endlich 2002: 31): on the face of it, it is evidently true that Stolpersteine are actually installed precisely at that specific location. However, perhaps Endlich wrote more than she may have been aware of. In his 2010 *Stumbling Blocks: A Decentralized Memorial to Holocaust Victims*, Michael Imort mentions that the Stolpersteine differ from more traditional and centralized monuments, in that 'they are dispersed in multiple across everyday locations' (2010: 235). Also, just outside the front door or entrance door to present play grounds and schools, universities and workplaces may function as Stolpersteine locations. Above, the discussion began with the lonely or abandoned Stolpersteine (Chapter 4), which may now be continued: with the idea of a cartography of the past *in mente* the question is, in the end, which pathway and front door the Stolpersteine actually relate to. If Demnig is true to his project, the locations are not necessarily everyday – at least not in the contemporary understanding of it.

In towns and cities that have long since been abandoned, either because everybody was exterminated (true for many places in Eastern Europe), or because the inhabitants managed to escape, someone can stumble upon victims of Third Reich exterminations. However, if this kind of stumbling remembrance over abandoned or lonely Stolpersteine is no longer tied to a present resident's dwelling and life or to any in fact, does this not – on Heidegger's premises at least – rupture the actualization of the gift of dignity that the Stolpersteine were supposed to give via the *hier wohnte* [here lived]? Who hears the cry that comes from the past in the vehicle of these monuments if they are left for no resident or no pedestrian nor citizen to hear; if the structure of a present being and a former dwelling is somehow separated?

The question is not merely academic: the Stolpersteine for Konrad Brzezek and Max Schmidt, at the corner of the very busy crossroads in the Berlin periphery, mentioned earlier in this chapter, would not seem to achieve the same level of commemoration as those in front of a present home or workplace. For such abandoned Stolpersteine, no present dwelling corresponds to their past dwelling. The quite extreme historicism, which has been mentioned several times by now, is recognized again in this cartographical clash between the Stolpersteine's use of the past and referentiality on one side, and their commemorative reality on the other. Because, whether or not some victims are likely to be more commemorated than others – that is, whether or not a previous home corresponds to a present – is completely random.

To use a formulation inspired by Jefferson Chase in the Boston Globe, quoted above in this regard, one could say that 'history has decided for you'. The concern is, though, if Ulrike Schrader's problematizations do not also touch upon this problem. There seem to be no principles for determining the differentiation between commemoration of victims installed at a present dwelling and home and those who are not – whether a potential sponsor might prefer to not have a Stolperstein installed in more-or-less deserted locations and would rather have one installed in the city centre, Schrader's point would indeed seem to extend also to this aspect: 'The naming memory [*Das namentliche Gedenken*] leads to an over-identification with one victim and to the exclusion of all others' (2006: 178).

It is not impossible that a far more devastating fate than what the present investigation has succeeded in pointing out may await these abandoned Stolpersteine, installed as they are on locations that once were everyday but are so no more. Although it is true that to a certain extent such monuments underline and testify to the horror of the event by representing abandonment and oblivion, one could ask how effective all this is if no body stumbles upon these victims of National Socialism and acknowledges this context that has been actualized in this manner. The historical emphasis needs commemorative support, no less than memory needs historical ground. If these monuments are to be successful the abandoned Stolpersteine pose a problem, especially on the premises of the Stolpersteine themselves. They need present dwelling in order to properly provide that which they believe to do: to give the victims back the dignity they lost.

If the intention of the Stolpersteine is applied to the utmost, and a Stolperstein therefore can be installed in front of a former home to which no present home corresponds, and if this 'address', furthermore, is in the wildernesses of the European landscapes in a settlement that no longer exists, this will leave commemoration to oblivion. Each and every address in these abandoned parts of Europe (and beyond), in having Stolpersteine installed, would at the same time conduct an installation of oblivion. The archive of extermination and annihilation would install itself in the shape of the victim's Stolperstein but would not merely, to which Imort alludes, have transformed cities and towns but even forests, wildernesses and outskirts into gigantic memory scapes that are forgotten in the very act of the Stolperstein's installation, and the ceremony surrounding that installation has faded away.

Although the victim's *Wohnort* [place of residence] is here being pulled forth from darkness, it can never be more than a ruin, the only things that 'have permanence', as Andreas Huyssen suggests (2003: 45). Ruins have left history and reside solely in the past; they do not engage with history's presentness, with contemporaneity. Just as was stated earlier in this chapter by Salomon Korn, it is a fundamental premise 'that every memorial in the end becomes the memorial of its own perishability' (1999: 60), that is, that a monument is in fundamental opposition to the ruin in acknowledging its historicity in the form of some kind of rituality and social practice. For the Stolpersteine, this practice is dwelling. The cartographical historicism, which in the first instance designated the radicality of the Stolpersteine in a splintering individualization of the urban memory scape, is what in the last analysis becomes one of the greatest challenges of the abandoned Stolpersteine.

However, at least the problem regarding the violation of the contemporary citizen's private sphere appears to be solved with these abandoned Stolpersteine. As a matter of fact, since these monuments seem to belong within the fixed spheres both of the public domain and of the past, no one lives anymore behind the boundary and in the private sphere of the Stolperstein, which as a consequence cancels the conflict between the past victim's and the present resident's dwelling. Nonetheless, this solution happens at the expense of the commemoration of the victim, who once again must linger in oblivion and remain isolated in the past.

Throughout, this chapter has underlined the extent to which the Stolpersteine specifically tie dwelling to a certain victim's life and death, and that the monuments set in motion fundamental boundaries and dichotomies, such as the difference between public and private, state and home. In this connection, the Stolpersteine establish a specific link between the victim's dwelling on the one hand and the victim's fate on the other. The Stolpersteine are aimed to symbolize a dwelling *before* the Third Reich, and a fate *after*, and as a consequence of, the Third Reich.

It would therefore appear to be the intention of the Stolpersteine to first establish a case of normality, by stating a dwelling regarding the individual victim in question via the central heading *hier wohnte* [here lived] and then to say something about the victim when such a normality was replaced by the Third Reich. As such, both the heading *hier wohnte* [here lived] and the specific location illustrate a particular dwelling that relates to the period *before* the Third Reich, pointing in the direction of a dwelling, which was made impossible *after* the Third Reich was established, all of which the five fates are intended to illustrate. Earlier in the present book (Chapter 2) the most important boundary that posed problems for the Stolpersteine was argued to be that between normality and exception. On behalf of the Heidegger exegesis, this critique can be further elaborated: the Stolpersteine describe the victim's annihilation in terms of a normality, which, in fact, does not appear as a description of annihilation at all but is performed via a perfectly normal set of vocabulary from the world of ethics and law. The victim's *death* is described via the same degree of normality as the *life* of the victim. Just as the victim's life is commemorated in the normality via the *hier wohnte* [here lived], so too is the victim's death and fate, especially in the two fates that indicate the victim as *tot* [dead] or *ermordet* [murdered]. The transition of a citizen living in a home and in a city (*hier wohnte* [here lived]) to the citizen's deportation from home and life into likely annihilation beyond death is difficult to be testified by the Stolpersteine.

A crucial problem for the Stolpersteine in this connection becomes, in fact, not the wish to commemorate both life as well as death of the victim, but instead that both are intimately bound to a specific location (the victim's home), which ties together both dwelling and annihilation in the name of normality leaving the extremity that characterizes the victim's fate unsymbolized. If the Heidegger exegesis conducted above is correct, the corresponding interpretation of the Stolpersteine has shown that they have effectively cut of the victim's relation and tie to its undead death, and instead the Stolpersteine keep insisting that the victim's life, once lived in a home, ended with a death that the victim could die. The Stolpersteine represent life and dwelling in Berlin on the same side of normality's boundary as extermination and dwelling's suspension in Auschwitz.

It has been underlined again and again that the only way to maintain an ethical responsibility towards commemoration of the victims of Third Reich extermination and annihilation, is to recognize not only the humanity of the victims (perfectly rendered in the victim's name and *hier wohnte* [here lived]), but to the same extent to not forget the inhumanity to which they were reduced and under which they were exterminated. What happened to the victims concerns the suspension of dwelling and being, the suspension of life and death towards the stage of Muselmann and annihilation. Since the Stolpersteine wish to symbolize the victim's way *from* home *to* the camp – that is, as the ultimate crossing of a boundary from the dwelling of *hier wohnte* [here lived]) to the victim's fate – the monuments are at the same time obligated to insist on the immense transition and, indeed, suspension of dwelling altogether at the moment of deportation. The victim's annihilation, what the Stolpersteine call fate, therefore needs to be captured by a language that respects this extremism.

Perhaps the poetical descriptions of some victims' fate via fate unknown [???] and escaped in death [*Flucht in den Tod*] are actually examples of such a language. Unfortunately, they appear more as euphemisms than actual attempts at recognizing the extremism of the event, which is Third Reich extermination.

CHAPTER 5

Contextualizing the Stolpersteine

Using the Bible

This chapter will try to thematize, to a greater extent than has been possible till now, the way in which the Stolpersteine could be said to initiate a certain use of the past. In particular, the aim is to analyse how the monuments use central models from Christianity in order to commemorate victims of the Third Reich. In doing so, this chapter will also deal with the question of the perpetrator, and with guilt and innocence in connection with the exterminations as presented in the literature on the Stolpersteine.

The word Stolperstein is, in fact, a Biblical term appearing in both the Old and New Testaments, and of no small importance. Kirsten Harjes partly mentions these philological–theological goods in her article on the Stolpersteine (2005: 144), although she restrains herself from analysing what the construction of a commemorative monument for victims of the Third Reich could mean for them; in the next pages, I shall attempt to present such an answer. Contemporary German distinguishes between a *Stein des Anstoßes* [stumbling block] on the one hand and a *Stolperstein* [stumbling stone] on the other. Luther's translation of the Biblical term is 'Stein des Anstoßes' (Is (LUT) 8:14), which has become traditional and thus appears in today's edition of the German Bible (Is (SCH) 8:14). '*Der Stein des Anstoßes*', the great Duden explains, is '*die Ursache der Verärgerung* [The stumbling block is the cause of the irritation'], and refers to the Bible, '*nach* [according to] *Jesaja* 8:14'. A Stolperstein, the dictionary continues, is instead a '*Schwierigkeit, an der etwas, jemand leicht scheitern kann* [a difficulty of some sort that can easily make somebody fail']. Whereas contemporary German distinguishes between a moral or ethical account and a kind of obstacle, such a distinction is not to be found in the Bible.

The term Stolperstein appears in slightly varied versions in different parts of the Old Testament. In the Septuagint, for example, it is initially called a *λίθον προσκόμματι* [stumbling stone], but this is clarified and redefined as a *πέτρας πτώματι* [a stone upon which to stumble] (Is (LXX) 8:14), which The King James Version translates into 'a stone of stumbling' (Is (AV) 8:14). Later, in Isaiah (Is (LXX) 28:16), it is even mentioned as a *λίθον πολυτελῆ* [a precious stone]. In the New Testament, the term Stolperstein appears three times: once in the Gospels and twice in the Epistles. In the Gospel of Matthew, the evangelist follows Isaiah's lead in defining the stone as the 'most important stone [*κεφαλὴν γωνίας*]' (Mt (NT) 21:42): the cornerstone.

In Paul, two occurrences are to be found, also modelled on Isaiah. One is in the First Epistle to Peter where – as in Matthew – it is defined as the precious cornerstone [*λίθον ἀκρογωνιαῖον ἐκλεκτὸν ἔντιμον*] (1 P (NT) 2:6). The second is in Paul's Epistle to the Romans, and is the most important one in regard to the Stolpersteine because here the juridical sphere is at centre, just as it is in Demnig's monuments. The stone here takes the role, in the scope of the whole epistle, of interpreting the law as justice and salvation through faith of the individual (R (NT) 1:16f.). The stumbling stone is described in words that are by now familiar, that is, as a corner stone and a rock over which one may stumble ['*λίθον προσκόμμαος καὶ πέτραν σκανδάλου*'] (R (NT) 9:33).

Paul's Epistle to the Romans centres on the apostle's discussion of faith *versus* works, reinterpreting the problem of law along the model of each individual's relation to God. The dilemma between faith and works, Jochen Flebbe notes in his commentary, is what constitutes the context of the Stolpersteine in Paul structuring the 'question of Israel as the question of God [*Gottesfrage*]' (2008: 269). In the end, to Paul, this determines who will be free to carry the burden represented by the stumbling stone: the one who believes will not stumble. It is significant that the Stolpersteine monument philologically and theologically refers to a term that plays a central role in determining who are among the chosen people and who are not, that is who believes in God and who does not.

It is not easy to see how the case regarding victims of Third Reich exterminations concerns questions of faith, and although the context of the epistle is rather interesting too, it contains, if not direct problems, at least a moral dilemma. Because, to Paul, his contemporary Jews were rather sceptical towards the question of their God, and he found inspiration in the non-Jews (the Gentiles) who appeared to better understand the issue (R (NT) 3:29). Considering that the term Stolperstein refers to a rather sceptical and negative picture of Jews – historic Jews, one might add, in the context of Paul – one could ask, all things considered, whether such a term at all is suited for commemorating the extermination of millions of victims of whom six million were Jews.

In both the Old and the New Testament, these stones of stumbling are surrounded by a considerable amount of violence as part of defining the relation to God. The passages around the Isaiah reference are as follows:

> Sanctify the Lord of hosts himself; and let him be your fear, and let him be your dread. And he shall be for a sanctuary; but for a stone of stumbling [*λίθον προσκόμματος*, LXX] and for a rock of offence [*πέτραν σκανδάλου*, LXX] to both the houses of Israel ['the lasting house of Jacob', LXX], for a gin and for a snare to the inhabitants of Jerusalem. And many among them shall stumble, and fall, and be broken, and be snared, and be taken. Bind up the testimony, seal the law among my disciples. (Is (AV) 8:14–16)

When later Matthew mentions the stumbling stone, it is as part of the explanation of who shall inherit the kingdom of God. The reference is, again, to Isaiah 28:16. However, this explanation follows in the verse immediately after: 'Therefore say I unto you, the kingdom of God shall be taken from you, and given to a nation bringing forth the fruits thereof. And whosoever shall fall on this stone [sc. stone of stumbling] shall be broken: but on whomsoever it shall fall, it will grind him to powder' (Mt (AV) 21:43f.).

In the New Testament, Paul, on the contrary, omits the references to violence and hypothetical evils. Instead, he draws attention to the existence of the possibility of escaping shame, not violence. The whole passage explaining why Israel, according to Paul did not obtain justice, reads: 'Wherefore? Because they sought it [justice (*δικαιοσύνην*), NT] not by faith [*πίστεως*, NT], but as it were by the works of the law. For they stumbled at that stumbling stone [*λίθον προσκόμματος*, NT]. As it is written: behold, I lay in Sion a stumbling stone and rock of offence [*λίθον προσκόμματος καὶ πέτραν σκανδάλου*, NT]: and whosoever believeth on him shall not be ashamed [*καταισχυνθήσεται*, NT]' (R (AV) 9:32f.).

The Pauline question of God and justice, faith and works, is what constitutes his question of the law, and 9:30–3 – where the term Stolperstein occurs – is so important to the whole of Paul's Epistle to the Romans that Flebbe, in his commentary, calls it a transitory paragraph: 'God, who is constituted by a group of salvation alone, has established Israel as a stumbling stone in the face of the announcing salvational *νόμος* [law]. This explains Israel's lack of salvation [*Heillosigkeit*] in comparison with the contemporary salvation of the Gentiles. In this anticipating and concluding function the verses 30–3 clearly present themselves as a transitory paragraph' (Flebbe 2008: 347).

Paul, by evidently substituting law with shame (as he does by way of another citation from Isaiah 8:14 and 28:16) can argue that while divine punishment – for which the stumbling stone has now appeared as a metaphor – originally took the form of violence (as in Isaiah 8:14) it now takes the form of shame. Seeking justice [*δικαιοσύνην*] through faith, the seeker will not stumble upon the stone for he will not be ashamed. Thus, Paul does not overthrow the law, but interprets it anew: 'Do we then make the law [*νόμον*] inoperative [*καταργουμεν*] through faith? No! We preserve the law' (R (NT) 3:31. Cf. Agamben 2000: 140).

What Paul deals with in his letter to the Romans is therefore, in fact, a quite classical problem between law and justice that cannot easily be reduced to a specific circumstance in ancient Judaism's confrontation with (what today is known as) Christianity. For instance, in Sophocles' drama *Antigone*, Antigone wishes to bury her dead brother, Polyneices, as the laws of ritual and ceremony prescribe. However, since he was killed in a civil war in the course of which he attempted to conquer Thebes, its new king, Creon, insists that according to the law he may leave Polyneices on the battlefield. In a similar way, it seems that Paul's idea is to transpose questions of justice from the sphere of law to the sphere of ethics (i.e. to the sphere of shame), where the Stolperstein, with its context and Biblical history, is used to illustrate this particular question.

The specific details surrounding the aftermath of the Third Reich exterminations are, to say the least, quite different from those of Greek drama and myth and the question of God in Paul. However, common to all these events – setting aside the evident differences between them – is that they all point to a sphere in which the law appears to have insufficient applicability, and therefore to once again question the relation between jurisprudence and history as well as the belief that the latter can be reduced to the former.

'The past is never dead. It's not even past'

As has been pointed out several times above, Marlis Meckel's (2006) idea of giving the victims their names back is probably a variant on Demnig's same slogan that with the Stolpersteine '*bekommt das Opfer seinen Namen wieder*' [the victim will get its name back] (Demnig 2002: 13). Demnig has found part of this idea in the Talmud: '*Ein Mensch ist erst vergessen, wenn sein Name vergessen ist*' [A human being is only forgotten if its name is forgotten]. The gift economy of the Stolpersteine is – as its very name – thus immediately placed in a religious frame of reference. The purpose of the Stolpersteine is easily recognized: these individual monuments ensure that the victims are not forgotten, and remembering their names represents this commemorative task.

Something similar to Demnig's slogan is found yet again in Meckel, who ends her short, two-page introduction to her book on the Stolpersteine with a citation from American author William Faulkner and his 1951 *Requiem for a Nun* (Act I, Scene 3) that is translated into German: 'das Vergangene ist nicht tot, es ist nicht einmal vergangen' (Meckel 2006: 14). The original American citation would then read 'the past is not dead. It's not even past'. Nevertheless, the original text reads: 'The past is never dead. It's not even past' (Faulkner 1951: 92). Meckel transforms 'never' into 'not'. So, what is really being said of the past? How Demnig (and also Meckel) uses or, perhaps, misuses, history and Faulkner and why, most importantly, this is of crucial importance to the form of commemoration in the Stolpersteine are questions that will structure the rest of this chapter. This will allow a closer description of the kind of restoration that the Stolpersteine provide of the victim, as well as of the past.

Faulkner's American original allows hearing a slight ambiguity not possible in this case in German: on the one hand, the past is not over; on the other the past is not even past – all depending, so to speak, on the interpretation of the past. In German, the first possibility has been chosen (*vergangen* [past] instead of *Vergangenheit* [the past]). Under the index entry 'history and Faulkner' in the *Critical Companion to William Faulkner*, Fargnoli and co-editors write: 'Past and present clash eternally in Faulkner's fiction' (Fargnoli et al. 2008: 404). The quotation from *Requiem for a Nun* certainly confirms this, making it therefore not at all unlikely that Meckel – considering the German translation – had something similar in mind when she chose it as the slogan and ultimate statement for her introduction. It even seems to capture Demnig's point of view.

Faulkner's short story from 1951 continues from his earlier work, *Sanctuary* (1931), its major theme being the complexity of evil, but is now placed in a scenario where past actions continue to have a strong effect in the present. In *Requiem for a Nun* the young college student Temple, who bears responsibility for the death of her own infant child, a crime for which her black maid, Nancy, is convicted, portrays this. The complicated sequence of events means that Nancy is guilty of manslaughter, but that guilt is difficult to establish legally: although Nancy actually does kill the child, by holding a blanket over its nose and mouth, William Howe Rueckert notes, nonetheless: '[t]he overt motive for Nancy's act is to prevent Temple from running away with yet another petty gangster (Pete), abandoning her family' (Rueckert 2004: 275). And what would seem more reasonable than (as in a Greek tragedy) to murder a child to prevent this?

Rueckert has an answer:

> Nancy's motive is to preserve the family and redeem Temple from her corrupt ways. Having tried all the other ways she knows of, she commits this shocking act of infanticide […]. To preserve the family she [Nancy] destroys the youngest female member of it; to redeem Temple, she kills her baby, or the innocent generative new female life that has come from Temple's own corrupt body'. (Rueckert 2004: 275)

Although Nancy is convicted of this crime and later executed, the act 'achieves Nancy's purpose. Temple does not run away with Pete' (Rueckert 2004: 275).

However, what to Nancy appeared to be a good idea at the time has now turned into a nightmare for Temple, who lives with a tremendously bad consciousness. Temple feels that she is, in fact, the guilty one. For Temple the past is, hence, not past – in both meanings of the word: it is neither over, nor is it sealed off from the present. This could be said to be true to the extent that the past is almost turned into the present for her. Temple's moral scruples lead her to confess her wicked ways to none other than Nancy herself just before she is to be executed. The stoical Nancy calmly forgives her, and even comforts Temple, encouraging her to trust in God. Fargnoli and his colleagues explain the dilemma in this Faulknerian historical drama the following way:

> Suffering is a major theme of *Requiem for a Nun*. The acceptance of all human suffering as the consequence of living is central to the novel. In *Sanctuary*, Faulkner shows the inevitability of evil, its pervasiveness and its potential presence within us all – even a seemingly innocent 17-year-old college student [Temple]. In *Requiem*, Faulkner attempts to show that evil can, in fact, be resisted, but that suffering is the price we pay (or the reward we get) for succumbing to it. But through suffering and the recognition of one's guilt [Temple's], there is spiritual redemption. (Fargnoli et al. 2008: 234)

In this light, Meckel's choice of quotation appears to be the following: *Requiem for a Nun* is paradigmatic for the Stolpersteine, because Faulkner's book, and the citation, in particular, centres on guilt and punishment, responsibility and truth, all intertwined in the form of a difficult and very particular case of calumny and unjust verdict. Fact and truth, reality and cause, almost drift between Temple and Nancy, illustrating this. In an almost Kafkaesque manner, this was the method by which Faulkner criticized a deeply unjust and racist legal system to which the American society of the 1950s served as model.

If applied to the case of the Stolpersteine, which Meckel does, the use of Faulkner could also, perhaps, be said to touch upon a fundamental problem that concerns the question of the perpetrator in the Third Reich exterminations, a challenge that has been mentioned persistently above (Chapters 2 and 3): 'Nancy Mannigoe is innocent of murder, although not of homicide, because of her motives and the absence of malice aforethought' (Fargnoli et al. 2008: 234). The three acts structuring the short story therefore concern – in a sense that, perhaps, would have pleased Michel Foucault – the three central institutions in a democratic state of law and its separation of powers: the courthouse, the government building and the prison facilities (Rueckert 2004: 287). In Faulkner, all these components thus seem to exist to provide a paradigm for the Third Reich exterminations.

It is not at all impossible that what the conclusion to Meckel's strategy quoting Faulkner might amount to – 'The past is never dead. It's not even past' (Faulkner 1951: 92) – is that it raises the question of the perpetrator. Who, in Faulkner, is juridically guilty? Nancy was not the one responsible, which was Temple. When it comes to the exterminations, the question becomes even more acute: is the perpetrator a Temple or a Nancy, that is, one morally and ethically responsible, or the one juridically guilty and convicted? Is it the one behind the scene of the crime or the one directly responsible, that is, the Eichmanns or the Himmlers, the SS guards or the *Sonderkommando*, those who voted for the NSDAP back in the winter of 1932 or the party members?

It is clear that, with the Faulkner quotation, Meckel places the Stolpersteine in a juridical sphere on the one side concerning the question of guilt and perpetration, and in an ethical–theological frame of reference, on the other, concerning forgiveness and redemption. This is, indeed, largely in harmony with the Stolpersteine, which seem to do something similar. On these monuments it is stated, as has been underlined several times, that the *Schicksale* [fates] of the victims were variously '*tot* [dead], *ermordet* [murdered] and *Flucht in den Tod* [escaped in death]' (Demnig 2015: 4).

Nonetheless, in somehow establishing a paradigm under which the National Socialist past and the exterminations presided over by the Third Reich might be located, Meckel's use of Faulkner is not accurate. The Third Reich victim was, once again to quote Agamben, a *homo sacer*, a naked life whose manslaughter did not amount to homicide, and whose 'whole existence is reduced to a naked life stripped of every right' (2005a: 205).

Nevertheless, calumny could perhaps be understood here as the wrongful accusations against the Jews and the other victims, just as Nancy was wrongfully accused of an act for which Temple, although indirectly, bore the ultimate responsibility. But it is still important to keep in mind that the circumstances concerning perpetrator and victim in the Third Reich are fundamentally different from the conflict Faulkner describes in *Requiem for a Nun*.

In Faulkner, Nancy is executed by the state because a court of law found her guilty of murder, an illegal action. Temple feels ethically responsible because she believes that her corrupt actions and indecent life forced Nancy to commit homicide as the only way to save and redeem Temple and her family. No court of law found the Jews or any other victim annihilated by the Third Reich guilty. The Jews were exterminated because they were Jews. The *Endlösung* is not a juridical phenomenon! What the Third Reich developed, as argued in the previous chapters, has nothing to do with jurisprudence and everything to do with political strategies in a zone of biopolitical and durative state of exception – again, in total opposition to Faulkner's universe where, as quoted above, Nancy is innocent 'because of her motives and the absence of malice aforethought' (Fargnoli et al. 2008: 234). Nancy is hardly comparable to the National Socialists.

Concerning the degree of victimhood in Faulkner, to Rueckert (2004: 275) this is perfectly captured in the infanticide. However, here as well as concerning the exterminations, one could ask what such victims really were innocent of? Could Temple's baby have been guilty? Could the Jews, the communists, the handicapped and all the other victims have been guilty? Is victimhood in these cases at all a question of guilt and innocence, or is it not rather something that remains reserved for the perpetrator? The consequences for the use of Faulkner in terms of commemoration seem to be that through the Stolpersteine contemporary Germans live redeemed but in suffering as they carry the responsibility (like Temple) for someone else's deeds (like Nancy).

Although it is at first glance commendable to state that victims of the Third Reich were innocent, further reflection shows that this is actually a rather problematic point: only if someone could also be guilty would such a line of argument be meaningful; if everyone is innocent, no one is innocent, to the same extent that if everyone is guilty, no one is guilty. The problem is, therefore, what the victims of extermination could possibly be innocent of? Of what could they have been found guilty? The question itself, along with its unreasonable premises, vanishes. Jews and homosexuals, communists and the disabled, etc. were no more innocent than they were guilty: they could not even be part of such categorizations. To engage in such a discussion concerning victims of extermination is not only inappropriate and cruel, it more importantly fails to acknowledge the true fate of these victims, which was far more extreme and violent than juridical categories of guilt and innocence allow to acknowledge. The Third Reich victims were – as was argued by Arendt, Heidegger Klemperer, Levi and Agamben above – beyond jurisprudence and politics, theology and ethics. This is what the analyses above of the state of exception, of the Muselmann and of naked life, have shown.

The calumny living in Temple's body, so to say, does not end with Nancy but with the redemption provided through Nancy who forms the requiem, thus thematizing central issues from the Christian universe. Not only is 'nun' a Christian term, but 'requiem' is too – signifying the first words in the Roman church's requiem mass: *requiem aeternam dona eis Domine* [Lord, give them eternal peace]; and even if the Christians have churches rather than temples, the name Temple does connote a religious sphere as well (Rueckert 2004: 276). Following the intention of Meckel's book, expressed to the full in the title – *Den Opfern ihre Namen zurückgeben* [*Giving the Victims Their Names Back*] (2006) – her strategy in the use of Faulkner seems to be that whatever wrong is done against the victims of the Third Reich, the monument can function as a vehicle for redemption, just as Nancy redeemed Temple, hence turning the confession from *Requiem for a Nun* into the ritual and ceremonial form of commemoration in the Stolpersteine.

The problem is that Meckel stretches the Faulknerian metaphor more than it can hold. Meckel simply transports Faulkner's complex juridical and psychological, moral and theological universe of calumny, guilt and verdict (Temple and Nancy) to the reality of the Third Reich and the commemoration of its victims, even though this event does not concern calumny, guilt or verdict in any of these instances. What is extraordinary in Meckel's quotation of Faulkner is, moreover, that she ignores that while the problem in Faulkner is how to make the past stay in the past (redemption), the problem the Stolpersteine try to solve is how to tie the past to the present (commemoration).

The Faulkner quotation experienced a renaissance in the 2010 *Vor meiner Haustür* [*Outside my Front Door*], a book about the Stolpersteine edited by Joachim Rönnerper. Also in this book, a literary–artistic paradigm was chosen as template for the Stolpersteine. Apart from Chapters 1 and 4, Rönnerper's book reprints a range of important and well-known writer's texts about the Third Reich, specifically concerning *Verfolgung, existentielle Beraubung und Exil* [Persecution, Existential Robbery and Exile], followed by a third chapter that 'summarises the tragedy of genocide and murder ((ed.) 2010: 7). The third chapter carries a familiar title: '*Die Vergangenheit ist niemals tot, sie ist nicht einmal vergangen*' [The past is never dead, it is not even past] (Rönnerper (ed.) 2010). And this time the German translation of the Faulkner citation is correct (cf. Faulkner 1951: 92).

The criticism that has been raised against Meckel's use of the Faulkner quotation as a paradigm for the Stolpersteine can similarly be applied to Rönnerper, and so there is no reason to repeat this. However, it is interesting that, in an even stronger sense than Meckel, Rönnerper – using the correct Faulkner citation – states that not only is the past *not* over (as Meckel did), but that the past is *never* over. Even stronger than Meckel's, Rönnerper's use of Faulkner pushes into the extreme the conception of the past regarding the commemorative culture, as the citation is somehow meant as the key to unlocking the status of the past that the Stolpersteine commemorate. Contrary to Meckel, Rönnerper does not seem to believe that commemoration of Third Reich victims can ever end by, for instance, giving the victims their names back. Instead, as perhaps suggested by the fact that Temple can only find her requiem through her continued faith in the Lord, so too the Stolpersteine to Rönnerper appear to be continuous acts of commemoration. This was also the result of the analysis conducted above concerning the element of eternalization in the Stolpersteine (Chapter 4). In Rönnerper there is no difficulty in tying the past to the present; this difference almost seems not to exist. However, Rönnerper has other worries, and these are expressed in yet another literary–artistic paradigm.

In Rönnerper's third chapter – bearing the Faulkner quotation – quotations from Imre Kertész and Primo Levi also appear. One finds passages from Kertész's 1975 *Fatelessness* and from Levi's 1947 *If This Is a Man*. Regarding Levi, the passage is from the chapter '*Sul fondo*' [At the Bottom]. However, in Moshe Kahn's German translation, which seems to be the one Rönnerper uses, the chapter has undergone some translator's artistic creativity, thus involving a headline that the original does not carry: '*Mein name ist 174517*' [My name is 174517] (Rönnerper (ed.) 2010: 77), referring to Levi's number, which was tattooed on his forearm in Auschwitz. More seriously, the missing question mark in the title of Levi's book, which above was proven to be so significant (Chapter 2), has now been supplied, while the 'if' (the *Se* in the Italian original) has not been translated at all. The German title simply reads *Ist das ein Mensch?* [*Is This a Man?*] (Levi 1988). As a consequence, in Kahn's translation, Levi's book now appears completely contrary to what Levi decided to proclaim via his title and, indeed, to the entire scope of the book and the analyses of humanity's suspension in the camp. Kahn has now made it a real question of whether Levi and the other inmates – especially the Muselmänner – were actually human beings.

Both Levi and Kertész were deported to Auschwitz in 1944, though the latter was later moved to Buchenwald. Kertész survived and, like Levi, he chose the art form of literature as the medium through which he preferred to tell his experiences. Nonetheless, a significant difference exists between Kertész and Levi, between *Fatelessness* and *If This Is a Man*, through which Rönnerper without any further distinction nonetheless intends to illustrate persecution, existential robbery and exile: while the first book is not at all an unlikely story, it is fiction nonetheless. The main character of *Fatelessness*, the Hungarian youngster György, is invented and never existed – no matter how probable his endless suffering in the camp is. Even if millions of victims are likely to have experienced what György experienced in the novel, their experiences were real ones. György's, though realistic, are not. This, of course, does not mean that all the historical circumstances mentioned in the book are completely fictitious, nor that important insight cannot be achieved via literature and fiction when it comes to the Third Reich exterminations. It does mean, however, that as Kertész has chosen the form of a novel, that is, of fiction, he is, in a completely different way from Levi, bound by what Carlo Ginzburg called the principle of reality (Ginzburg 1992. Cf. Chapter 2).

Naturally, a grain of aesthetics is always present whenever commencing a process of writing. This is true also in Levi's texts and one of his most gifted biographers, Ian Thompson (2003: 245f.), does not fail to mention this, and neither is Ginzburg in disagreement. Ginzburg quotes Vidal-Naquet in writing that 'we have been aware of the fact that the historian *writes*, and that he produces a space and a time while he himself remains included in space and time. But (Vidal-Naquet continues) we must not dismantle ourselves from the old conception of "reality" in the sense Rilke evoked a century ago regarding "as it actually happened"' (Ginzburg 1992: 533).

Not distinguishing, as Rönnerper does, between Kertész's (realistic) fiction on the one hand and Levi's memory of a past reality on the other, corresponds to not taking into account the importance of the principle of reality – a lack which, in Assmann's theory of cultural memory, for instance, proved to be so devastating (cf. Chapter 2). A fundamental difference simply exists between the fictional novel about a probable sequence of events and the probable account of facts that might seem fictional due to their horror but are very real nonetheless. Although Kahn's translation involves a constructive element in the form of a headline referring to Levi's number 174517 that was tattooed on his forearm, Kahn's choice involves a direct reference to reality. Not only does Levi *refer* to a reality (as does Kertész); Levi's renderings are witness accounts and therefore *bound* by reality (something which for Kertész is not necessarily the case). As Assmann is unable to deal with the difference between fact and memory, so too Rönnerper seems unwilling to accept the difference between witness literature (Levi) and novel (Kertész).

Nonetheless, in his short, three-page introduction, Rönnerper is not afraid to address the question of the aestheticization of reality and the difference between fact and fiction. This is done through the use, yet again, of a quotation, this time from the German translation of Kertész's *A Breath-long Silence, While the Fire Squad is Reloading Their Guns* (1998):

> Of the Holocaust, this unbelievable and unforeseeable reality [*Wirklichkeit*], we can only form a true conception with the aid of the aesthetic power of imagination [*ästhetischen Einbildungskraft*]. The conception of the Holocaust as such is, however, such a monstrous endeavour, such an overwhelming spiritual task, that it exceeds the capacity of those who struggle with it. Because the Holocaust has taken place, the conception of it seems difficult. Instead of being a figure of the imagination – in the shape of invented allegories, literary fictions – the Holocaust manifests itself as a heavy and rigid load, like the fragile stone blocks of Mauthausen. (Kertész cit. in Rönnerper (ed.) 2010: 8)

It is clear that Levi has chosen a very different approach from Kertész. To Levi, his memory of life, or rather of life captured on its threshold with death, has little to do with the power of aesthetic imagination (but, as mentioned, very much to do with aesthetic style). To Levi, what he experienced in Auschwitz is not incomprehensible, but needs to be told. At the very beginning of his book on Auschwitz and Levi's quality and status as a witness, Agamben calls to attention the fact that some never speak of Auschwitz; quoting Levi, he then writes: 'Yet some, on the other hand, speak about it incessantly, and I am one of those' (Levi, cit. in Agamben 1998: 14).

As a matter of fact, not much of aesthetics is found in the writings of Levi (who was a chemist) – at least not in comparison with just a couple of passages from Kertész. While beautifully written, Levi's writing appears descriptive, scientific and 'objective', so to speak. On that account, it is clear why Rönnerper, in this regard, has chosen a quotation from Kertész rather than Levi when attempting to aestheticize the reality of the exterminations, however brutal. One primary consequence follows from this: using Kertész, the fundamental incomprehensibility of Auschwitz and of the camp is expressed (a favourite theme in the literature on the camp and the Third Reich) and so the reality of the exterminations must be aestheticized in order to comprehend the event ('we can only form a true conception with the aid of the aesthetic power of imagination [*ästhetischen Einbildungskraft*]', as Kertész wrote).

Rönnerper's position now appears as a paradox, considering that the Stolpersteine do not at all express that the exterminations are incomprehensible. Rather the contrary: the Stolpersteine attest that the event is in fact so comprehensible that it can even be understood in quite ordinary vocabulary from ethics and the state of law, something to which the five fates all testify. For instance, the victims, as the symptomatic description declares, were *ermordet* [murdered].

Concerning the specific crime of the camp, Agamben writes that it is as 'if Auschwitz were something like a Gorgon's head that one cannot – nor want to – see at any cost, something so unheard of that one tries to make it understandable by bringing it back into categories which at the same time are both more extreme and more familiar: life and death, dig nity and indignity' (1998: 75). In aiming to become the vehicle that will give the victim his or her name back, the Stolpersteine apparently must bring deportation and annihilation back into categories that are far more familiar (murder, suicide, etc.) even though at the cost of a reduction or fictionalization of reality.

Guilt and Responsibility

The discussions concerning responsibility and guilt, survivor and perpetrator, that the Stolpersteine have set in motion in one way or another, in fact had a kind of climax many years before anyone had conceived of the Stolpersteine. Just after the end of the war, as early as 1946, Martin Heidegger's colleague in philosophy at Freiburg, the psychiatrist Karl Jaspers, wrote *The Question of German Guilt*. In this book, Jaspers reflects on questions that concern Germany in the period immediately after the Third Reich. The general theme of the book is quickly introduced, and the second line reads: '*Our* guilt […]' (Jaspers 1946: 7, italics added). Although, as Jaspers specifies, some feel guilty while others feel mere innocence, in any case an accusation is at stake. Hence, it is only natural, he continues, that it is important to make it clear 'whether this accusation is true or untrue and in what sense' (Jaspers 1946: 7).

With these formulations, Jaspers clearly places the *Schuldfrage* [question of guilt] in the realms of law, which is hardly surprising considering that this is the realm in which guilt is also normally found. However, Jaspers does not stop here for, in the end, what is at stake is nothing but 'the inner inversion [*der inneren Umkehrung*]', and Jaspers is not slow to let his reader know that he therefore touches 'on the mixture of concepts' (1946: 8), as the law does not involve such inwardness. What quickly becomes evident is that the business of Jaspers' book will be to transport an otherwise juridical question of guilt into a moral or ethical discussion – to some extent similar to what Faulkner five years later will do in *Requiem for a Nun* – given the extraordinary status that Jaspers not surprisingly believes is the matter in the case of the Third Reich and the exterminations. Law must be expanded or, so to speak, 'ethicalized'.

After Jaspers has defined criminal guilt in a couple of quick phrases as a crime pure and simple, political guilt as 'the actions of statesmen and in the citizenship of a state', moral guilt as the actions one commits as an individual and where the '"sentence" is one's own consciousness' (1946: 10f.), Jaspers reaches the fourth, most difficult and most interesting definition of guilt: *Metaphysische Schuld* [metaphysical guilt]:

> A solidarity exists between human beings as far as human beings, something which makes each and every person jointly responsible for everything that is unjust [*Unrecht*] and all injustice in the world, especially for crimes that were committed in his contemporaneity or with his knowledge. If I do not do what I can in order to prevent this, then I am complicit [*mitschuldig*]. If I have not put my life at stake in order to prevent the murder [*Ermorderung*] of others but instead stood by, in a certain way I feel a guilt that is not properly understandable legally, politically and morally. That I am still alive, when something like that has happened, is placed as an irredeemable guilt upon my shoulders. As human beings, we arrive at a boundary [*Grenze*], if luck does not spare us from the situation where we must choose: either to put our life at stake without purpose, because it would be without prospect of success, or to remain alive because success is impossible. That somewhere between human beings the unconditional [*das Unbedingte*] applies – only to live together or not to live at all, if a crime is committed against one or the other, or if it concerns the sharing of physical living conditions – this is what constitutes the substance of its essence [*die Substanz ihres Wesens*]. However, that this does not exist in the solidarity between all human beings – that is, not between citizens or even between smaller groups – but instead remains limited in the most narrow human ties; this is what makes this guilt of us all. Authority is God alone. (Jasper 1946: 11)

Summarizing the four most important points of this quotation:

A) Everyone has a responsibility for everything unjust and illegitimate in the world, regardless of whether it is actually followed by a specific deed, because there is a solidarity between humans as humans.
B) Survival is a metaphysical guilt that does not depend upon an action, but that someone else was annihilated instead of you.
C) Metaphysical guilt is a category separate from criminal, political and moral guilt. ('Justice', Jaspers later specifies, 'can only concern a guilt in the sense of crime and political liability, not moral or metaphysical guilt' (1946: 16)).
D) Metaphysical guilt constitutes a kind of Fall of Man, of which God is the sole judge.

Metaphysical guilt, therefore, is the term Jaspers suggests in order to make the Third Reich deportations and exterminations understandable. It is significant that when Jaspers mentions the consequences of metaphysical guilt as a kind of metaphor for the application or use of traditional law, he determines it as 'a transformation of the human self-consciousness before God' (1946: 15). To Jaspers, the matter appears to be that God and history become one and the same, and that the latitude for human responsibility overall is determined from this fundamental pair.

An interesting, though nonetheless brutal, consequence of Jaspers' theory, is that victim as well as perpetrator, Jew as well as SS officer, are all bearers of equal degrees of metaphysical guilt. It is true that the tendency to place the Third Reich exterminations in the realms of the sacred and of religion also characterizes Jaspers' thinking, because the metaphysical guilt transforms profane time into divine time, making, as just mentioned, human history the place for God's divine government of the world. In the light of Jaspers' thinking, the task in the pages to come will be to further discuss the Stolpersteine's placing of the victim's annihilation in the realms of jurisprudence, which at least also to Jaspers would appear not to embrace the full magnitude of the event.

One of the quite extreme formulations concerning questions of guilt in connection with the Stolpersteine comes from Monica Richarz, to which reference has been made several times above: 'The stones mark everyday places of everyday life – yet these are places in which people who were neighbours became victims. They, *therefore*, also point *directly* to the question of who were the perpetrators and who stood by and watched' (Richarz 2008: 329, italics added). A careful reading of this quotation elicits the following line of reasoning: because each Stolperstein is placed at an address where a victim of deportation and annihilation used to live or work, it *therefore* – meaning as a logical consequence of this fact – not only represents the victim in question, but points *directly* at the question of both the perpetrators and those who stood by and did nothing. Since the Stolpersteine are laid throughout the European continent and even beyond, the installation of guilt via this monument is, according to Richarz, substantial.

Richarz's argument is surprising. It is well known that the Stolpersteine contain no trace whatsoever of who the perpetrator was, nor of 'who stood by and watched'. But is it true that the Stolpersteine contain traces of the *question* of the perpetrator and passive bystanders? Richarz herself is rather silent on the matter, and her argument consists entirely of underlining the fact of the victim's home as that which alone points directly to the question of perpetrator and bystander. Although the Third Reich was responsible for each victim's deportation and, most likely, annihilation, whereby the monument thematizes a knowledge that the pedestrian stumbling across this monument must possess beforehand, it is hardly a question but, quite on the contrary, a very solid fact. This strategy in the Stolpersteine, also, is what makes pedestrians stumble that is, wonder and reflect on what they read and experience.

What in the end does point to the question of who the perpetrator was, is not, in fact, constituted by the victim's place of residence [*Wohnort*], as Richarz argues. Instead, this question arises from the fact that in most cases the Stolpersteine state that the victim in question was *ermordet* [murdered], without identifying the perpetrator. This aspect was briefly discussed above (Chapter 2), and it is now possible to address this important matter once more. The strategy of not identifying the perpetrator is what prompts the question: who was the victim's perpetrator? It is thus not at all unlikely that the Stolpersteine are actually intended to symbolize the fact that in many cases the perpetrators really were unknown and that the exterminations were part of an *anonymized*, bureaucratic form of government, just as Hilberg suggested years ago in his landmark book, *The Destruction of the European Jews* (1961).

Not answering who the perpetrator is in particular in the usage of *ermordet* [murdered], the Stolpersteine could be said to, perhaps, perform their utmost stumbling function of raising the question of and commencing the discussion on who was responsible, who carried the guilt and where it ends – if ever. Although the Stolpersteine have the unfortunate tendency to describe the victim's fate juridically, it is not impossible that the monument, on the other hand, could at least be said to succeed in provoking a discussion of the question of the perpetrator, so that the Stolpersteine hence make citizens and pedestrians reflect on and contemplate these difficult questions themselves.

Just as interesting is the responsibility that, according to Richarz, can reasonably be expected from a citizen living in the Third Reich. Later on in her article, Richarz repeats her above argument, but leaves the idea that the Stolpersteine could point to the question of guilt and responsibility, and she now stresses that 'nobody put a stop to it [deportation]' (2008: 335). Not only is it difficult not to notice the indignation in Richarz's writing on these lines; it is just as difficult to find an answer to what it is that Richarz may have in mind that these bystanders could or should have done. At least it is certain that by now Richarz has accused practically everyone: the unknown individual perpetrator, the neighbours and the bystanders.

At the end of her article, Richarz approaches the questions of responsibility once more, but now addresses it more firmly in connection to the past and how the Stolpersteine work commemoratively – circumstances that have now accumulated in her argument:

> As has been shown here, the memorial stones project has a striking pedagogical and psychological dimension to it. It can also be interpreted as an attempt at self-therapy by the descendants of the perpetrators. [...] For some of the descendants, the little memorial stone can thus ease the burden and change their perception of modern day Germany. At the same time it also enables today's Germans to engage positively with the biggest crime against humanity in their history. (Richarz 2008: 336f.)

Richarz is probably right concerning the guilt that is felt on the part of the descendants. Nonetheless, it does strike one as particularly odd that Richarz feels no need to discuss why contemporary Germans feel any need for self-therapy for deeds committed seventy years ago in their fathers' or grandfathers' generation. One could ask, thus, whether or not particular monuments should rather have as their proclaimed task to free these descendants from any feeling of guilt, rather than to affirm it, that is, to let the deeds and their responsibility remain in the past, while the ethical obligation to commemorate the victims is reserved for the present.

Moreover, since Richarz correctly defines Third Reich deportations and exterminations as the greatest crime against *humanity* in the twentieth century – thus actually establishing a platform to take the questions of guilt to a higher and more principled level – it remains a mystery why only Germans are relevant in such a discussion. Austria, the Netherlands and Hungary already had stones installed when Richarz published her article. Moreover, was it not also, from the beginning in the 1990s, one of the central, important and decisive aspects of the Stolpersteine project to include all of Europe and even beyond, that is, to insist that the Stolpersteine constitute 'an art project for Europe' with the intention to install these monuments throughout the continent where European victims, and not just German victims, used to live? It would at least seem to be too narrow a focus on the premises of the Stolpersteine to simply omit their European and supranational character in order to focus exclusively and limitedly on Germany and the Germans. As a result, Richarz's discussion of these complicated matters appears to change little in the diagnosis that Jaspers made seventy years earlier when he discussed the 'accusation against Germany and the Germans', a guilt that 'is stated with indignation, with horror, with hatred, with contempt' (Jaspers 1946: 7).

Janet Ward, Professor of History at the University of Oklahoma, shares Richarz's analysis and speaks uncritically and without hesitation of 'fears about a collective loss of *inherited responsibility* for the Holocaust', and later of 'the post-war representation of a national or collective guilt' (2009: 145; 154). If read in the sphere from which these terms are taken – namely jurisprudence – Ward does little more than present her reader with a *contradictio in terminus*. If Ward intends these formulations to be understood metaphorically rather than as strictly juridical conceptualizations, she, in any case, does not explicate this peculiar strategy.

With Richarz and Ward, the interpretation of the Stolpersteine and their relation to contemporaneity appears, thus, to have been taken back to where it began: to Jaspers and at the crossroads of jurisprudence and politics, religion and ethics. Again, the desire is recognized, by these scholars at least, to change the barriers and conceptualizations for (and inside) these disciplines themselves when it comes to understanding the Third Reich, its crimes and the commemoration of its victims. Concerning this specific scholarly enterprise (which is also found in Meckel and Rönnerper), it is almost as if conceptual stringency and argumentation become unnecessary for the benefit of creating a certain zone of literature that shares substantial features with fiction, thus becoming the preferred style of writing in the field of commemoration.

Jaspers' 1946 book may therefore in many regards be read as a problematization of Richarz's and Ward's arguments (and thus implicitly also of Meckel's and Rönnerper's) regarding the Stolpersteine and their representation of responsibility and guilt, survivor and perpetrator, and to which it is therefore advantageous to return once more. Jaspers' book is not, as shown, about those who are guilty, in the juridical meaning of guilt, but is essentially about those who are metaphysically guilty – those citizens whose 'crime' was to be German or, rather, to be human. Jaspers' distinction between political and criminal guilt on the one hand and metaphysical guilt on the other is 'predicated on the liberal distinction between public and private in that it circumscribes a private sphere of personal (moral and metaphysical) accountability that is not subject to public scrutiny', Andrew Schaap writes in *Guilty Subjects and Political Responsibility: Arendt, Jaspers and the Resonance of the 'German Question' in Politics of Reconciliation* (2001: 751f.). 'To declare a collective guilty', Jaspers writes in opposition to the authors mentioned above, 'that is an error' (1946: 20). Towards the end of his book, Jaspers again points to the problem of a position like Richarz's and Ward's: 'Everywhere the complaints become accusations. But against whom? In the end *everyone against everyone*' (Jaspers 1946: 88, italics added).

It is not at all impossible that the philosopher is indirectly referring to Thomas Hobbes' famous *dictum* from his *Leviathan* in its Latin phrasing: *bellum omnium contra omnes* [the war of everyone against everyone] (Hobbes 1966c: chapter XIV), which Hobbes uses to explain the state of nature, which according to Agamben should be read as a paradigm for the state of exception (cf. Chapter 2). Jaspers' use of Hobbes could be motivated by the fact that as part of Germany's so-called denazification after 1945, Schaap explains, the Allied forces had a poster put up all around Germany with the wording: 'You are guilty' (Schaap 2001: 749). It definitely seems to be the case that Jaspers' worry is that if everybody is accused, then the innocent will also be accused, thus drawing everybody into a gigantic calumnious event.

In a similar way, considerations on inherited responsibility, collective guilt and accusations against the unknown, as these thoughts are presented in Richarz's and Ward's discussions of the Stolpersteine, end with putting everyone on trial as well as freeing everyone. Richarz and Ward are perhaps even more radical than Stefanie Endlich, who supported the commemorative repetition of Third Reich biopolitics by the Stolpersteine forcing their way into the private sphere of contemporary citizens (cf. Chapter 4). It is quite astonishing that Richarz's juridical vocabulary is not used against the perpetrator (whoever he or she was), but instead is formulated in the shape of a psychologism that internalizes and transposes the juridical vocabulary into a 'psychological dimension' that can be used 'as an attempt at self-therapy by the *descendants* of the perpetrators' (Richarz 2008: 336, italics added). Thus, in at least one perspective Richarz shares Endlich's idea of letting commemoration force its way into the private life of contemporary citizens.

In his book, Jaspers refers to Hannah Arendt's 1945 *Organised Guilt and Universal Responsibility* (Jaspers 1946: 61). Under the heavy influence of Martin Heidegger, in many matters Arendt shares with Jaspers' (who was her *Doktorvater*) points of view. Arendt writes:

> Just as there is no political solution within human capacity for the crime of administrative mass murder, so the human need for justice can find no satisfactory reply to the total mobilization of a people for that purpose. Where all are guilty, nobody in the last analysis can be judged. For that guilt is not accompanied by even the

> mere appearance, the mere presence of responsibility. So long as punishment is the right of the criminal – and this paradigm has for more than two thousand years been the basis of the sense of justice and right of Occidental man – guilt implies the consciousness of guilt, and punishment evidence that the criminal is a responsible person. (Arendt 1964b: 150f.)

In harmony with Jaspers' argument concerning a collective German guilt (accusations of everyone against everyone), that when everyone is guilty the innocent are also guilty, Arendt's concern is – perhaps rather surprisingly – from the point of view of the perpetrator: Arendt calls attention to the fact that, with the charge of a collective German guilt, the perpetrators are acquitted. To some extent, this can be said to introduce Arendt's later, famous doctrine of the banality of evil, further developed in her 1963 *Eichmann in Jerusalem* (1964a). Heinrich Himmler's subordinates, Arendt explains already in her text from the 1940s, 'are not Bohemians nor fanatics, nor adventurers, nor sex maniacs, nor sadists, but first and foremost jobholders, and good family men. [...]. When his occupation forces him to murder people he does not regard himself as a murderer because he has not done it out of inclination but in his professional capacity. Out of sheer passion he would never do harm to a fly' (Arendt 1964b: 152–4). Arendt pushes this insight to its brutal consequence: those who participated 'in Himmler's organization [...] are not even all natural murderers [...]. You must understand', an SS member spontaneously told a former schoolmate of his to whom he had just given the certificate of release, 'I have five years of unemployment behind me. They can do anything they want with me' (Arendt 1964b: 153).

Although Schaap's faithful reading of Jaspers and Arendt does underline that 'collective accountability for state wrongs should be conceived in terms of a political responsibility that does not imply blame' (2001: 758) (nor, as a consequence, can it imply a juridical conception), Schaap nonetheless fails to mention an evident coincidence between the two authors that relates them to one another as the sides of a Möbius bond: the clash between victims as perpetrators (Jaspers) and perpetrators as victims (Arendt), the clash making the innocent guilty, and making the guilty innocent. In the first instance, calumny is committed just as a false acquittal has taken place in the other – it is a kind of calumny 'turned upside-down'. Jaspers and Arendt agree upon the fact that the whole idea of juridical guilt and responsibility regarding the Third Reich exterminations in the end is far from justice, and will in any case either falsely accuse or falsely acquit.

Jasper's book was quite influential, Schaap shows. It probably contributed to a telling event, namely 'in the displacement of a collective reckoning with the past to the private sphere, where it became a psychological issue of personal healing rather than a properly political concern' (Schaap 2001: 754). Thus, perhaps it is necessary to turn once more to Richarz's psychologism? For her arguments incontestably share their wording with Jaspers' mention of metaphysical guilt in the accusation '"You are guilty" [*Das ist eure Schuld*]: You carry the guilt of having stood by passively when these crimes were committed – here, a metaphysical guilt is indicated' (Jaspers 1946: 27). Despite the similarity in these phrases, some quite substantial differences exist between Richarz's and Jaspers' conception of passive bystanders and the question of guilt and responsibility. Jaspers' point is not, in the end, psychological but, as he writes, metaphysical or, in other words, philosophical.

It is important to take note of the historical difference between the two texts. Jaspers wrote straight after the war, when these passive bystanders, whoever they were, were actually alive and were neighbours in flesh and blood of those who used to live next door but did so no more. These citizens had experienced and survived the Third Reich. Richarz writes in our time, when practically none of the actual bystanders are alive. The former writes on issues that his fellow contemporary citizens had experienced; it is not commemoration literature. The latter writes on issues that her contemporary citizens have not experienced; it is commemoration literature and concerns the descendants.

When discussing Jaspers above, it was suggested that to expect individuals to have prevented anything regarding deportation and extermination would have been unreasonable. This is what constitutes the philosopher's idea of metaphysical guilt as the guilt of being human, thus carrying the responsibility of the other whom one could not save. The juridical machine that constituted criminal and political guilt breaks down here, because it cannot address the event. It is likewise vital for the understanding of Jaspers' idea of metaphysical guilt that its precondition is constituted by a shared contemporaneity between victim and the carrier of metaphysical guilt: the existence of a potentiality to do that always already ends in not doing. Such a potentiality requires a shared contemporaneity between those who perished and those who did not. In Jaspers, to speak of an inherited guilt would make little sense. Reconsidering Richarz's position, it becomes obvious that she breaks this contemporary bond between victims and bystanders. In the end, Richarz effectively transports a metaphysical guilt, along with its presumption of the shared contemporaneity, away from its rightful sphere of the *oikos* (what Schaap called a psychological issue of personal healing), and into the sphere of the *polis*, thus mixing it up with criminal and political guilt.

On the premises of the Stolpersteine, Michael Imort suggests something similar to what Richarz intends. At least he is probably right when arguing that readers of the engravings on the Stolpersteine are actually expected to be affected, as they 'must stoop down a bit to be able to read – and thus perform what can be seen as a respectful bow to the victim' (Imort 2010: 235). However, following Schaap, such a kind of respect is not without problems: it could run the risk of being turned into a forced public grief, or attempts at creating a feeling of being *betroffen* [affected], which, in any case, does not tie in with Jaspers' conception of metaphysical guilt:

> To be *betroffen* suggests a subjective state of guilt, shame, embarrassment, speechlessness and contriteness. However, a public expectation of such sincere expression means that utterances about the past become vulnerable to being questioned according to the true understanding of the actor, which is veiled by his or her words. The demand for sincerity shifts the emphasis of political life away from contesting and debating the significance of past events, to conforming to a ritualistic mode of behaviour that is intended to convey that actors have properly 'come to terms with the past'. (Schaap 2001: 763)

Rather than the Stolpersteine actually displacing law into ethics or sentimentality completely, they constitute a whole in which law and ethics, sentimentality and feelings, proper guilt and metaphysical guilt, all appear inseparable. The Stolpersteine do utter quite strong opinions on the Third Reich and, at the same time, they do strangely, conform to a ritualistic mode of behaviour that is not always fortunate. Imort's idea of the 'respectful bow to the victim' could, just as Schaap warns, simply end in a commemorative performance that gives only the impression of sincerity.

In *Remnants of Auschwitz*, Agamben discusses some of these difficult theoretical and juridical challenges in his analyses of the Third Reich. In his book, the genealogy of these concepts points in the direction of Jaspers and Arendt as well as to the problems that were identified in Richarz and Ward above: 'In every age, the gesture of he who assumes a juridical guilt of which he is innocent has been considered noble', while, Agamben continues, 'the assumption of a political or moral responsibility without juridical consequences has always characterized the arrogance of the mighty [...]' (1998: 22). On the previous page, Agamben exemplifies Adolf Eichmann who, as his lawyer Robert Servatius repeated, 'feels guilty in the eyes of God not the law' (Agamben 1998: 21), and therefore ought not to be prosecuted. Until the end, Eichmann preferred '"to hang himself publicly" in order to "set the young Germans free from the weight of guilt"', ultimately with the result that 'the penitent assumption of moral responsibility is at every occasion invoked for relieving the juridical one' (Agamben 1998: 21).

On this ground, Agamben comments on the substitution of law with ethics:

> The confusion between ethical and juridical categories (with the logic of remorse which it implies) is here absolute. This confusion stands at the origin of numerous suicides committed to subtract oneself from trial (and not only from part of criminal Nazis), in which the implicit assumption of moral guilt would redeem from the juridical one. It is worth remembering that the Catholic doctrine is not the one primarily responsible for this confusion knowing, on the contrary, a sacrament whose scope is to liberate the sinner from guilt [*colpa*]; but instead secular ethics (in its well-meaning and pharisaic version which is the dominant one). After having constructed the juridical categories into ethical supreme ones and hence having irreparably confused the cards, this confusion would like to still put into play its *distinguo*. But ethics is the sphere that knows neither guilt nor responsibility: ethics is, like Spinoza knew, the doctrine of the beatified life. Assuming a guilt and a responsibility – which, sometimes, can be necessary to do – signifies stepping out of the field of ethics to enter in that of law [*diritto*]. The one who have had to make this difficult step, cannot pretend to go back through the door that has just closed behind him. (Agamben 1998: 22)

Now it more or less begins to be clear in what way these considerations, and indeed the complications whose threads this chapter has tried to disentangle, are relevant to the current investigation of the Stolpersteine monument. From this quotation, it is evident that any assumption of responsibility without (juridical) consequences seems rather costless and perhaps also irrelevant – Jaspers and Arendt would seem to believe so, Richarz and Ward less so. The Kafkaesque universe to which Faulkner's *Requiem for a Nun* also testified is, in Agamben, paradigmatically found in Eichmann. The critique that Jaspers and Arendt delivered on the possibility of a juridical understanding of the exterminations gave way to an ethical position that Jaspers called metaphysical guilt and which Agamben locates in Spinoza's theological ethics of the beatified life. Metaphysical guilt, as shown above, is similarly not without theological connotations, and from a theo-philological point of view it would have been interesting had the monument chosen, as Paul in fact did (cf. Chapter 5), to relocate the question of justice from the sphere of law to that of ethics, which, in Agamben's words, knows neither guilt nor responsibility.

In contrast to Paul's analysis and use of the Stolpersteine is that of Joachim Rönnerper, who maintains a rather harsh interpretation of the monument. In the shape of an aphorism, Rönnerper expresses his verdict on those who do not stumble upon the Stolpersteine: 'He who does not stumble, does not walk [*Wer nicht stolpert geht nicht*]' (Rönnerper, cit. in ibid. (ed.) 2010: 7). The violence of separatism, which according to Paul divided humans into those who fell upon the stone of stumbling and those who did not, and which Paul replaced by an all-inclusive reinterpretation of that law by transforming it into ethics, is now reinstalled by Rönnerper. In Rönnerper, the separatism does not divide those who hold the true law from those who do not, but those who recognize the Stolpersteine and those who do not. Nonetheless, the consequences of this separatism are just as violent as its Biblical predecessor: those who are humans, who walk and stumble, and those who are not considered humans, and thus do not walk.

Of course, this necessitates the question: what is the creature that does not stumble and, *therefore*, does not walk? Clearly Rönnerper's aphorism is metaphorical. The question is, however, why such extremism is necessary when it comes to commemorating Third Reich victims of extermination.

Rönnerper is not on his own, however, and this sort of radicalism is far from unusual. The idea that the Stolpersteine can give the victims their names back (Demnig; Meckel), that they contain evidence of who the bystanders were (Richarz) or that the monuments cite the former biopolitical form of government (Endlich) are just a couple of examples mentioned in this chapter that all testify to a contemporary commemorative extremism and brutality that, despite its unquestionably good intentions, belittles the fate of the victim along with the reality of the human catastrophe of Third Reich extermination for contemporary commemoration.

CHAPTER 6

Art as Ritual Normalization of the Past

Mytho-historical Memory

The Stolpersteine are proclaimed to be an 'art project for Europe' [*Kunstprojekt für Europa*] (see Figure 3). However, it is not entirely easy to describe how to understand such a form of art, which aims at being a monument that can fulfil a commemorative task. As well, the materiality of the Stolpersteine seems to be both profane and sacred – installed as they are in profane, public spaces while paraphrasing the writing on a tombstone – thus leaving the vocation of rituality beyond any ordinary sense of sacred or traditional rituality. In the course of this book, the ritual and religious elements have been addressed, sometimes *en passant*, sometimes with more rigour. In this chapter, the task will therefore be to consolidate these thoughts regarding the Stolpersteine. Where, in the history of religion, is one to look for categories of understanding in order to grasp such a strange form of art and such a peculiar memorial?

The suggestion in this final chapter is to follow Italian philosopher Mario Perniola's interpretation of the *ancilia* of the archaic Roman religion. Granting these *ancilia* the status of a paradigm will provide some useful strategies by which, as is the hypothesis for this chapter, it is possible to learn more about the art and rituality embedded in the Stolpersteine. The chapter ends with a discussion of Agamben's analyses of the oath, that is, 'the verbal act destined to guarantee the truth of a promise or of an assertion' (2008: 26), proving its strict relevance to the monuments and their engravings, whose form of commemoration appears to hover between ascertaining a fact and constituting a gift or forming a promise. In this way, the scope is to answer the crucial question raised in Chapter 3: what are the

Stolpersteine doing, if they are neither stating something completely true or accurate nor something completely untrue or false concerning the Third Reich and the victims of extermination as a means of commemoration?

The analysis will centre, yet again, on the five fates [*Schicksale*] mentioned on the Stolpersteine:

> Possible descriptions of fate are: DEAD [*TOT*] or MURDERED [*ERMORDET*]; for unclear cases: FATE UNKNOWN. Instead of suicide we write ESCAPED IN DEATH [*FLUCHT IN DEN TOD*]. We do not use the concept 'missing' [*verschollen*], and just as rare is the concept 'death' [*TOD*] since this suggests a natural death. Equally rare is the use of the concept 'Emigration' or 'left the country' [*Auswanderung*]. Instead, we write ESCAPED [*FLUCHT*] + YEAR + TARGET COUNTRY. (Demnig 2015: 4)

The questions concerning the rituality of the Stolpersteine cannot relate merely to 'the ceremonial laying of the stones' (Richarz 2008: 326), but must address the stones in their, so to speak, religious entirety. If memory takes on the form of a sort of 'civil religion', then what is the nature of this religion regarding the Stolpersteine? How are extermination and annihilation to be understood when, as Demnig explains, these must 'be experienced. Very personally and everywhere' (Demnig cit. in Conradi 2005)? A starting point is found in A. V. Seaton's 1996 *Guided by the Dark*, in which the author describes a phenomenon that, in fact, is rather old: death tourism or, in Seaton's words, thanatourism. Seaton defines it as follows: 'Travelling to a location wholly, or partially, motivated by the desire for actual or symbolic encounters with death, particularly, but not exclusively, violent death, which may, to a varying degree be activated by the *person-specific features* of those whose deaths are its focal objects' (Seaton 1996: 240, italics added).

Seaton describes two main elements in his definition of thanatourism:

> 1. It is a behavioural rather than essentialist definition, which defines Thanatourism by the traveller's motives rather than by an attempt to specify the discrete features of the traveller's destination.
> 2. It recognises that Thanatourism is not an absolute form but exists across a continuum of intensity according to a) whether it is the single motivation or exists with other motivations b) the extent to which the interest in death is person-centred or generalised. The purest form of Thanatourism is travel motivated exclusively by fascination with death in itself, irrespectively of the person or persons involved. It is not initially focused on the dead as individuals or collectives with

> differentiated features (though it may come to be so), but on the forms or scale of death in itself (e.g., visits to graveyards, catacombs, scenes of disaster [...]). At the other extreme is Thanatourism in which the dead are both known to, and valued by, the visitor (e.g., a visit to a war memorial commemorating a dead relative). The more differentiated and comprehensive the traveller's knowledge of the dead, the weaker is the purely thanatouristic element. (Seaton 1996: 240)

'Germany's challenge lies', Birgitte Sion concludes more specifically on Seaton's ideas in her article on the Berlin Memorial to the Murdered Jews of Europe, 'in the promotion of the memorial to tourists connected to the victims, tourists connected to the perpetrators, and tourists with no connection to the Holocaust at all' (Sion 2010: 248). Seaton's diagnosis of death tourism evidently touches on similar challenges concerning the Stolpersteine, especially when he mentions the journey to a location for individual deaths. However, when Seaton mentions the book depository in Dallas and the Tower of London as examples, it is evident that at stake are single, specific locations of death tourism (1996: 241).

As such a specific and isolated location Sion treats the Memorial to the Murdered Jews of Europe. To Seaton, it is clear that thanatourism is a journey away from home, which one can choose or not choose. To the same extent, the opposite is evident: the higher the scale on which one is met with a death to which one cannot travel, but which on the contrary presents itself immediately, the more the difference between home and away is blurred, the more the touristic element in thanatourism is reduced to the point where one does not travel to the sites of death, but is confronted by them.

The Berlin Memorial to the Murdered Jews of Europe, with its massive scale and bombastic architecture, is not unknown to other forms of memorials. For instance, the Vietnam Veterans Memorial in Washington is 8,000 m^2. To a greater extent than Seaton's own examples (the book depository and the Tower of London), death has been installed in the city itself with these two monuments. If this is true, then the challenge of which Sion speaks cannot simply consist of a 'right' or 'better' promotion of the memorial culture for tourists. The task must likewise consist both of determining the limits of commemoration in an attempt to locate an equilibrium between the dead and the living, as well as discussing the scales and locations of such a commemoration.

With the Stolpersteine, these problems and challenges would seem to culminate. However, Seaton's analyses and Sion's diagnosis both seem unequipped to handle such omnipresence of death and to deal with the monument's success (or failure) in terms of commemoration. For could it not be said that the Stolpersteine in fact suspend death tourism as any travel or journey, any coming or going, is always already touristic? Hence, it must be asked what this major monumental expansion of death to the whole of the European continent (and beyond) really means, and what its consequences are.

The idea that a closer study of the Third Reich and National Socialism is in some way connected with a work on rite and myth is not at all a new or original idea. In fact, this idea seems rather old. Nonetheless – and rather surprisingly – Kristen Harjes writes without much ado that the Stolpersteine 'successfully appeal to the contemporary association of authentic memory with an avoidance of ritual', constituting 'a rejection of ritualized forms of memory' (2005: 149; 144). This is done, it might be added, without explaining why authenticity is incompatible with rituality or why rituality is at all avoided by the Stolpersteine. Contrary to Harjes, the concern on the pages to come is instead to work with the hypothesis that central elements from Roman archaic religion in the shape of the *ancilia* on crucial points might actually tighten Seaton's definition of thanatourism in the context of the Stolpersteine, and thus finding a 'behavioural rather than essentialist definition' (Seaton 1996: 240); moreover, perhaps, even to adjust Sion's diagnosis and to better describe the challenges that the memorial culture faces contemporaneously concerning the Stolpersteine.

In any case, the referentiality – however this may be structured by rituality and myth, reality and memory – is particularly precarious for the Stolpersteine. It is obvious that, whatever the nature of this rituality, it carries a referentiality that is, by necessity, factual, and which the Stolpersteine also point out. The Stolpersteine refer to the historic period 1933–45. However, thinking on the considerations that have been raised above (cf. Chapter 2), could myth – so important in the Christian tradition – play a no less significant, if perhaps negative role, in commemoration, while hopefully never denying the reality of the exterminations of millions and the annihilation of the individual? Stricter than maintaining a rituality based on pure myth, as do some religions, is the case where the fact of annihilation is mythologized in order to suit forms of commemoration of the victims of National Socialism.

Although the Stolpersteine do refer to an unquestionable event, this book has underlined that the descriptions of that event have not always been fortunate. Instead, the descriptions tend to normalize the past, something that was discussed in relation to the five fates above (cf. Chapter 1). In this book, this has been conceptualized as *history as problem*, that is, that the Stolpersteine do not sufficiently distinguish between fact and reality on the one side and normative descriptions and commemoration on the other. However, since the descriptions are nothing like a refutation of the event but, instead, a normalization, such a circumstance is precisely the reason why it may be instructive to turn to Perniola's idea of the precedence of the ritual to further explain the nature of such a strange case of normalization. Hence, it will be argued that two pairs of Roman concepts from Perniola's investigations are relevant regarding the Stolpersteine: *ars* and *urbs*, *ritus* and *caerimonia*.

The starting point for the Italian thinker and his thoughts and hypotheses on Roman archaic religion is that the distinctions between sacred and profane, myth and ritual, are practically erased, so Perniola informs, for politically significant reasons found in Rome's *pignus imperii* [guarantor of power] (1980: 29). Clifford Ando formulates something similar in his 2008 *The Matter of the Gods: Religion and the Roman Empire*, when he writes that 'much of Roman ritual, and many strands of Roman religious literature, do, in fact, situate the gods in this world'; moreover, Ando continues, 'many focalize such relations upon a particular visible manifestation of the divine, namely their cult objects' (2008: 21). To Ando, as to Perniola before him, it likewise appears difficult to isolate the rite to a strictly sacred sphere.

As early as 1954, the German philologist Karl-Heinz Roloff described in his article *Ritus* how the philological components of the Latin term *rite* consist of two meanings that are difficult to distinguish: '1. is the quite broad meaning of general customs [*Sitte und Brauch*], 2. is specialized in the sacred field' (Roloff 1954: 40). Perniola begins his article on rite and myth by stating that this distinction equally does not exist in what he calls contemporary postmodern society: 'the mythic tale – with its idealization and emotional implications, its reference to an archetypical dimension of the existence – makes room for the *performance*, for an action that unites in itself the nature of execution and exhibition; being disenchanted and repetitive, technical and strategic it presents, thus, substantial similarities [*similitudes*] with the rite' (Perniola 1981: 19).

It is important to understand that to Perniola, Roman archaic religion is simply a privileged laboratory for understanding rituality (or performativity) in contemporary society, something Perniola had already done in *The Society of Simulacra* published the year before. The task of this author is more modest: it consists simply of asking how such a study of the Roman rite may unearth something about the Stolpersteine.

Perniola uses an interesting example to illustrate his point, which may also be used in this investigation. According to tradition, Plutarch tells in his *Parallel Lives* writing about Rome's second king, Numa Pompilius (753–673 BC, following Romulus who ruled from 715 BC), the blacksmith Mamurius Veturius was considered to be Rome's first artist. After the first *ancile* had fallen down from heaven into the hands of Numa, Plutarch explains, he let Mamurius make eleven other *ancilia*. These copies were completely identical to the original, hence making it impossible to distinguish them from each other: 'So he [Numa] assembled all the chief craftsmen then in Rome, to prove which of them would take upon him to make one like unto that [the original *ancile*]. Every man despaired to perform it. Howbeit, one called Veturius Mamurius (the most excellentest workman that was in those days) did make them all so suit-like, that Numa himself did not know the first target, when they were all laid together' (Plut. *Num.* 13:3, translation: Perrin).

Although Plutarch insists on the account, 'if any would enterprise to steal it, he should not tell which of them to take for the right target' (*Num.* 13:3), another matter seems more relevant, Perniola argues. Because, what really makes Mamurius' work so intelligent and Numa's idea so clever does not concern its originality – as it was a copy – nor its protection against theft. Instead, it is the cancellation of the extravagant value of the original: the cancellation of the prototype (Perniola 1980: 30).

The English term art, as well as the corresponding terms in French (*art*), Italian (*arte*) and many other Romance languages, all derive from the Indo-European root **ar–*, which signifies an order, a 'well-structured, sacred order [*Ordnung*] [...], series, sequence, number', Roloff suggests, in reference to the etymology Julius Pokorny had already established (Roloff 1954: 62). *Artus* [segmentation] shares the same root as *ritus*, leading to the contemporary term ritual, Roloff continues (1954: 62). As Perniola explains, in referring to Émile Benveniste: 'The *jus* is precisely an *ars*, that is, an *ars* that "*in sola prudentium interpretatione consistit*" [consists only of interpretation by the foreseeing ones]; if one keeps in mind that *ars* and *ritus* derive from the same root as *ar–*, designating an order, the ceremonial repetition then imposes itself as one of the cardinal points of Roman thought' (Perniola 1981: 25).

The Latin citation Perniola brought attention to in the citation just above refers to Pompinius (second century AD), of whom nothing is known. The citation, however, figures in a book entitled *Enchiridium*, concerning the origin of law, and is also part of Justinian's famous *Digest* (D.1.2.3.12), which figures in the *Corpus Iuris Civilis* [*Body of Civil Law*] for which Emperor Justinian I was responsible, around 530 AD (Tellegen-Couperus 2008: 96). Rather than the Roman ritual illustrating or bringing the myth to life, as in, for example, the Eucharist, the rite cancels the myth and makes it irrelevant. Instead, it presents the participants with an order – even legal, it seems – rather than an ideological entity (e.g. as Jews or Christians) to which to belong; an order, one might add, built not upon identity, but instead on plural activity. *Ritus* is, Roloff writes, 'the act itself, it is almost "ceremonial" in our meaning, that is, the outer effort in the cult' (1954: 41).

Thinking on Mamurius's ritual – at least as Perniola presents the matter – it is therefore nothing like the Greek *poiêsis* or *technê* – a divine inspiration and creation from absolute nothing. Instead, the *ritus* concerns the artistic handling and shaping of an object already at hand and present. There is no *creatio ex nihilo* in the Roman world, nor is there any transcendent, divine object. Roman religion is concerned neither with the *Ursprung* [origin] of the *urbs* nor with the foundation of the city, but concerns how to ritually preserve a (legal) order and the structures of society.

The energy by which the Roman authors, from Cicero to Livy, describe and celebrate the origins of Rome, Perniola explains, 'does not succeed in hiding the disturbing past of the city, which has not had a true origin but only a beginning' (1980: 28). The *urbs*, Richard Sennett adds in his book about the city in Western civilization, did not even have a real divine origin to which its citizens had to belong (2002: 106–21). The only origin ascribed to the Roman citizen was the fact that he was born into a world that itself had no origin, no birth – just like the city. Rome can perhaps best be described as a collector of orphans and wanderers (even of an emperor such as Augustus) whose common point of reference does not consist of a collective historical starting point – *the* origin, *the* language.

The Roman people, thus, do not constitute a people in the common sense of the term, born into a nation to which they are bound (from the Latin *nascor*: to be born). To its citizens and peoples Rome was a *Gemeinschaft*, a *communitas* [community]. On arrival, one's past was forgotten with the promise of a Roman future, a collector of similar action. One might say, perhaps, that what united Roman citizens was the constructed and collective memory that the *ancile* really had fallen from heaven, leaving any new citizen to be welcomed in the form of ritual participation and commemoration of the twelve *ancilia*. '*Romanae spatium est urbis et orbis idem*' [Roman space and city are identical], Perniola quotes the Latin poet Ovid (1980: 31). Unlike the Greek *polis*, the Roman *urbs* is a spatial principle of organization, not of identity: 'If *πόλις* is translated into Latin by *civitas* [city], a Greek term indicating *urbs* [city] does not exist' (Perniola 1980: 30). The *communitas* is constructed ritually by way of the *ancilia* without ascribing the myth (or, rather, the different myths or origins that the immigrants had brought with them) much ontological ground. The original *ancile*, whatever of it once existed, is absorbed by the contemporary Roman ritualization.

In Rome, authority and hierarchy were related to history. Great men such as Numa lived in Rome. They were not created by a goddess or by a holy spirit. Unlike the Greek pantheon in which Poseidon and Athena represent divine origin, urban ontology and identity, such ideas were altered by the Romans towards a much more practical and, so to say, 'useful' direction. Rome was founded not by gods, but from a war between humans – Romulus and Remus; not upon myth, but on politics. What concerns

Rome's beginning should be related to the very political survival of the city, to its maintenance and not to any mythical or theological truth. This is why, according to Plutarch, Numa had the twelve *ancilia* 'go skipping and leaping up and down the city' (Plut., *Num.* 13:3). As Anna Ferrari notes in her lexicon the procession of the *ancilia* were even accompanied 'by songs and dances in honour of Mars' (1999: 47), thus in a ritual honouring of the god of war, that is, of continuous political expansion rather than the identity between members in a religious community. Religion and politics in ancient Rome were so intimately connected that they appeared inseparable.

Rome is established again and again in a continuous construction of itself through its mytho-historical past, lying, as Plutarch describes, on the threshold of reality and myth: the myth of the first and original *ancile* on the one side, the fact and ritualization of all the twelve *ancilia* on the other. The shields may be considered, thus, as a *mytho-historical fact* founded ritually by way of ritualizing the memory of the divine origin of the *ancile* into the profane commemoration of the *ancilia* over and over again. It is against this background that the attempt will now be to try and show how Perniola's thoughts on Roman archaic religion may concern the Stolpersteine, and whether it is at all possible to come closer to the point Seaton tried to make regarding the role of death in modern society. Having done so, it will be possible to determine the religious dimension of commemoration regarding the Stolpersteine.

History's *relegere*

An important aspect when trying to make relevant any comparison between the Roman *ancilia* and the German Stolpersteine is that both seem to prefer to not give particular attention to the difference between fact and myth, memory and history, in their ritual liturgical practice and unification – naturally, all of this in a very special sense, which the following pages will try to determine more precisely. In any case, it is clear that differences between nationalities, nations, cities, languages, religions etc. are all minimized or united via the Stolpersteine. In that connection, it is interesting to note what Perniola writes concerning the artistic production of the twelve *ancilia*, so closely tied to politics: 'This segmented production involves a plurality of objects in a mutual ordered relation. But this order, to which the artistic operation is connected, neither has any mythological contents nor, in fact, a mere technical functionality. It consists, rather, in the construction of a system of references involving several parts each capable of fulfilling different purposes' (Perniola 1980: 30).

Three points in this aesthetic theory of the *ancilia* correspond to the Stolpersteine:

Ancilia		*Stolpersteine*
1. Rome: main city of reference as the capital *urbs*.		1. Berlin: capital and main *Führerstadt*.
2. The artistic reproduction of myth (the *ancile* fell from heaven).	⇔	2. The artistic reproduction of fact (the extermination of millions of victims).
3. A ritual order as a system of references (specific times of the year) constituting a commemorative past that in contemporaneity is acknowledged via the materiality of the objects.		3. A commemorative order of a system of references (the homes of the victims) constituting a commemorative past that in contemporaneity is acknowledged via the materiality of the objects.

The aspect of the model that concerns the *ancilia* will first be explained, after which some parallels with the Stolpersteine can be made. Rome is the capital *urbs* where the *ancile* falls into Numa's hands, and is carried around for public worship in Rome, along with the other eleven *ancilia*. All twelve shields form the ritual: both the original prototype (the myth, the past *in vivo* [living]) as well as the copies of that event (its 'history', its fact). When the difference between original and copy is logically erased due to the complete identity between all twelve shields, so too is the difference between the myth of the original's divine and mythological origin on one hand, and the profane and historical fact of the eleven shields made by Mamurius on the other.

If myth and fact cannot be told apart, as in the case of these twelve shields, history becomes mythologized just as myth becomes historicized, which is to say that the difference between myth and fact dissolves itself ritually, leaving reality on the threshold of the two. In other words, more than just that these shields install oblivion – they erase any difference between divine and profane, myth and fact, history and memory. The myth of the original *ancile* is dressed in fact through the rituality of the copies of the *ancile* constituting the political formula for guaranteeing the Roman *urbs*.

What the *ancilia* thematize, and what makes them paradigmatic in relation to the Stolpersteine, thus, is of course not the divine as problem. Instead, the *ancilia* illustrate something about the annulment of the difference between a history of the past and a memory of the past, in a way that would seem to challenge Carlo Ginzburg's insistence on the principle of reality, which was discussed above in relation to Jan Assmann's theory of cultural memory and the Third Reich exterminations. It could be advantageous, therefore, to recall Assmann's words by which the Egyptologist explains cultural memory (cf. Chapter 2):

> For cultural memory what counts is not actual history but only remembered history. One could also say that in cultural memory actual history becomes transformed into remembered history and, thus, into myth. Myth is a foundational history, a story that is told in order to enlighten a contemporary time of its origin. Completely independent from the question of its historicity, the Exodus is the foundational myth of Israel: as such it is celebrated in the Pesach celebrations, and as such it belongs to the cultural memory of the people. Through memory history becomes myth. Without being unreal history, on the contrary, first becomes reality [*Wirklichkeit*] in the sense of an ongoing normative and formative power. (Assmann 2007: 52)

As for the Stolpersteine, the procedure Assmann explains is absolutely correct: the historical event of National Socialist extermination and annihilation does not disappear in the ritual cultivation of its memory no more than the *ancile* prototype disappeared in its ritual cultivation. Such a comparative approach would be too strong and far from being in harmony with what has been established as the case for the *ancilia*. Rather, to use a formulation that would have pleased Assmann: the history on which the Stolpersteine insist (the extermination of millions) in their ritualized memorialization becomes the formative force of memory and turns history into remembered myth in shape of the five fates.

There is no doubt that the Stolpersteine do function like this, but the questions one must raise are really of another scale. If the intention of the Stolpersteine, in Demnig's own words, is to give back to the victim that which he or she had lost ('the victim gets its name back' (Demnig 2002: 13)) in a juridical and ethical reconstruction of the victim as citizen and human being, why does Demnig then state that the Stolpersteine are *describing* a historical state of affairs? There can be no question that, for Demnig, the five fates are descriptive terms by which the Stolpersteine are intended to indicate a true state of things (Demnig 2015: 4). Moreover, does it not strike as rather odd that the means by which the Stolpersteine intend to restore the victims' lost juridical and ethical status is by way of understating the fact and brutality of their extermination using ethical and juridical jargon?

If one now tries to answer one of the central questions directed towards the Stolpersteine, that is, whether they are *describing* or *commemorating* a fact (or perhaps even both) – the answer is anything but easy. The question is crucial, because without historical ground commemoration of victims of the Third Reich loses its footing.

The challenge with which the Stolpersteine battle, as does, in fact, any monument dedicated to the victims of Third Reich exterminations, is how to ethically commemorate (the victims) while insisting on not forgetting Auschwitz (the circumstances surrounding their individual annihilation). At this point of the present analysis, it largely appears that rather than insisting on the success of this – admittedly, almost insurmountable – task, the Stolpersteine deny the very existence of such a double task. As a result, the Stolpersteine appear to be a case of cultural memory so that – precisely as Assmann writes – 'actual history becomes transformed into remembered history and, thus, into myth' (2007: 52).

Naturally, if this is true, then the Stolpersteine's form of commemoration is that by describing a fact they commemorate the victim. In other words, the wish to represent the victim's fate historically (to *describe*) turns out to dress the fact of the victim's annihilation in the clothes of a myth stating that the victim *de jure* was murdered and suffered death, when *de facto* something *far worse happened to the victims*. This critique has been made many times on different grounds throughout the present book, but before a further analysis is made of the hopeful link between the Stolpersteine and the historical reality – whatever its nature – it is necessary to investigate whether there is a ritual connection between the *ancilia* and the Stolpersteine that, perhaps, could be said to act descriptively as well as commemoratively.

The Roman religion was based upon the cult of public objects, of which the *ancilia* are ample indication, and at the same time it is clear that this was something Numa used politically in order to govern the Romans. The Stolpersteine, in their turn, seem almost to materialize this kind of rituality to the letter: the memorial stones are installed just outside people's homes on the threshold of *polis* and *oikos*, house and city, the private life of the human being and the public life of the citizen as this was analysed in Chapter 4. Yet unlike the *ancilia*, which were carried along the highways and byways of the Roman *urbs*, the German memorial is installed, once and for all, outside a private residence (this is at least the most common practice) at a specific European location and even beyond.

For instance, on Via della Reginella 2 in the old Jewish quarter in Rome, it is clear that, although pedestrians can also 'stumble' upon the stones, the intention is first and foremost to tie the monument closely to the former home and its current residents, who will then be the ones primarily performing the stumbling act of commemoration (see Figure 4). Something similar could perhaps even be said of Stolpersteine installed in front of playgrounds, schools or other institutions devoted to education and research, where every child's act of play, or every pupil's and student's learning, must begin or end with a commemoration of the Third Reich exterminations. In fact, the commemoration is tied to a certain and contemporary occupation and activity, that is, to the practice of dwelling or working, just as was shown via Heidegger above (cf. Chapter 4).

Figure 4. Stolpersteine. Jewish Quarter, Rome, May 2012.

It is clear that, since the Stolpersteine on Via della Reginella 2 are placed as near as possible to the front door, the cult of public monuments goes on even though the residents in this apartment are simply arriving or leaving their block. Every time they walk on or over the Stolpersteine, they commemorate – whether they want to or not. It has nothing to do with faith or belief, but with the action as such, the participation itself. Also, this is an effect of the breaking down of boundaries between public and private, man and citizen, profession and Being, which was also was analysed above in relation to Heidegger's discussion of the boundary [*Grenze*] (cf. Chapter 4), which here in the case of the Stolpersteine seems to have the scope – or at least the effect – of ritually automating commemoration. It appears that this form of commemoration does not only challenge the dichotomy between public and private, perhaps even evocating a desired collapse, most importantly for this chapter it also raises the question of the public character of rituality and commemoration.

In his *On the Nature of The Gods* Cicero describes one of the main features of the Roman cult as *relegere*:

> Persons who spent whole days in prayer and sacrifice [*precabantur et immolabant*] to ensure that their children should outlive them were termed 'superstitious' (from *superstes*, a survivor), and the word later acquired a wider application. Those on the other hand who carefully reviewed and so to speak retraced all the lore or ritual [*qui autem omnia quae ad cultum deorum pertinerent diligenter retractarent et tamquam relegerent*] were called 'religious' from *relegere* (to retrace or reread) [*sunt dicti religiosi ex relegendo*] […]. (Cic. *N. D.*, II, xxviii, 72)

Rackham notes in his translation that scholars disagree over the etymological origin of religion as *relegere*. Cicero, readers are taught by Lewis and Short, elsewhere connects it with *ligare* 'to tie, bind, bind together, bind fast' (Lewis and Short 1879).

In any case, Perniola has chosen – at least initially – to follow Cicero's etymology that is described here in the quotation. Roman archaic religion, hence, is characterized by a significant repetitive element that forms its rituality, Perniola explains, so that one could say it is effectively an *anti-mythologized ritual* (1980: 32). Nothing but human action keeps the ritual intact, justifies it and keeps it alive. Belief is toned down and rituality is stimulated – unlike, say, the Jewish or Christian religion, the Roman religion is in no need of any transcendent guarantee for its existence. It lives on participation alone and is thus in opposition, Ando explains, to Augustine and his fellow Christians, who nonetheless were right in denying 'that pagan divinities had a metaphysical status equivalent to that of the true God' (2008: 27) – a point also made by George Dumézil.

Considering that many words in the Roman archaic rituals 'were incomprehensible to the priests who recited them' (Perniola 1980: 32), it only becomes more obvious – despite the importance of the priests as authorities – that the Roman cult was, to a large degree, actually founded upon an act of essentially blind repetition and action, rather than on any deeper meaning to or reflection on the recited words and even of the deities. Sometimes, words were actually recited in order to forget or even to suppress their meaning, and in this way to force an oblivion of such potential meaning by means of memorizing a blind, semantic operation. To Dumézil, Perniola makes clear, the Roman pantheon is best compared to 'a world with almost immovable shadows, a twilight crowd in the midst of which it is difficult to detect any precise contours' (Dumézil cit. in Perniola 1981: 24).

Many gods have no other personality, Dumézil continues, 'than their name, which is sometimes a group name, in short no other way of existence than the cult which is provided for them' (1974: 49f.). These characteristics of maintaining a ritual order via participation and blind repetition certainly appears to be the case for the *ancilia*:

> This emptying, this separation of the rite from the myth is the very condition for such an order, and can solely operate on this condition provided that the prototype is repeated so well that it is dissolved. The efficiency is not bound to the ritualization of an *Urhandlung*, but to its disappearance and destruction. […] this tendency is under no circumstances concerned with a text reading or an explanation of its subject matter but, on the other hand, concerns an external perfect repetition, dissolving the meaning of the text […]. (Perniola 1980: 32)

Does the Stolpersteine monument contain a similar repetitive character and, furthermore, could it similarly be said that they are dissolving the meaning of the text engraved upon them? Regarding the Stolpersteine in Berlin's Friedrichshain-Kreuzberg quarter for instance (mentioned above in another context (Chapter 1)), the goal was to install one stone for each deportee, just as Demnig had imagined for his project: 'Between 1996 and

2004, 350 stones were set in the sidewalks of the districts of Friedrichshain and Kreuzberg alone', Jennifer Jordan states, 'with the aim of eventually installing a stone for each of the 2000 people from these districts who died at the hands of the Nazis' (2006: 192). In this connection, Ulrike Schrader's comment perfectly describes what above has been defined as a central aspect of Roman rituality: 'The recognisability via the brand name, which indeed is already established, leads to a strange and gracefully high motivated joy of discovery, and the "Oh my God here's another one!" is the triumph of the song of praise that follows the project. *The name on the stone and the further inscription no longer needs to play a role*' (Schrader 2006: 178, italics added).

Following Schrader's argument and tying it in with the analysis of the originality of the *ancile* (the prototype) that was dissolved in the multitude of the eleven other *ancilia*, so too could the name and identity of the single individual victim disappear in the mass of the thousands and, eventually, millions of other Stolpersteine. If the comparative approach of the *ancilia* is true (at least Schrader's comments would seem to support this hypothesis), a Stolperstein in a Berlin pavement in Friedrichshain-Kreuzberg naturally runs the risk of reducing and anonymizing the victim in the midst of hundreds of Stolpersteine, whereby a reading of a victim's name is repeated so many times that it loses its extraordinary character and individuality as a victim of annihilation.

At least one phenomenon could seem to underline this interpretation and even to support Schrader's conclusion: polishing Stolpersteine. The event *Berlin putzt Stolpersteine* [Berlin polishes Stolpersteine] was organized in commemoration of the *Kristallnacht* of the evening of 9 November 1938. Journalists of the *Berliner Morgenpost* wrote that Minister of State for Culture, André Schmitz from the German Social Democrats (SPD), 'had urged Berliners to care about the Stolpersteine, and at once he led the way with a good example: in the Passauer and Marburger Straßen, Schmitz, with prominent support, polished the memory signs' (Kellerhoff and Gandzior 2013). In magazines and elsewhere, a small cardboard flyer and a polishing cloth were even provided, hence encouraging citizens to effectively commemorate by polishing. The Berlin Stolpersteine homepage announced *Stolperstein-Putzt-Spaziergänge* [Stolpersteine-Polish-Walks] and also made available a detailed programme for each of Berlin's districts. In April 2017, further Stolpersteine-Polish-Walks were organized in Berlin, Hamburg and many other cities.

Seaton's idea of thanatourism, which would also seem to lie at the very basis of the Stolpersteine (although in a much more extreme fashion), becomes explicit by this commemorative event: a grand ritual voyage throughout the German *urbs* is now undertaken to the different *Wohnorte* [places of residence] and Stolpersteine houses commemorating victims of the Third Reich. One could argue that in this ritual act of commemoration the act itself and, hence, the memorial stones as objects become almost more important than the victims, thereby risking that the victim's name really does disappear into oblivion. Thus, it is noteworthy that Kellerhoff and Gandzior do not thematize the importance of the *victims* but, instead, maintain that what it is all about is 'to care about the *Stolpersteine*' (2013, italics added).

Again, as so many times before, the Stolpersteine challenge standard and perhaps even quite evident conditions and circumstances surrounding the commemoration and rituality of a monument. Even though the Stolpersteine take hold on everyday life activities, transforming them into acts of commemoration, each Stolperstein *does* bear the name of the individual victim, which any 'commemorative cleaner' is bound to be confronted with and thus stopping the otherwise repetitive element and the forgetting of who the individual victim was. In this way, it could be argued that this suggested commemorative practice is not blind after all but shares, rather, quite common features with the maintenance of a burial place for instance.

In contrast to the *ancilia*, each Stolperstein does bear a mark of identification (in the form of the victim's name), thus distinguishing one from the other and preventing anonymizing the individual victim into a mass of victims. Is the idea, then, to argue for the *ancilia* as a paradigm for the Stolpersteine refuted, or is it possible that it could still be useful? Before it is possible to answer that question, it is necessary to say something more about the Roman conception of history.

To the Romans, history itself was sacred, and also constituted the place for human action and rituality, as in the case with the *ancile*. To the Romans, history was not a Fall, nor the actions of the Lord or of his delegates, and likewise Roloff explains, 'there is also no merely transcendent "sacredness"' (1952: 107). Above it has already been shown, at least partially, that in Rome rather than myth taking on the leading role in a tale on divine substance, ritual becomes the organizational form and structure for law and politics, and in this way structures Roman religion. What Cicero called the ceremony of the gods [*caeremonia deorum*] is, Roloff writes, 'no dead sacredness, but instead a sacredness that will be made the point of departure, contents and goal for human "acts" [*Handlungen*]' (1952: 124). Concluding on this passage of Roloff's text, Perniola writes the following:

> A sacred offering that is not motivated by an intimate and spiritual devotion, and which furthermore is addressed towards divinities of whom nothing is known, constitutes an incomprehensible madness. Nevertheless, this madness constitutes the basis itself of the ancient Romans' religion and mentality. Most astonishing is that in ancient Rome, exteriority and ceremony, rite without myth and faith were not formulated in terms of a historical process, nor were they the expression of the decadence and breathlessness of a religion that had lost every connection to the real experience from which it was born. Quite the opposite: these characteristics are found at the origin of Roman culture and they constitute the central intuition upon which the Roman conception of the divine, of the human and of time is founded. (Perniola 1981: 22)

One could therefore speak of 'the *ceremoniality of time*' [la *cérémonialité du temps*], Perniola suggests, that is, 'the calendar, a formal structure of days, months and feasts that always return, but without preventing the historical activity of man' (1981: 25). In fact, Perniola continues, the calendar lays out specific points of reference and the actions (the rituals) that go with them although, 'without saying *a priori* what these elements must contain, and it does not *a posteriori* transform their contents into sacred history' (1981: 25). This form of circular ritual practice is what constitutes the political and juridical sphere.

Caeremonia appears to be that by which secular objects such as the *ancilia* are made sacred, tying in with the politico-juridical sphere over and over again. Whereas myth concerns a single act, ritual is repetitive. However, *caeremonia*'s relation to the juridical is not to be understood as *lex* [law] but, Perniola specifies, as a form of justice, 'in the sense of *jus*, that is, of a rigorously technical character of the rite, that is, a procedure in which the magistrates and parties have roles rigorously determined by tradition' (1981: 24). Roloff explains this more precisely when he writes that although *ritus* occurs eleven times in Cicero there is no trace of the term in the letters, which is to say, not in everyday language. On the contrary, it appears in the political sphere: seven times in *On the Laws* alone (Roloff 1954: 46):

> Hence, Numa establishes laws and norms for specific tasks that condition the deity, that is, certain things and acts are thereby made sacrosanct – the only means by which norms of law [*Rechtsnormen*] can be enforced upon a primitive people [...]. The sacred include not only the heavenly gods: also the *manes* [spirits of the death] must claim their right or, rather, are included in the sacred legal exchange [*Rechtsverkehr*]; also here sacred norms exist. (Roloff 1952: 121f.)

It is crucial that Roloff's analysis shows that at centre of Numa's political use of the *caeremonia* regarding the *ancilia* is the imposition of legal norms [*Rechtsnormen*] through a significant element of ritual repetition. 'This means', Perniola explains, 'that the mandatory nature of the ceremony did not depend upon the participants' adhesion to its [the legal norms'] contents, but to the magistrates' ability *to reattach the particular case to the general and abstract form of the rite*' (1981: 24, italics added).

Ius obtained its justification through the ritual, and together they constituted the *caeremonia*, which thereby tied the juridical inseparably tight to the ceremony. In this way, Roman religion understood as ritualized ceremony formed the juridical and *vice versa*, which together constituted Roman law. In a similar way, therefore, as Carl Schmitt viewed the ordering of space as 'the structure-determined encounter of order and location' (1950: 48) – that is, of an ordering and of a localization; Perniola suggests that the calendar really is the paradigmatic description for Roman rituality where similar acts are repeated year after year.

The analysis so far has suggested that, contrary to the (original) *ancile* and to the (collection of) *ancilia*, each Stolperstein is identified, and can – at least as a monument in the urban or otherwise inhabited spheres of life – thereby reject oblivion: the *hier wohnte* [here lived] and the victim's name are precisely such marks of identification. Furthermore, the Stolpersteine-Polish-Walks prove that possibilities of a more practical nature also exist for maintaining the individuality of the victim in question. Schrader's argument, that the victim will run the risk of disappearing in the commemorative act due to the enormous quantity, appears to be too harsh.

Nonetheless, since it has been ascertained that the Stolpersteine could be said to be a ritualization and, at the same time, an activation of the juridical and political order – first and foremost in the shape of the five fates – Schrader's position needs, perhaps, more careful attention. The fact that the Romans created such an order *in actu*, whereas the Stolpersteine imply it *post festum*, is irrelevant in this matter. What is decisive, though, is that what is inferred, created and maintained in both the *ancilia* and the Stolpersteine is a normative order of a political, ethical and juridical nature. As a means for ritual cultivation of Rome and the Romans, the order of the *ancilia* faces no problem. However, this guarantee is not certain when what is being ritually cultivated is the lives of former citizens and the memory of each individual victim's annihilation.

Thinking back on the model above, the *ancilia* constituted a ritual reproduction of myth (that the *ancile* had fallen from heaven) into fact (the collection of all twelve *ancilia*), while the Stolpersteine constitute an artistic reproduction of historical fact (the extermination of millions of victims) into a practice of commemoration (of the individual victim). While the Roman religion was free towards the myth, letting only the ritual determine the contents of the ceremony, the outset for the Stolpersteine is (hopefully) not mythic but factual. The monument is therefore bound by one specific calendar and one specific historical event, which would have been incomprehensible to the Roman mind.

So when, in Rome, the original event disappears by way of a ritual act of commemoration that works inseparably from the maintenance of a political order, the clash between myth and fact, memory and history, is what constitutes the formative force of the *ancilia*. The price the Stolpersteine could be said to pay – if the hypothesis that their religious paradigm is the *ancilia* of Roman religion – is considerable. Because, if the original event disappears, that is, the fact that the individual victim was annihilated, it is anything but certain that commemoration of Third Reich extermination will be successful: it is not at all certain that the ethical commemoration of the individual's deportation and annihilation is successful or honourable if the victim's fate is historically understated, underestimated or even unimportant.

This is why it is so difficult to describe whether the Stolpersteine are describing (as they claim they do) or whether they are only performing an act of commemoration isolated from history (which would be a strange position, as the *primus motor* on each stone is declared to be the name of a victim in flesh and blood and the historical period 1933–45). If anything, the Stolpersteine represent a threshold or third plateau between factual commemoration and constructed commemoration, between commemorating the victim's *hier wohnte* [here lived] and the victim's fate (murdered, death, etc.).

The crucial question, which has been mentioned several times throughout the present book, can therefore be approached anew: if the engravings of the five fates represent a *relegere* and an absence of distinction between reality and myth, fact and memory – and therefore do not state historical facts but rather a ritual normalization of the anti-normal – what, then, is the nature of that which the Stolpersteine state? What is, from the point of view of the philosophical archaeology this author has suggested, the linguistic status of these engravings? What is, so to speak, their link to reality, if not historical or factual?

The Oath and the Sacrament of the Political

In what way do the engravings on the Stolpersteine constitute a *use of history*? Throughout this book it has been argued that an understanding of Third Reich deportation, extermination and annihilation is impossible to accomplish in juridical or political, ethical or religious terms; it should instead be interpreted as the result of a biopolitical and durative state of exception, wherein victims were produced as naked life and potential Muselmänner, rather than that they died or were executed as dignified subjects of law.

Naturally, the problem presents itself: if the Stolpersteine seriously use such juridical, political, ethical or religious terminology regardless, how is it to be understood? What is this *abracadabra* whereby each occasion on which someone stumbles upon a Stolperstein starts up the engine of this ceremonial construction, claiming that law and ethics existed in the Third Reich and that this may therefore constitute the historical ground and frame of reference upon which to base commemoration? In other terms, what is the nature of this special linguistic function of utterances juridical, political and ethical governing, so to say, this transformation or, indeed, this creation transforming the victim who was deported and annihilated in the camp into a subject of law and ethics? Put differently, what do these terms mean when their meaning is neither denotative nor connotative, and thus can be based on neither fact nor metaphor alone? An answer to these questions will focus on the oath, and allow coming just a little closer to understanding the consequences of placing the victims in the state of law and in an ethical universe in the shape of the five fates.

From the beginning of the Roman tradition, the oath [*iuramentum*] was connected with a certain object and its use. Something similar was the case with the rite regarding the twelve *ancilia* – especially considering that Mamurius' art was, in fact, something rather more craftsman-like than artistic. Even Demnig himself says something of the sort about the Stolpersteine: 'My professional title can most accurately be rewritten as sculptor' (Demnig 2002: 9). In this regard, Perniola introduces interesting reflections regarding some passages from Caesar's *Gallic War* and the term *gravissima caeremonia* [serious ceremony]:

> When Caesar at last tells of the scheme designed against him by the Carnutes and other people from Gaul (in *Gallic War*, VII, 2), he tells us that they will renounce the exchange of hostages in order not to break their alliance, but that they will demand that all the military emblems be united in a bundle, and that all utter the oath [*fassent le serment*] that they would not separate themselves from the others once the war had started. Caesar defines such an act as a *gravissima caeremonia*, since the emblems, thus united, had acquired a sacrosanct power that was objective and independent from the belief of man, hence replacing very effectively the exchange of hostages. […] In Caesar's text there is no trace whatsoever of any allusion to a manifestation of the divine. All the attention of the Carnutes is focused on the act they dress themselves to begin, on the necessity to found this historical act – full of risks and unknown

> factors – and on the obedience to the *gravissima caeremonia* of the emblems united in a bundle. This ceremony is not a feast organized for the occasion of the alliance, but the objective guarantee, extremely serious and demanding, of that same alliance. (Perniola 1981: 22–4)

The formulation 'utter the oath' [*fassent le serment*], translates Caesar's '*ut iureiurando ac fide sanciatur*' (Caes. *Gal*, 7.2.2), in which *iuramentum* [oath] and *fides* [faith] are recognized respectively. In Latin, another word is sometimes used for oath: *sacramentum*. The institution of the oath is probably very old, figuring as early as in the *Corpus Iuris Civilis* (*Dig*. 22.3.25, cf. Lewis and Short 1879). The oath is even found in the Bible, where God speaks through oaths, and in the central Christian ritual: in the Eucharist, bread becomes flesh and wine blood, but only through the sacrament: 'This is the body of Jesus Christ. This is the blood of Jesus Christ'. In a less serious context, most have heard the word *abracadabra*, the magic formulation that for instance transforms the empty adult hand into a hand presenting a piece of candy to the child.

In all cases, the oath is, apparently, what makes things come true. The interest now, since the special kind of ritual and ceremony tied to the Stolpersteine have been analysed, is to try to determine the meaning these stones acquire as religious objects on account of their engravings, especially of the five fates of dead [*tot*], murdered [*ermordet*], fate unknown, escaped in death [*Flucht in den Tod*] and escaped [*Flucht*] (Demnig 2015: 4), and thus to try to investigate to what extent these monuments could be said to constitute a commemorative sacrament.

In Agamben's 2008 *The Sacrament of Language. An Archaeology of the Oath*, he mentions the central text from Cicero, *De natura deorum*, which Perniola also used and which was quoted and discussed above. Agamben gives the following explanation for what makes an object religious, that is, makes it a *res religiosa* [religious artefact]: 'A *res religiosa*', Agamben explains, 'is deprived from profane use and from commerce; it can neither be sold nor imposed as servitude; it cannot be given away, accepted as security or serve as part of any kind of stipulation', and in general, 'the religious object, as is the sacred, bound by a range of ritual precepts making them inviolable, and which must be strictly kept' (2008: 33ℵ. Cf. Agamben 2005b: 85). This type of explanation can be recognized from the analysis of the *homo sacer* figure above (cf. Chapter 2), a being who was also excepted from sacred and profane law through the formulation *sacer esto* [be sacred]. The oath appears to be the linguistic utterance that places any given object or subject in another context or sphere.

Citing Cicero's *De officiis*, Agamben asks what the contents of the oath really are: 'Concerning the oath, one must understand not what fear it infuses, but what force it has (*non qui metus sed quae vis sit debet intellegi*). The oath is really a religious affirmation (*affirmatio religiosa*), and that which you have promised in a solemn form and confirmed, as had you almost God as witness, you must keep' (Cic. *Off.*, III, cit. in Agamben 2008: 32). Thus, what is essential is not the wrath of the gods, 'but the trust (*fides*)' (Agamben 2008: 32), for this is what constitutes the force [*vis*] of the oath.

This is similar to what Caesar explained to be the case with the Carnutes: in the oath – as with *homo sacer* – traditional differentiations between sacred and profane appear to enter upon a threshold of indistinction. Hence, it seems that a *res religiosa* [religious object] may be a malediction or a ban (as with the utterance *sacer esto* [be sacred]), as well as something rather positive though the strict observance of formulas and ritual regulations (as in Caesar's *gravissima caeremonia* [serious ceremony]). Most importantly, in both cases the human being is directly affected and is at the centre of the oath: either negatively as in the constitution of the *homo sacer* through the utterance 'be sacred'; or positively, as in the ceremony Caesar explained, and which united oath and faith, materializing in the assembling of the military ensigns and military success.

It is important to notice that in both cases the effect depends completely on the fact that a certain and specific set of linguistic regulations is at hand. In this sense religion is, therefore, nothing but the keeping and observations of these rituals and ceremonies: it is a *relegere*. Cicero in fact concurs with modern researchers, Agamben writes – and Perniola appears to be just such one – and can thus 'relate the etymology of religion to the verb *relegere*: to carefully observe' (Agamben 2008: 34א). As proof, Agamben delivers the same citation that lay at the ground of Perniola's rendering of *relegere*: namely, the central passage from Cicero's *de Natura Deorum*, which reads: '*Qui autem omnia quae ad cultum deorum pertinerent diligentur retractarent et tamquam relegerent, sunt dicti religiosi ex relegendo* [those on the other hand who carefully reviewed and so to speak retraced all the lore or ritual were called "religious" from *relegere*, to retrace or re-read]' (Cic. *N. D.*, II, xxviii, 72, cit. in Agamben 2008: 34א).

It is now possible to draw some preliminary conclusions concerning the basic components of the oath that will prove themselves relevant to the current scope of analysing the engravings on the Stolpersteine:

A) to obtain *vis* [force] the oath [*iuramentum*] requires an authority (e.g. the sovereign in the constitution of *homo sacer*); but
B) the oath can also be used to form a kind of social pact, as in the example of the Carnutes;
C) the oath is a collusion between trust or belief and reality, which is what realizes its effects – that is, that the *homo sacer* really is a *Friedlos* [outlaw] or that the gathering of military ensigns will actually form the alliance and provide victory.

By creating a new field of application, a new reality seems to exist simply by way of proclaiming this reality, that is, simply by the concept being used in a new and perhaps even alien field. In this way, the oath could seem to have a lot in common with John Austin's speech act theory. It was Austin's idea that enunciations had impact on reality, to such an extent that some could even be said to create reality. It is of particular interest in the present context that Austin's favourite examples are mostly from jurisprudence and religion. He argues that, for instance, it is the pronouncement of a given conviction in a court of law, or a woman's 'I do' in a matrimonial ceremony, that creates a reality due to the simple fact that it is these words themselves that respectively put the criminal in jail and turn the woman into a wife (Austin 1992: lecture I and II).

Even though Agamben's philosophy of language differs from Austin's (the idea of the witness and the testimony would have been too far-fetched to Austin) and relies more on Benveniste, the summary above does appear to contain at least some of Austin's key considerations nonetheless – especially when Agamben declares the oath to constitute a *performative* utterance:

> The self-referring in the performative utterance is unquestionably decisive. This self-reference is not only exhausted by the fact that the performative, as Benveniste makes clear [in *The Expression of the Oath in Ancient Greece*, 1948], turns itself into reference

> as far as it refers to a reality constituted by the performative itself. Rather, it must be admitted that the performative's self-reference always is constituted by a suspension of the normal denotative character of language. The performative verb is, in fact, necessarily constructed together with a *dictum* which, in itself, is of a purely denotative kind, and without which it remains empty and ineffective (*I swear* has no value unless it is followed by – or follows – a *dictum* which makes it complete). This denotative character of a *dictum* is suspended and, at the same time, disputed in the very moment in which it forms part of a performative syntagm. In this way the utterances 'yesterday I was in Athens' or 'I will not fight the Trojans' cease to be denotative if preceded by the performative *I swear*. The performative, thus, replaces the denotative connection between word and fact with a self-referential connection which – in cancelling the denotative – establishes itself as the determining fact. Here, the model for truth is not the correspondence between word and thing, *but the performative model in which the word inevitably realizes its own meaning*. As the law in the state of exception suspends its own applicability only in order to found its own validity, in the same manner language too suspends its denotation via the performative only so that language may now found its own existential bond to things. (Agamben 2008: 75f., final italics added)

Summarizing this citation in four points, it may be said that a performative utterance, paradigmatically found in the oath, carries the following characteristics:

A) The performative suspends the denotation of a concept, and
B) breaks down the connection between concept (say, murder) and reality, although resting on the latter nonetheless (say, the fact that the victims of the Third Reich are exterminated).
C) The performative depends on neither truth nor falsehood, but on a *vis* [force] that instead realizes its own meaning.
D) The performative is comparable to the state of exception that likewise suspends the norm so that it, by its very own expression, may tie in with humans and things.

Based on these four points it is now possible to ask how, then, the *Schicksale* [fates] of the victims (dead [*tot*], murdered [*ermordet*], fate unknown, escaped in death [*Flucht in den Tod*] and escaped [*Flucht*] (Demnig 2015: 4)) can be said to constitute such performative utterances.

Remembering the Stolpersteine that were mentioned at the beginning of this book may prove to be instructive. At first glance, there seems to be nothing performative about what is read: Max Pander really did disappear; and Bertha Oppenheimer did in fact survive and manage to reach the USA – at least nothing motivates us to doubt these assertions. Nevertheless, the case seems to be all the more problematic for the other victims to whom attention was also drawn, as they augur a differentiation in the realms of extermination and annihilation itself, as was also discussed: Stein and Frank, so their Stolpersteine display, were murdered; Bloch is dead; Pollack escaped in death. The reasons for these fates to contain serious problems concerning their ability to *describe* the historical event have already been amply investigated earlier in this book and need no repetition here. However, since these utterances are also intended to form the very special gift of giving the victims their individual names back, as Demnig intends to do via these monuments, and therefore not only to be descriptive, this changes the status of these utterances on the Stolpersteine.

It seems that at stake in the Stolpersteine engravings is the religion of the oath [*religio iusiurando*], as discussed in regard to Cicero above. It could therefore be argued that if 'the victim will get its name back' (Demnig 2002: 13), it is because each time the *dictum* of *hier wohnte* [here lived] begins a process of commemoration that in the end suspends the denotative and connotative meanings of the five fates (dead [*tot*], murdered [*ermordet*], fate unknown, escaped in death [*Flucht in den Tod*] and escaped [*Flucht*]), thus turning them into performative utterances. Adding to the probability of this interpretation is that, according to Benveniste, Austin himself is not sure whether one can simply say that certain words, utterances and phrases really are performative in themselves (although one can, as Agamben did, argue for the centrality of certain ones), 'and finally', Benveniste continues, 'nor are we in possession of a certain criterion' (Benveniste 1966: 269). In any case, it is interesting to note that the Stolpersteine live up, to the letter, to the criteria of performativity that Benveniste specifies for Austin's theory: '[…] it is often accompanied by indications of the date, location and names of the person' (Benveniste 1966: 273).

Following the strategy of a performative, as explained by Agamben, the five fates of the Stolpersteine therefore become the *iuramentum* [oath], which opens up to a suspension of the meaning of the terms such as *ermordet* [murdered], and *tot* [dead] – that is, a description of facts and reality – for the sake of constructing the victims in the normality of the state of law and ethics. The act of replacing the victim in the city from which he or she was once brutally deported is performed once already by way of the specific location for the victim's deportation (*hier wohnte* [here lived]). However, the wish expressed through the Stolpersteine to commemorate the victim with dignity is so great that they must also performatively replace he or she in the state of law and ethics. However, this solution does not come without problems. There is no doubt that the Stolpersteine stand upon the reality of deportation, extermination and annihilation. Nevertheless, it is precisely this ground the Stolpersteine cultivate by way of an 'ethicalization' and 'juridicalization' in the shape of the performativity of each victim's fate. Doing this, the monument abandons the fundamental differentiations between reality and memory, history and commemoration and could be defined as a *commemorative performative*. Moreover, the performative pulls the victim away from the scene of history in performatively giving back a dignity and a fate that focus exclusively on the victim's humanity, while setting the historical anchoring aside, that is, the victim's annihilation and inhumanity to which he or she finally succumbed.

If this is true, then the Stolpersteine manage to commemorate the victim's humanity, but it no longer rests upon the fact of the victim's annihilation, but on the sole fact that the victim was once a human being. If it be admitted that commemoration of the victims of the Third Reich must stand upon historical ground – that is, must show the transition from humanity in inhumanity, from subjectivity to its destruction, from life and death to their mutual obstruction and impossibility – then the Stolpersteine would seem to face a severe problem.

It is clear, in any case, that the Stolpersteine do not share the belief that this book has tried to present with the readings of Agamben, Arendt, Heidegger, Hilberg, Klemperer and Levi: *that which was taken away from the victims of extermination can never be given back*. Understanding and, perhaps, more importantly admitting and acknowledging that impossibility and consequent limitation of any form of commemoration including the Stolpersteine, is what a remembrance of humanity's inhumanity could have brought, and without which Auschwitz would not run the risk of being forgotten.

Conclusion

The results of this investigation of the Stolpersteine can be presented in terms of three overall conclusions.

1.

Commemorating victims of the Third Reich is problematic: if the reality of Auschwitz is absent, the risk is that the linkage between that extremity and the fates of the victims is lost; on the other hand, if the reality of Auschwitz is over-represented, the risk is that the commemoration will fail to give voice to the individuality of the victims. The task of interpreting the Stolpersteine as an instance of *history as problem* thus turns out to be double: on the one hand it consists in analysing the theoretical challenge of the aporia between history and memory, history and representation, reality and language; on the other hand, from an ethical point of view, the *commemorative* success has to be understood in terms of the Stolpersteine's success in giving witness to Auschwitz' non-language, that is, to present the victims' humanity in the midst of the inhumanity of Auschwitz in which they found themselves.

The analyses advanced in the first chapters show that Demnig's idea of giving the victims their names back, that is, to replace the victims in the community from which they were once deported, is to be found in particular in the five fates that stem from the spheres of law and ethics: dead [*tot*], murdered [*ermordet*], fate unknown [???], escaped in death [*Flucht in den Tod*] and escaped [*Flucht*]. The monument insists that it actually *describes* what happened to the victims. Since the five fates, *causa sui*, are different, the consequence is that the Stolpersteine differentiate between various degrees of deportation, extermination and annihilation but without establishing criteria of qualification between them. This book has argued that some central facts about the historical period between 1933 and 1945 and the Third Reich make it difficult to defend such a commemorative strategy if commemoration is to be *historically* founded. The exterminations, if juridically conceivable at all, are grounded in the domain of constitutional rather than civil law. The perpetrators were not civilians but state officials. Nonetheless, for the Stolpersteine the Third Reich exterminations took place within a space of normality, and the juridical term murder is apparently understood universally (which therefore transports it beyond the spheres of law, since no universal term for murder exists). Third Reich annihilation is, to the Stolpersteine, another type of murder.

Taking a point of departure in Agamben's *homo sacer* project, it was argued that the nature of victimhood in the Third Reich is something very different, and cannot be understood from the spheres of law or ethics but, instead, via the term naked life. The Muselmann in the camp is this life at its most extreme and final stage; he is the integral witness of Auschwitz, of Jews, communists, homosexuals, Sinti and Roma, etc. The Muselmann is the paradigm for the camp, because this figure constitutes the utmost destruction of subjectivity and humanity, which is the ultimate purpose of the camp and every detainee's potential end. Along with Agamben arguing with Arendt, Heidegger, Klemperer and Levi, it has been discussed that what made the camp so evil was not extermination or even annihilation (facts), but instead the state towards which the camp (potentially) reduced all the detainees, after which life could be swept away as though it were not human. The ethical space of the camp to which commemoration must give voice is neither silence nor death, neither law nor ethics, but Hurbinek's non-language: *Matisklo.*

Something far worse than murder or faulty ethics happened to the victims of the Third Reich.

Through Agamben's comment on Schmitt's work, it was shown why and how the Third Reich cannot be understood in Schmitt's conceptualizations of the state of exception, because to him the state of exception must never leave the sphere of law. The Third Reich was simply something completely different in every aspect, which Schmitt's 1933 *State,*

Movement, People clearly showed in 'juridicalizing' the Third Reich via a similarity of the species [*Artgleichheit*] – a term that evidently has nothing to do with law but everything to do with an attempt to give legal ground to a very special branch of National Socialist racism. The Third Reich did not concern law's ever greater absorption of life in the form of state institutions such as prisons, hospitals etc. Rather, the Third Reich suspended the law, and what appeared was the camp and naked life, neither a simple space of confinement nor a convicted felon. And when this is the case, Schmitt's theory cannot operate. For the same reason, although the Third Reich and the camp seem obvious for a Foucauldian analysis, neither can Foucault's notion of biopolitics grasp the event of the exterminations and victimhood.

Using Agamben's *homo sacer* project, complementary as well as critical to the works of Schmitt and Foucault, it was argued that Third Reich biopolitics had the normalized production of naked life at its centre, that is, life that can be killed without committing homicide and without this entering into the sphere of the sacred. Just like the *homo sacer*, the figure from ancient Roman law who lost his juridico-political clothes in the oath *sacer esto* [be sacred], so too is the biopolitical subject in the Third Reich an individual stripped of legality and humanity, left naked to be annihilated as if he were not a human being. This is what constitutes the Third Reich as a biopolitical and durative state of exception. The analyses hence conclude that a placement of victimization and form of government in the realms of the law, as the Stolpersteine do, tends to simplify and understate a reality that was far more extreme.

Chapter 3 therefore ends by posing one fundamental question: why do the Stolpersteine situate victims of the Third Reich in a juridical and ethical sphere, when it is so obvious that they were subjected to far more extreme measurements? Only after having considered the fates as neither denotative nor connotative does a solution slowly begin to present itself, which surprisingly shares common features with the results concerning the engraving *hier wohnte* [here lived], which, nonetheless, is very denotative.

2.

The engraving *hier wohnte* [here lived] is most often displayed on the Stolpersteine, indicating the home of each victim. Using Heidegger's central text, *Building Dwelling Thinking*, the meaning of dwelling in relation to the Stolpersteine is analysed. To Heidegger, dwelling is the space where the human being comes to light and constitutes itself. Dwelling and Being are coexistential, and the form of life capable of building a home unites them. In terms of commemoration, the *hier wohnte* [here lived] thus performs a beautiful memorialization of the victim and his or her past home in the midst of the contemporary city or landscape. By contemporary reference to the victims' past home, the Stolpersteine achieve their most decisive meaning and function, at the same time manifesting a strong use of history. However, since a Stolperstein in most cases has been installed directly in front of a contemporary home, although still on public ground, it is located on the very threshold of private and public, *oikos* and *polis*. This use of the past testifies to a use of property unheard of in other forms of commemoration. Considering the unquestionable success of the Stolpersteine, it is interesting that very few sponsors of the Stolpersteine live in Stolpersteine houses.

In this way, the Stolpersteine test and challenge the fundamental boundaries of liberal society, and the responsibility each contemporary citizen in this way is forced to carry on behalf of the sponsors of the Stolpersteine. Demnig himself believes this aspect to be a necessary part of commemoration of Third Reich victims. European citizens must be forced to commemorate because, as Demnig explains, otherwise such specific memory would not be possible. Harjes underlined the problems involved in this, a criticism that was followed in discussing the violence of this cartography, which paradoxically reproduces central aspects of the Third Reich's form of biopolitical government as it forces its way into the private life of the citizen, making especially the residents vehicles for government politics of commemoration. Although Endlich interestingly noticed this commemorative strategy, contrary to Harjes, she found such a historical citation appealing, and thus left her discovery untreated regardless of the quite severe problems this poses for commemoration. It could be said that commemoration becomes biopolitical because the difference between private and public, *oikos* and *polis*, collapses, making dwelling the state's concern rather than the citizen's.

3.

The purpose of the last two chapters is to find an answer as to why the Stolpersteine insist on placing victimhood in the spheres of law and ethics, when the monument's *hier wohnte* [here lived] already places the victim in the city and in the spheres of normality from which he or she was deported, in most cases to be annihilated.

The analysis took its point of departure in Meckel and Rönnerper's uses of Faulkner, Kertész and Levi and discussed the question of the perpetrator. Richarz followed the idea of a guilt that would ultimately disregard the difference between perpetrators and descendants of perpetrators – largely corresponding to Faulkner's calumnious universe in *Requiem for a Nun* – although one of the definite successes of the Stolpersteine is that they do not mention either perpetrators or bystanders, thus pointing, in fact, in the direction of Jaspers and his idea of metaphysical guilt. It was argued that Ward took up the thread from Richarz, but went even further in underlining that the Stolpersteine must be viewed as the natural and commemorative inheritance of the Third Reich's deportations and exterminations, thus speaking of an inherited responsibility. It became clear, hence, that placement of guilt in the traditional realms of law turns out to be less meaningful and, effectively, to lead to the installation of autocalumnia in the Stolpersteine where ethical responsibility and guilt would tend to lose their anchoring in reality.

While it could be said to be true that the Stolpersteine actually do raise questions of guilt and perpetrator, this is not done via the insistence of the *hier wohnte* [here lived] but, instead, via the five fates. A core reason for the Stolpersteine to place the victim in the realm of the law could be, perhaps, to underline the fact of an unknown perpetrator. While an effective strategy of commemoration, the analyses have underlined, however, the difficulties in all this: the perpetrators in the Third Reich were something far more extreme than simple murderers, something which also Arendt's reflections of the perpetrator, as well as Jasper's term of metaphysical guilt, support. Third Reich crime is only with difficulty captured by law. The commemorative strategy of the Stolpersteine would have been more in harmony with history and limited the gap to memory had the monuments refrained from explicit juridical and even ethical terminology. Because *something far worse than murder or faulty ethics happened to the victims of the Third Reich.*

In the last chapter, an interpretation key is therefore sought that could somehow provide an answer as to why the Stolpersteine insist on using juridical and ethical vocabulary regarding the fate of each individual victim. A solution was to some extent found when analysing the engraving as a *commemorative performative*. A paradigm was found in the Roman *ancilia* that ritualized and normalized the divine and mythical origin of the *ancile* and created a threshold of indistinction between the two. Similarly, the Stolpersteine, in their turn, ritualize the historical fact of the extraordinary exterminations by normalizing them via the five fates. The reason for such a mytho-historical construction of victimhood was found in Demnig's paradigmatic formulation that, with the Stolperstein, the victim will get his or her name back thereby symbolically *restoring* dignity to the victim. The only sphere capable of providing such dignity and of giving back that which each victim once lost is that of law and ethics, according to the form of commemoration found in the Stolpersteine.

This author argues that the solution was only partial, as *hier wohnte* [here lived] and, for instance, *ermordet* [murdered], reflect conditions from the same sphere of normality, despite the fact that the latter is brutal and violent, the other not. Just as the *hier wohnte* [here lived] subtly expresses the victim's place in society before the National Socialist government, the five fates – some more than others – to the same extent normalize the deportation, extermination and annihilation. As a consequence, the Stolpersteine inscribe Auschwitz (the biopolitical and durative state of exception *par excellence*) in the same referentiality of political and juridical normality and humanity as that of the victims' homes and residences before the Third

Reich was established. Although the commemorative performative allows commemoration to suspend the denotative and connotative meanings of the five fates, the Stolpersteine suspend what Ginzburg called the principle of reality. In this way, the Stolpersteine pull the victim away from the grounds of history, restoring the victim's humanity exclusively, but without being able to include the victim's annihilation.

Commemoration consists of a double task: the historical task of never forgetting the reality of Auschwitz, and the ethical task of commemorating its victims based on this reality. From those who were deported and exterminated, the Stolpersteine insist that commemoration can give the victims back what they lost. This book has tried to show that something was taken from the victims that can never be given back.

Bibliography

Agamben, G. (2008). *Il sacramento del linguaggio. Archeologia del giuramento. Homo sacer II, 3*. Rome and Bari: Laterza.

—— (2007). *Il Regno e la Gloria. Per una genealogia teologica dell'economia e del governo. Homo sacer II, 2*. Vicenza: Neri Pozza.

—— (2005a). *Homo sacer. Il potere sovrano e la nuda vita*. Torino: Bollati Boringhieri.

—— (2005b). *Profanazione*. Rome: Notte tempo, 2nd edn.

—— (2004). *Stato di eccezione. Homo sacer II, 1*. Torino: Bollati Boringhieri, 1st edn 2003.

—— (2000). *Il tempo che resta. Un commento alla Lettera ai Romani*. Torino: Bollati Boringhieri.

—— (1998). *Quel che resta di Auschwitz. L'archivio e il testimone. Homo sacer III*. Torino: Bollati Boringhieri.

ALEX: *ALEX, Historische Rechts- und Gesetzestexte Online* (Deutsches RGBL, 1922–1945, Teil 1 & 2) <http://alex.onb.ac.at/cgi-content/alex-iv.pl>.

Ando, C. (2008). *The Matter of the Gods: Religion and the Roman Empire*. Berkeley: University of California Press.

Anne Frank Guide. 'The Persecution of the Roma and Sinti' <http://www.annefrankguide.net/en-us/bronnenbank.asp?oid=15978> accessed 16 September 2015.

Arendt, H. (1964a). *Eichmann in Jerusalem: A Report on the Banality of Evil*. New York: Penguin Classics, revised edn.

—— (1964b). 'Organised Guilt and Universal Responsibility'. In J. Kohn (ed.), *Essays in Understanding*, pp. 121–32. New York: Schocken Books.

—— (1964c). 'What Remains? The Language Remains. A Conversation with Günter Gaus'. In J. Kohn (ed.), *Essays in Understanding*, pp. 1–23. New York: Schocken Books.

—— (1962). *The Origins of Totalitarianism*. Cleveland and New York: Meridan Books, 7th edn.

Aristoteles. *Politica* (*Pol.*). In G. R. Crane (ed.), Perseus Digital Library <http://www.perseus.tufts.edu/hopper/>.

Assmann, J. (2007). *Das kulturelle Gedächtnis. Schrift, Erinnerung und politische Identität in frühen Hochkulturen*. Munich: C. H. Beck, 6th edn.

Austin, J. L. (1992). *How To Do Things With Words*. Oxford: Oxford University Press, 2nd edn, reprint.

Bassler, S. (2013). 'Der Fall Erbslöh – Materieller Schaden durch Stolpersteine?'. In R. Redies (ed.), *Zehn Jahre Stolpersteine für Stuttgart. Ein bürgerschaftliches Projekt zieht Kreise*, pp. 65–7. Stuttgart: Markstein Verlag.

Bendersky, J. W. (1983). *Carl Schmitt. Theorist for the Reich*. Princeton, NJ: Princeton University Press.

Benveniste, É. (1969). *Le vocabulaire des institutions indo-européennes. 1. Économie, parenté, société*. Paris: Les Editions de Minuit.

—— (1966). *Problème de linguistique générale.* Vol. I. Paris: Gallimard.

Berenbaum, M. and Skolnik, F. (eds) (2007). *Encyclopaedia Judaica*, 2nd edn. Vol. 14. Detroit, MI: Macmillan Reference.

BGB: Bürgerliches Gesetzbuch <http://www.gesetze-im-internet.de/bgb/index.html>.

Bibles:

King James Version (AV). In <http://www.biblegateway.com/>.

Luther's Bible (Lut). In <http://lutherbibel.net/>.

Novum Testamentum Graece (NT), ed. B. and K. Aland, J. Karavidopoulos, C. M. Martini, B. M. Metzger, 27th revised edn. Stuttgart: Deutsche Bibelgesellschaft, 2001.

Septuaginta (LXX). *Id. est Vetus Testamentum graece iuxta LXX interpretes*, ed. A. Rahlfs and R. Hanhart, revised edn. Stuttgart: Deutsche Bibelgesellschaft, 2006.

Biella, B. (1998). *Eine Spur ins Wohnen legen: Entwurf einer Philosophie des Wohnens nach Heidegger und über Heidegger hinaus*. Berlin: Parerga Verlag.

Blasius, D. (2001). *Carl Schmitt: Preußischer Staatsrat in Hitlers Reich*. Göttingen: Vandenhoeck & Ruprecht.

Borgmann, T. (2011). 'Stolpersteine dürfen bleiben', *Stuttgarter Zeitung*, 18 March.

Broszat, M. (1969). *Der Staat Hirlers. Grundlegung und Entwicklung seiner inneren Verfassung*. Munich: DTV.

Burleigh, M. and Whippermann, W. (1991). *The Racial State. Germany 1933–1945*. Cambridge: Cambridge University Press.

Bussmann, H. (1990). *Lexikon der Sprachwissenschaft*, 2nd completely reworked edn. Stuttgart: Alfred Kröner Verlag.

Caesar, J. C. *De bello Gallico* (*Caes. Gal*) (original and English translation), ed. W. A. McDevitte and W. S. Bohn (1869). 'Caesar's Gallic War'. New York: Harper & Brothers. 1st edn in G. R. Crane (ed.), Perseus Digital Library <http://www.perseus.tufts.edu/hopper/>.

Caplan, J. and Wachsmann, N. (eds), *Concentration Camps in Nazi Germany. The New Histories*. London: Routledge.

Chare, N. (2006). 'The Gap in Context: Giorgio Agamben's Remnants of Auschwitz', *Cultural Critique*, 64 (Autumn), 40–68.

Chase, J. (2004). 'Stumbling over the Holocaust', *Boston Globe*, 11 April.

Cicero, M. T. *de Natura Deorum* (*N. D.*). Original and English translation by H. Rackham. Edinburgh: St Edmunsbury Press, reprint 2000.

—— *De officiis* (*Off.*) (original and English translation), ed. W. Miller (1913). Cambridge, MA and London: Harvard University Press. In G. R. Crane (ed.), Perseus Digital Library <http://www.perseus.tufts.edu/hopper/>.

—— 'De Senectute' (*Sen.*), in *De Senectute De Amicitia De Divinatione* (English translation), ed. W. A. Falconer (1923). Cambridge, MA and London: Harvard University Press. In G. R. Crane (ed.), Perseus Digital Library <http://www.perseus.tufts.edu/hopper/>.

Conradi, M. (2005). 'Steine in den Weg gelegt', *Berliner Zeitung*, 15 October.

Demnig, G. (2015). *Schritte zum Verlegen von STOLPERSTEINEN* <http://www.stolpersteine.eu/>.

—— (2002). 'Am treffendsten läßt sich meine Berufsbezeichung mit Bildhauer umschreiben'. In G. Demnig, M. Düspohl, S. Endlich, A. Hallen, H. Lieser (eds), *Stolpersteine. Dokumentation, Texte, Materialen. Für die von den Nazis ermordeten ehemaligen Nachbarn aus Friedrichshain und Kreuzberg*, pp. 9–24. Berlin: Neuen Gesellschaft für Bildende Kunst.

Doremus, A. and Ball, H. (2004). 'La théologie politique de Carl Schmitt', *Les Études philosophique*, 1 (January), 65–104.

Dreier, H. (2001). 'Die deutsche Staatsrechtslehre in der Zeit des Nationalsozialismus'. In J. Ipsen (ed.), *Die deutsche Staatsrechtslehre in der Zeit des Nationalsozialismus. Europäisches und nationales Verfassungssrecht. Der Staat als Wirtschaftssubjekt und Auftraggeber*, pp. 10–147. Berlin and New York: De Gruyter.

Drobische, K. and Wieland, G. (1993). *System der NS Konzentrationslager 1933–1939*. Berlin: Akademie Verlag.

Dumézil, G. (1974). *La réligion romanine archaique. Avec un appendice sur la religion des Étrusques*. Paris: Payot, 2 edn.

Durantaye, L. de la (2009). *Giorgio Agamben: A Critical Introduction*. Stanford, CA: Stanford University Press.

Echterhölter, R. (1970). *Das öffentliche Recht im nationalsocialistischen Staat*. Stuttgart: Deutsche Verlags-Anstalt.

Edelheit, A. J. and Edelheit H. (1994). *History of the Holocaust. A Handbook and Dictionary*. Boulder, CO: Westview Press.

Endlich, S. (2002). 'Ein "dezentrales Monument"? Anmerkungen zu einem ungewöhnlichen Denkmalskonzept'. In G. Demnig, M. Düspohl, S. Endlich, A. Hallen, H. Lieser (eds), *Stolpersteine. Dokumentation, Texte, Materialen. Für die von den Nazis ermordeten ehemaligen Nachbarn aus Friedrichshain und Kreuzberg*, pp. 29–36. Berlin: Neuen Gesellschaft für Bildende Kunst.

Fargnoli, N., Golays, M. and Hamblin, R. W. (eds) (2008). *Critical Companion to William Faulkner. A Literary Reference to His Life and Work*. New York: Facts on File.

Faulkner, W. (1951). *Requiem for a Nun*. New York: Random House.

Ferrari, A. (1999). *Dizionario di mitologia greca e latina*. Torino: Unione Tipografico-Editrice Torinese (UTET).

Fings, K. (ed.) (2007). *Stolpersteine. Gunter Demnig und sein Projekt. Gunter Demnig and his Project*. Köln: Hermann-Josef Emons Verlag.

Flebbe. J. (2008). *Solus Deus. Untersuchungen zur Rede von Gott im Brief des Paulus an die Römer*. Berlin: Walter de Gruyter.

Foucault, M. (2004). *Sécurité, territoire, population. Cours au Collège de France. 1977–1978*. Paris: Éditions Gallimard, Éditions Seuil.

—— (2001). *L'Histoire de la sexualité 1. La volonté de savoir*. Paris: Éditions Gallimard.

—— (1997). *'Il faut défendre la société'. Cours au Collège de France 1976*. Paris: Éditions Gallimard, Éditions Seuil.

Franke, D. (2008). *Stolperstein. Ein Film von Dörte Franke*. Hangarf & Ufer Filmproduktion.

Fritsche, P. T. (2014). *Stolpersteine – Das Gedächtnis einer Straße*. Berlin: Wissenschaftlicher Verlag.

Funke, M. (1987). 'Republik im Untergang. Die Zerstörung des Parlamentarismus als Vorbereitung der Diktatur'. In K. D. Bracher, M. Funke and H. A. Jacobsen (eds), *Die Weimarer Republik 1918–33. Politik. Wirtschaft. Gesellschaft*, pp. 505–31. Düsseldorf: Droste Verlag.

Gaffiot, F. (1936). *Dictionaire abrégé latin français illustré*. Paris: Librairie Hachette.

Gentile, E. (2012). *É fu subito regime. Il fascismo e la marcia su Roma*. Rome and Bari: Laterza.

Georgi, S. (2011). 'Transcultural Remembrance: Stolpersteine, Silent Promises, and the European Capital of Culture Ruhr. 2010'. In C. C. Waegner, P. R. Laws, G. de Laforcade (eds), *Transculturality and Perceptions of the Immigrant Other: 'From-Heres' and 'Come-Heres' in Virginia and North Rhine-Westphalia*, pp. 28–47. Newcastle: Cambridge Scholars.

Gibbon, E. (1996). *The History of the Decline and Fall of the Roman Empire*. Vols I–VIII. Oxford: The Folio Society, 3rd printing.

Ginzburg, C. (2000). *Miti. Emblemi. Spie*. Torino: Einaudi.

—— (1992). 'Unus testis. Lo sterminio degli ebrei e il principio di realtà', *Quaderni storici*, 80/a, XXVII (2) (August), 529–48.

—— (1991). 'Checking The Evidence: The Judge and the Historian', *Critical Inquiry*, 18 (1) (Autumn), 79–92.

Goebel, A. (2004)'Neue Diskussion über die "Stolpersteine"', *Süddeutsche* Zeitung, 14 June.

Gruner, W. (ed.) (2008). *Die Verfolgung und Ermorderung der europäischen Juden durch das nationalsozialistische Deutschland 1933–45, Bd.1: Deutsches Reich 1933–7*. Munich: R. Oldenbourg Verlag.

Harjes, K. (2005). 'Stumbling Stones. Holocaust Memorials, National Identity and Democratic Inclusion in Berlin', *German Politics and Society*, 23 (1) (Spring), 138–51.

Heidegger, M. (2001). *Sein und Zeit*. Tübingen: Max Niemeyer, 18th edn.

—— (2000) 'Bauen Wohnen Denken'. In id. *Vorträge und Aufsätze*, Gesamtausgabe (GA) 7, pp. 145–64. Frankfurt am Main: Vittorio Klostermann.

—— (1996). 'Brief über den Humanismus'. In id. *Wegmarken*, Gesamtausgabe (GA) 9, pp. 313–64. Frankfurt am Main: Vittorio Klostermann, 2nd edn.

—— (1994). 'Die Gefahr'. In id. *Bremer und Freiburger Vorträge*, Gesamtausgabe (GA) 79, pp. 46–67. Frankfurt am Main: Vittorio Klostermann.

—— (1982). *Parmenides*, Gesamtausgabe (GA) 54, Frankfurt am Main: Vittorio Klostermann.

Hilberg, R. (1996). *The Politics of Memory. The Journey of a Holocaust Historian*. Chicago: Ivan D. Ree.

—— (1985). *The Destruction of the European Jews*. New York: Holmes & Meier.

Hobbes, T. (1998). 'The Citizen'. In B. Gert (ed.), *Man and Citizen (De Homine* and *De Cive)*, pp. 87–388. Indianapolis, IN and Cambridge: Hackett Publishing Company, 3rd printing.

—— (1966). *Leviathan, or The Matter, Forme, & Power of a Common-wealth Ecclesiastical and Civill*. Harmondsworth and Middlesex: Penguin Books, reprinted 1974.

Hobsbawm, E. J. (1995). *The Age of Extremes. The Short Twentieth Century 1914–1991*. London: Abacus.

Huyssen, A. (2003). *Present Pasts, Urban Palimpsests and the Politics of Memory*. Stanford, CA: Stanford University Press.

Imort, M. (2010). 'Stumbling Blocks: A Decentralized Memorial to Holocaust Victims'. In B. Niven and C. Paver (eds), *Memorialization in Germany since 1945*, pp. 233–42. New York: Palgrave Macmillan.

Jaspers, K. (1946). *Die Schuldfrage. Ein Beitrag zur deutschen Frage*. Zürich: Artemis-Verlag.

Jordan, J. (2006). *Structures of Memory. Understanding Urban Change in Berlin and Beyond*. Stanford, CA: Stanford University Press.

Kantorowicz, E. H. (1997). *The King's Two Bodies. A Study in Medieval Political Theology*. Princeton, NJ: Princeton University Press.

Katzman, L. and Paulix, G. (2005). 'Against Forgetting: The Memorial Art of Gunter Demnig', *Art Papers*, 6 (November/ December).

Kellerhoff, S. F. and Grandzior, A. (2013). 'Gedanken in Berlin – Jauch und Raabe putzen "Stolpersteine"', *Berliner Morgenpost*, 9 November.

Kershaw, I. (1993). '"Working Towards the Führer". Reflections on the Nature of the Hitler Dictatorship', *Contemporary European History*, 2 (2) (July), 103–18.

Kertész, I. (1975). *Fatelessness.* New York: Vintage.

Klemperer, V. (1975). *LTI. Notizbuch eines Philologen*. Leipzig: Reclam Verlag.

Knittel, S. C. (2010). 'Remembering Euthanasia: Grafeneck in the Past, Present, and Future'. In B. Niven and C. Paver (eds), *Memorialization in Germany since 1945*, pp. 124–33. New York: Palgrave Macmillan.

Korn, S. (1999). 'Die Tafeln sind zerbrochen. Über die Darstellung des Unvorstellbaren, das Vergessen und den Streit um das Holocaust-Denkmal in Berlin'. In M. S. Cullen (ed.), *Das Holocaust-Mahnmal. Dokumentation einer Debatten*, pp. 49–60. Zürich: Pendo Verlag.

Levi, P. (1989a). *Se questo è un uomo*. Torino: Einaudi.

—— (1989b). *La tregua*. Torino: Einaudi.

—— (1988). *Ist das ein Mensch? Die Atempause*. Munich: Carl Hanser Verlag.

—— (1984). *Ad ora incerta*. Milano: Garzanti Editore.

Lewis, C. T. and Short, C. (1879). *A Latin Dictionary.* Oxford: Clarendon Press. In G. R. Crane (ed.), Perseus Digital Library <http://www.perseus.tufts.edu/hopper/>.

Lindenstraße <http://www.lindenstrasse.de/>.

Loewenstein, K. (1936). 'Law in the Third Reich', *The Yale Law Journal*, 45 (5) (March), 779–815.

Marion, E. (2006). 'The Nazi Genocide and the Writing of the Holocaust Aporia: Ethics and Remnants of Auschwitz', *MLN*, 121 (4) (September), The Johns Hopkins University, 1,009–22.

Meckel, M. (2006). *Den Opfern ihre Namen zurückgeben. Stolpersteine in Freiburg.* Freiburg and Berlin: Rombach Verlag.

Mehring, R. (2005)'.Carl Schmitt om Martin Heidegger – den katolske "skærper" kritiserer nationalsocialismens "neutraliserer"', *Slagmark. Tidsskrift for idéhistorie*, 43, Aarhus, 39–44.

Nietzsche, F. (1999). 'Die fröhliche Wissenschaft ("la gaya scienza")'. In G. Colli and M. Montinari (eds), *Sämtliche Werke, Kritische Studienausgabe in 15 Bänden.* Munich: Walter de Gruyter, 2nd revised edn, vol. 3, pp. 343–651.

Niewyk, D. L. and Nicosia, F. R. (2000). *The Columbia Guide to the Holocaust.* New York, Chichester and West Sussex: Columbia University Press.

Noack, P. (1993). *Carl Schmitt. Eine Biographie*. Frankfurt am Main: Verlag Ullstein.

Perniola, M. (1981). 'Le rite et le mythe', *Traverses*, 21–2, 19–27.

—— (1980). 'Ars e urbs', *Rivista di estetica*, 4, 27–34.

Pfeifer, W. (1989). *Etymologisches Wörterbuch des Deutschen*. Berlin: Akademie Verlag.

Plutarch. *Numa Pompilius* (*Num*). In P. Bernadotte (ed.) (1914), *Plutarch's Lives. With an English Translation*. Vol. 1. Cambridge, MA: Harvard University Press; London: William Heinemann. In G. R. Crane (ed.), Perseus Digital Library <http://www.perseus.tufts.edu/hopper/>.

Pöggeler, O. (1990). *Der Denkweg Martin Heidegger*. Tübingen: Verlag Günther Neske Pfullingen, 3rd extended edn.

Pokorny, J. (1959). *Indogermanisches Etymologisches Wörterbuch*. Vol. 1. Bern and Munich: Francke Verlag.

PSM-Data Geschichte <http://www.zum.de/psm/index1.php>.

Radies, R. (ed.) (2013). *Zehn Jahre Stolpersteine für Stuttgart. Ein bürgerschaftliches Projekt zieht Kreise*. Stuttgart: Markstein Verlag.

Richarz, M. (2008).'Stumbling Stones. Marks of Holocaust Memory on German Streets'. In L. B. Strauss and M. Brenner (eds), *Mediating Memory. Challenges and Trends in the Jewish Encounter with the Modern World. Essays in Honor of Michael A. Meyer*, pp. 325–37. Detroit, MI: Wayne State University Press.

Roloff, K. H. (1954). 'Ritus', *Glotta*, 33 (1–2), 36–65.

—— (1952). 'Caeremonia', *Glotta*, 32 (1–2), 101–38.

Rönnerper, J. (ed.) (2010). *Vor meiner Haustür. 'Stolpersteine' von Gunter Demnig. Ein Begleitbuch*. Gelsenkirchen: Arachne Verlag.

Rueckert, W. H. (2004). *Faulkner from Within: Destructive and Generative Being in the Novels of William Faulkner*. West Lafayette, IN: Parlor Press LLC.

Schaap, A. (2001). 'Guilty Subjects and Political Responsibility: Arendt, Jaspers and the Resonance of the "German Question" in Politics of Reconciliation', *Political Studies*, 49, 749–66.

Schmitt, C. (1994a). *Die Diktatur. Von den Anfängen des modernen Souveränitätsgedankens bis zum proletarischen Klassenkampf*. Berlin: Dunker & Humbolt, 6th edn.

—— (1994b). *Politische Theologie. Vier Kapitel zur Lehre von der Souveränität*. Berlin: Dunker & Humbolt, 8th edn.

—— (1934). 'Der Führer schützt das Recht. Zur Reichstagsrede Adolf Hitlers vom 13. Juli', *Deutsche Juristen-Zeitung*, no. 15, 1 August, column 945–50.

—— (1933). *Staat, Bewegung, Volk*. Berlin: Dunker & Humbolt.

Schrader, U. (2006). 'Die Stolpersteine oder Von der Leichtigkeit des Gedenkens', *Geschichte im Westen*, 21, 173–81.

Seaton, A. V. (1996). 'Guided by the Dark: From Thanatopsis to Thanatourism', *International Journal of Heritage Studies*, 2 (4), 234–44.

Sennett, R. (2002). *Flesh and Stone. The Body and the City in Western Civilization*. London: Penguin Books.

Serup-Bilfeldt, K. (2004). *Stolpersteine. Vergessene Namen, verwehte Spuren. Wegweiser zu Kölner Schicksalen in der NS-Zeit*. Köln: Verlag Kiepenheuer, 2nd edn.

Sion, B. (2010). 'Affective Memory, Ineffective Functionality: Experiencing Berlin's Memorial to the Murdered Jews of Europe'. In B. Niven and C. Paver (eds), *Memorialization in Germany since 1945*, pp. 243–52. New York: Palgrave Macmillan.

Slettholm, A. (2011). 'Holocaust i nabolaget', *Aftenposten*, 9 September.

Snoek, A. (2010). 'Agamben's Foucault: An overview', *Foucault Studies*, 10 (November), 44–67.

Snyder, T. (2010). *Bloodlands. Europe Between Hitler and Stalin*. New York: Basic Books.

—— (2009). 'Holocaust: The ignored reality', *Eurozine* <http://www.eurozine.com>.

Tellegen-Couperus, O. (2008). 'Ehrlich's non-state law and the Roman jurists'. In H. van Schooten and J. Verschuuren (eds), *International Governance and Law. State Regulation and Non-state Law*, pp. 94–103. Cheltenham, MA: Edward Elgar Publishing.

Thamer, H. U. (2005). 'Beginn der nationalsozialistischen Herrschaft (Teil 2)', *Bundeszentrale für politische Bildung*, Bonn <https://www.bpb.de/>.

—— (1994). *Verführung und Gewalt. Deutschland 1933–1945*. Berlin: Wolf Jobst Siedler Verlag.

Thompson, I. (2003). *Primo Levi*. London: Random House.

Traverso, E. (2004). 'Storia e memoria. Gli usi politici del passato', *Novecento, per una storia del tempo presente*, no. 10, 9–26.

United States Holocaust Memorial Museum (USHMM) <http://www.ushmm.org/>. USHMM: 'German Jews during the Holocaust', *Holocaust Encyclopedia* <http://www.ushmm.org/wlc/en/article.php?ModuleId=10005357> accessed 16 September 2015.

Vattimo, G. (2008). *Introduzione a Heidegger*. Rome and Bari: Laterza, 18th edn.

Vogt, M. (1987). 'Parteien in der Weimarer Republik'. In K. D. Bracher, M. Funke, H. A. Jacobsen (eds), *Die Weimarer Republik 1918–1933. Politik. Wirtschaft. Gesellschaft*, pp. 134–57. Düsseldorf: Droste Verlag.

Ward, J. (2009). 'Sacralized Spaces and the Urban Remembrance of War'. In U. Staiger, H. Steiner, A. Webber (eds), *Memory Culture and the Contemporary City*, pp. 145–60. Basingstoke: Palgrave Macmillan.

Weber, S. (1992). 'Taking Exception to Decision: Walter Benjamin and Carl Schmitt', *Diacritics*, 22 (3–4), 5–18.

Wolz, H. D. (2010). 'Stolpersteine zum Gedanken an Nazi-Opfer aus dem Dorf', *Stuttgarter Nachrichten*, 5 October.

Website for Stolpersteine

Stolpersteine <http://www.stolpersteine.eu/>.

City and Other Homepages for Stolpersteine

Allmende Stetten <http://www.allmende-stetten.de/archiv-menu/61-07102010-stolpersteinverlegung.html> accessed 23 September 2015.

Berlin <http://www.stolpersteine-berlin.de/> accessed October 2015. <http://www.stolpersteine-berlin.de/de/orte-biografien> accessed 20 May 2015. <http://www.stolpersteine-berlin.de/de/spaziergaenge> accessed 21 September 2015.

Berlin putzt Stolpersteine <http://www.berlin.de/2013/veranstaltungen/9-1011-in-berlin/> accessed 21 September 2015.

Cologne <http://www.museenkoeln.de/nsdokumentationszentrum/default.aspx?s=1194> accessed May 2017.

Hamburg <http://www.stolpersteine-hamburg.de/> accessed October 2015.

Stuttgart <http://www.stolpersteine-stuttgart.de/index.php?docid=436&mid=72> accessed 23 September 2015.

Individual Stolpersteine

Aron, Berl Lot and Reisel Johanna Heme, born Bergman <http://www.stolpersteine-berlin.de/de/biografie/1544> and <http://www.stolpersteine-berlin.de/de/biografie/1545> accessed 20 May 2015.

Berg, Johanna <http://www.stolpersteine-berlin.de/de/biografie/1326> accessed 20 May 2015.

Bloch, Max <http://www.freiburg-im-netz.de/stolpersteine/stolpdoku.php?anzeige=blomax.jpg&reihe=name#Max_Bloch> accessed 16 September 2015.

Brzezek, Konrad <http://www.stolpersteine-berlin.de/de/biografie/2255> accessed 8 September 2016.

Frank, Anne <http://frauengeschichtsverein-aachen.de/?attachment_id=182> accessed 16 September 2015.

Frank, Edith and Anker, Emma <http://www.stolpersteine-neuruppin.de/#st> accessed 20 May 2015.

Liepmannssohn, Emil Louis <http://www.stolpersteine-berlin.de/de/biografie/1365> accessed 20 May 2015.

Oppenheimer, Bertha <http://www.schriesheim.de/fileadmin/Image_Archive/Stadtinformationen/Mehrueberuns/Flyer_Stolpersteine_2013.pdf> accessed 16 September 2015.

Pander, Max <https://de.wikipedia.org/wiki/Liste_der_Stolpersteine_in_Bochum> accessed 16 September 2015.

Pollack, Hans <http://www.stolpersteine-berlin.de/de/biografie/3032> accessed 16 September 2015.

Schmidt, Max <http://www.stolpersteine-berlin.de/de/biografie/3583> accessed 8 September 2016.

Stein, Edith <http://www.freiburg-im-netz.de/stolpersteine/stolpdoku.php?anzeige=steedi.jpg&reihe=Name> accessed 28 May 2015.

Trollmann, Johann 'Rukeli' <http://www.stolpersteine-berlin.de/de/biografie/2385> accessed 20 May 2015.

Index

FSC
www.fsc.org
MIX
Papier aus verantwortungsvollen Quellen
Paper from responsible sources
FSC® C141904

Druck:
Customized Business Services GmbH
im Auftrag der
KNV Zeitfracht GmbH
Ein Unternehmen der Zeitfracht - Gruppe
Ferdinand-Jühlke-Str. 7
99095 Erfurt